The Odes of John Keats

The Odes of John Keats

Helen Vendler

The Belknap Press of
Harvard University Press
Cambridge, Massachusetts, and London, England

This book is printed on acid-free paper, and its binding materials
have been chosen for strength and durability.

Library of Congress Cataloging in Publication Data

Vendler, Helen Hennessy.
    The odes of John Keats.

    Includes index.
    I. Keats, John, 1795–1821 — Criticism and interpretation.
I. Title.
PR4837.V43 1983   821'.7   83-158
ISBN 0-674-63075-0 (cloth)
ISBN 0-674-63076-9 (paper)

To Marguerite Stewart

Acknowledgments

It has been a privilege (which only others who have written on Keats can fully know) to have spent a portion of my life with Keats's words and thoughts constantly in my mind. I am grateful to those who helped in the writing of this book. First of all, I am indebted to the late Douglas Bush: it was his masterly introduction to the *Selected Poems* that took me from my first knowledge of Keats (a legacy from my mother) to a more adult one; and it was his life-mask of Keats that first showed me Keats's face. Walter Jackson Bate has given me a life-mask of Keats made at the same time as Douglas Bush's; the book has been written with the mask as Presider (as Keats called the picture of Shakespeare which he ornamented with tassels). The Department of English at Kenyon College encouraged me to begin this book by inviting me to give the John Crowe Ransom Memorial Lectures; the memory of the happy week spent at Kenyon remains for me in these pages. I wish to thank as well Princeton University, where these lectures were given as a Gauss Seminar; the audiences at Kenyon and Princeton and other universities all helped me refine my original tentative draft. The chapter on the ode *To Autumn* was delivered as a Beall-Russell Lecture at Baylor University in 1982. The Keats Museum at Hampstead and the Houghton Library of Harvard are resources to which I, like all writers on Keats, am indebted. This book was substantially completed during my tenure of a Senior Fellowship from the National Endowment for the Humanities, supplemented by a sabbatical leave and by research and typing grants from Boston University: much of the writing was done while I was an overseas Fellow at Churchill College of Cambridge University. I owe particular thanks to Sir William Hawthorne, Master of Churchill College, and to George and Zara Steiner for their kind hospitality to me during my college stay.

I am grateful to Harvard University Press for permission to quote both text and notes from *The Poems of John Keats,* edited by Jack Stillinger (1978): readers should consult that edition for bibliographical details encountered here in notes labeled "Stillinger's notes." Keats's letters are quoted by permission from the Harvard University Press edition by Hyder E. Rollins (1958). I quote from the *Collected Poems* of Wallace Stevens by kind permission of Alfred A. Knopf. The ambrotype of Fanny Brawne is reproduced by permission of the Curator of the Keats House and Museum in Hampstead; Keats's tracing of the Sosibios Vase is reproduced by permission of the Curator of the Keats-Shelley Memorial House in Rome. The two fragments from the Elgin marbles are reproduced by permission of the British Museum; Canova's Cupid and Psyche is reproduced by permission of the Louvre; and the death-mask of Keats is reproduced by permission of the National Portrait Gallery, England.

Finally, I wish to thank those close friends on whom my mind depends for daily sustenance, especially Marguerite Stewart, named in the dedication of this book. Many of my thoughts were hers first.

Contents

ILLUSTRATIONS

I deem
Truth the best Music.

— *Endymion,* IV, 772-773

They will explain themselves — as all poems
should do without any comment.

— Keats to his brother George,
2 January 1818: *Letters,* II, 21

Is *Criticism* a true thing?

— Keats's marginal comment to Dr. Johnson's
remarks on *As You Like It*

Introduction

Who found for me the grandeur of the ode,
Growing, like Atlas, stronger from its load?
To Charles Cowden Clarke, 62–63

THE odes of John Keats belong to that group of works in which the English language finds an ultimate embodiment. They will attract commentary in centuries beyond our own; each generation comes to them as Keats imagined generations of spectators coming to a Hellenic urn and finding, in turn, that it remained forever a friend to man. Our view of the odes has been shaped by several schools of criticism; before turning to what we know, I want to say in what spirit I add to this accumulation of learning and speculation.

Paul Valéry wrote that his way of translating Virgil's eclogues was to look at them "with the same critical eye as at French verse, my own or another's . . . Moreover, I thought that by thus imagining the still fluid state of a work now far beyond being merely completed, I could most feelingly share in the very life of that work, for a work dies by being completed. When a poem compels one to read it with passion, the reader feels he is *momentarily its author*, and *that is how he knows the poem is beautiful.*"[1] Although Valéry adds that this practice may appear "naive and presumptuous," he defends himself as the composing author of the emerging lines. For better or worse, I read under the same compulsion to "feel along the line" with the composing hand; in fact, I know no greater help to understanding a poem than writing it out in longhand with the illusion that one is composing it—deciding on this word rather than another, this arrangement of its masses rather than another, this prolonging, this digression, this cluster of senses, this closure.

This book, then, is a conjectural reconstruction of the odes as they are invented, imagined, put in sequence, and revised. Of course only a very few of the questions of their composition can be raised here. I quote Valéry again:

Think of everything that must go on inside a man who utters the smallest intelligible sentence, and then calculate all that is needed for a poem by Keats or Baudelaire to be formed on an empty page in front of the poet.

Think, too, that of all the arts, ours is perhaps that which co-ordinates the greatest number of independent parts or factors: sound, sense, the real and the imaginary, logic, syntax, and the double invention of content and form.[2]

Each set of relations in a poem invites comment; and sets of mutual relations between poems do the same. For the poet, the completion of one poem is the stimulus for the next; this is particularly true for poems in the same genre. But this stimulus is neither direct in its satisfactions nor easily perceptible from the finished work. I can scarcely hope that my conjectures here are all equally accurate; but to conjecture the reasons why the odes read as they do, and to con-jecture a sequence among them, is to offer them once more to the minds of others. Poems of course may be said to present themselves to all readers, just as musical scores present themselves to every eye. But (to borrow another idea from Valéry) just as the musical score requires an interpreter in the virtuoso or the conductor, so a text is of itself subject to "performance"; an inept presentation muddles a text just as it makes a score incoherent:

Thus a virtuoso is one who, by definition, gives life and real presence to what was merely a piece of writing at the mercy of all and sundry, and of their ignorance, awkwardness, or inadequate comprehension. The virtuoso makes the work flesh.[3]

How a work is best made flesh in commentary is not so clear as in the case of performance. But Valéry was speaking of both, criticiz-ing discussions of poetry that avoided the inner being of the work, its rigorous and fastidious choices, its succession of instinctive and conscious motions, its imperial control and its constant hazarding of disorder, its play of sensibility, its constant tension with tradi-tion. It is, often enough, only by seeing in a poem the choice that was *not* made that we understand the choice that has been made. The "erasures" that lie under the printed line are often deducible from previous poems or later ones, or from a parent poem in the tradition, or from the formula of common speech that is being avoided. If a study of Keats's authorial work in composing the odes offers, as I believe it does, new light on his mind and art, then a reading of the odes from this perspective cannot come amiss. It is generally agreed that classic literature can sustain many varying interpretations, since a work answers the questions that have been put to it, within the conceptual and contextual frame presupposed by those questions. I propose the conceptual frame of authorial choice and the contextual frame of the Keats canon (supplemented by some of Keats's sources).

The poet's first choice is the choice of theme: "I sought a theme and sought for it in vain; / I sought it daily for six weeks or so," says Yeats, allowing us a glimpse of the long searching for the first, and crucial, choice—the choice of subject (which may, of course, and often does, follow on the inchoate choice of rhythm, about which both Hopkins and Valéry have given testimony). It was in fact Keats's choice of subjects for the odes that originally perplexed me: why did he write on a quality (indolence), then to a goddess (Psyche), then to a nightingale, then on an urn, then on an emotion (melancholy), then to a season (autumn)? The usual critical accounts made these choices all seem relatively haphazard, depending on a nightingale in a plum tree or a visit to Haydon's studio or a walk to St. Cross; but I believe an artist's choices are never haphazard, though the occasioning motive may seem so.

The subsequent compositional choices (the angle of vision, the method of self-representation, the proportions of the treatment, the length and structural shape of the work, the level of diction, the registers of discourse, the manner of initiating, delaying, and resolving the work, and so on) all have metaphysical and ethical meaning for the artist, and therefore for us as well. It is a matter of some debate whether these meanings are at all recoverable. It seems to me a pragmatically useful critical hypothesis to suppose that they are—to suppose that we can reconstruct why Keats made the compositional choices that we see reflected in the final forms taken by the odes. Most artists have a limited "alphabet" of signification with which they work, and a rearrangement of familiar elements (like Cézanne's mountain or apples, or Chardin's kitchen vessels) creates a new signification. The primary context by which we appreciate the new arrangement is the whole body of work which preceded the creation of the new effort. My context for the odes is consequently all of Keats's previous work; but I believe that the most important context for each of the odes is the totality of the other odes, that the odes enjoy a special relation to each other, and that Keats, whenever he returned to the form of the ode, recalled his previous efforts and used every new ode as a way of commenting on earlier ones. We may say that each ode both deconstructs its predecessor(s) and consolidates it (or them). Each is a disavowal of a previous "solution"; but none could achieve its own momentary stability without the support of the antecedently constructed style which we now call "Keatsian." Keats was practicing a form of intrinsic self-criticism in continuing to shape the ode, time after time, to his own purposes; and this book, too, represents a form of intrinsic criticism by which "one poem proves another and the whole" (Wallace Stevens). The tale I tell here is the tale of a brief seven months in Keats's artistic life—a period extending from March to September 1819, from his first conception of the *Ode on Indolence* to his completion of the ode *To Autumn*. And I must add in honesty that the evolving tale I tell is not, strictly speaking, mine. It is, rather, one implicit in the work of Wallace Stevens.

As I became better and better acquainted with Stevens' poetry, I could hear behind many of his lines echoes of the odes of Keats. These echoes, too numerous to be related here,[4] haunted my ear when I went back to reread Keats. Under Stevens' implicit tutelage, I began to see the odes as a single long and heroic imaginative effort, in which Keats examined, in a sustained and deliberate and steadily more ambitious way, his own acute questions about the conditions for creativity, the forms art can take, the hierarchy of the fine arts (including the art of poetry), the hierarchy of genres within poetry, the relation of art to the order of nature, and the relation of art to human life and death. At the same time, Keats used the odes to investigate various formal problems: the implications of various structural shapes possible in lyric, from simple ones to the most complex polyphonic inventions; the formal result of emphasizing one rhetorical figure during the course of an ode; the effect of first-person, second-person, and impersonal self-representation. Keats was also, I believe, embodying in the odes a long inner conflict concerning the life of sensation and its proper language, and the life of thought and *its* proper language (whether allegorical, propositional, or representational). Finally, Keats was attempting in the odes "a system of salvation" (*Letters*, ii, 103) which had for him a religious seriousness.

Of course, many of these assertions are not new, and because Keats has attracted criticism more distinguished than that devoted to any other English author with the possible exception of Shakespeare, my gratitude to my predecessors goes beyond the usual bounds. I take for granted in what follows the many excellent books which have already been assimilated in our knowledge of Keats. The first generation of Keatsians were chiefly concerned with establishing Keats's texts and his biography — work which has continued into our day. We now have a reliable text for the poems, produced by Jack Stillinger. Two annotated texts, by Miriam Allott and John Barnard, have helped to disseminate knowledge of Keats's sources and his allusions to other poets (though many allusions remain to be noticed). Hyder Rollins' indispensable and monumental editions of Keats's letters and the papers of the Keats circle made possible the almost simultaneous writing of the three modern biographies — Walter Jackson Bate's critical biography, Aileen Ward's psychoanalytic life, and Robert Gittings' factually definitive account (all of these dependent on the often mistaken, idiosyncratic, but valuable earlier biographies, including that of Amy Lowell, whose bequest formed the nucleus of the Keats collection in the Houghton Library of Harvard University).

The story of Keats criticism is a complicated one, intertwined with the history of moral opinions of Keats. The notion of the ill-educated and even immoral Keats produced a form of patronizing criticism not absent even from Arnold; one of Amy Lowell's very American aims in writing her biography was to establish Keats as a greater writer (and a nobler man) than he had been thought by British critics suspicious of a writer who had not been university-trained and whose class origins were obscure. The argument for Keats as a thinker and religious guide distracted criticism for a long time. Middleton Murry's intense paraphrases took almost no notice of Keatsian genres or formal literary structures; and subsequent books (like Thorpe's *The Mind of John Keats*) rested, too, on the necessary defense of Keats as a poet of philosophical depth and substantial reading. Subsequent classic studies of Keats—most of them including long passages on the odes—have been more specialized, but they continue a thematic emphasis, adding (as the twentieth century advanced) the psychological to the philosophical, and concerning themselves with various well-defined problems: Keats's relation to art and artworks (Ian Jack); to the organic world of growth and form (Blackstone); to Romanticism (Bloom in *The Visionary Company* and de Man in his introduction to his *Selected Keats*); to religion (Ryan and Sharp); to the social world of manners illumined by the *Letters* (Ricks); to the ideas of his time about sensation, thought, and essence (Sperry); to metaphysical speculation (Wasserman); to myth (Evert); to the use of symbols for dialectic (Perkins); to metamorphosis (Gradman); and so on. The books which discuss poetic technique (Ridley, and Bate's *Stylistic Development of Keats*) do so on the minute levels of prosody and stanza form, rather than on the macroscopic levels of genre, proportion, and rhetoric.

One book very valuable to me—John Jones's *John Keats's Dream of Truth*—has approached Keats phenomenologically, examining his poetry of sensation in terms of its extraordinary empathetic power, and the struggle of this diction of sensation with Keats's "dream" of truth. No one interested, as I am, in Keats's language in its smallest units of phrasing can have failed to be influenced by Jones's uncanny grasp of Keats's way of feeling and seeing, and by his flexible shaping of an intellectual way of examining such elusive phenomena. Jones brilliantly emphasizes Keats's successes in the vein of sensation; I wish to emphasize Keats's success in the domain of poetic "thinking"—though by "thinking" in Keats I mean ultimately the architectural ordering of sensation in language. I must quote Valéry again:

> [It is not] by absence of mind and dreaming that one can impose on speech such precious and rare arrangements. The true condition of a true poet is as distinct as possible from the state of dreaming. I see in

it only willed inquiry, suppleness of thought, the soul's assent to exquisite constraints, and the perpetual triumph of sacrifice.

It is the very one who wants to write down his dream who is obliged to be extremely wide awake . . .

Whoever says exactness and style invokes the opposite of a dream; whoever meets these in a work must presuppose in its author all the labor and time he needed to resist the permanent dissipation of his thoughts . . . And the more restless and fugitive the prey one covets, the more presence of mind and power of will one needs to make it eternally present in its eternally fleeting aspect.[5]

It may be, as Jones argues, that for most of his life Keats was a better poet of sensation than of thought, in the usual meanings of those words; but Jones is more sympathetic to even the worst of Keats's attempts to grasp the infeeling of a moment than he is to Keats's attempts at architectonics. I should like to think that I trace in this book Keats's steps toward a poetry of thought with even a fraction of Jones's conclusive success in revealing to us Keats's explorations on the path of sensation.

There are three critics who have pursued lines of inquiry somewhat cognate to my own here. John Holloway, in his brief essay in *The Charted Mirror* on the odes of Keats, first suggested that the odes make up "a unified sequence"; but Holloway then treated the odes as expressions of one given mood, rather than as a sequence in which a later ode is a development of, or a contradiction of, or a consolidation of, former ones. Stuart Sperry (in *Keats the Poet*) says rightly that the odes have generally been read individually, and that "recent attempts to establish a basis for reading the odes as a group, for understanding the ways in which they interrelate with and qualify each other, have never been successful as individual readings" (p. 242). Sperry's own helpful but brief essay on the odes suggests that we should read them as Keats's greatest embodiment of a sense of irony and negative capability. Sperry treats chiefly the psychological attitudes he finds in the odes, and dwells on thematic detail; he is concerned, too, with what succeeds and what does not. I am more concerned with what Keats was attempting to embody and construct, and with what variety of technical means, than with general thematics or with local success or failure. Sperry does not discuss the reasons for the order of the varying topics of the odes, and by placing *Indolence* last he loses, to my mind, the appearance of a convincing sequence. He agrees (wrongly, I think) with Stillinger in positing a relatively general shape for all the odes—a shape of flight into transcendence and a descent from it—though Sperry sees the descent as one into irony rather than as one into ordinary daily reality (Stillinger's version). The third critic who has anticipated me to some degree is Gillian Beer, who in a brief article suggests that the odes concern themselves to some extent with the fine arts, and that the nightingale ode in particular is Keats's meditation on the art of music. In this we agree; but her article cannot go on to suggest how the idea might be developed.[6]

What has been neglected in the long critical emphasis on Keats's thoughts and feelings is (though it may seem odd to say so) a study of Keats as a poet. By this I mean the study of Keats as a maker of inexpressibly complex articulations of language in architectural form, works in which "the intention of making" controls what is said, works "in which the play of figures contain[s] the reality of the subject."[7] No writer on Keats neglects Keatsian imagery; but usually the images are considered for their thematic import, rather than as part of a network of combinatorial powers engaged in a constantly shifting set of relations. I believe that the Keatsian image-system is a compact (if luxurious) one, and that it is helpful to describe its basic elements and to see these elements in their various metamorphoses. To say, for instance, that the gardener Fancy, the nightingale, and the dead sculptor of the urn are all metamorphoses of a single element (the creative artist), or to say that the wine in *Nightingale*, the grape of Joy in *Melancholy*, and the last drops of apple juice in *Autumn* are transmutations of that elixir which also appears (as transparent juice) in *The Fall of Hyperion*, helps in understanding the way Keats's imagination went to work. Each ode is generated out of previous odes in part by image-transformations of this sort; we know where we are when we see what images Keats has chosen to transform, and into what new shapes he casts them.

Keats's language is so various that it exacts from us a division into sublanguages. Those I have taken up include the language of classical mythology, the language of eighteenth-century allegory, the language of architectural form, and the language of natural sensation. I believe Keats always had reasons for using or suppressing one or the other of these languages. The profound work of Geoffrey Hartman on eighteenth-century allegorical poetry takes this question much further than I can take it with Keats. Hartman's two revelatory articles (on *The Fall of Hyperion* and on the autumn ode) consider Keats's incorporation of and original departures from the technique of allegorical address in the epic and the ode.[8] But what I am chiefly interested in is Keats's authorial decision when to use, and for what reason to drop, the eighteenth-century allegorizing diction. The odes change their registers of diction so often (and always to some purpose) that these changes must solicit our questions.

The rhetorical figures that Keats used with great deliberateness in the odes can be described in many ways, and I have only touched the surface of an elaborate problem in deciding to propose here that each ode is governed by, even constituted by, one figure or trope (not necessarily a classical one). When I say, for instance, that reduplication is the constitutive trope of the *Ode to Psyche*, I do not mean that other tropes do not occur in the ode in subordinate roles; I simply mean that in *Psyche* things keep being reduplicated, thematically and verbally, and that it helps us to see the shape of the ode if we perceive its recurrent governing figure. These figures can be metaphorical (as in this case), or grammatical (the constitutive figure of the *Urn*, as I see it, is interrogation; it is questions that keep recurring in that ode, and that organize its shape), or syntactic (the governing figure of *Autumn* is enumeration, the figure of lists). Rough as such descriptions are, I believe they are useful. It is wrong to exact from heuristic notions a precision they cannot possess; I offer the notion of constitutive tropes only as something I myself find illuminating as a way into the poems. I believe that such figures have formal meaning (as reduplication implies a confidence in replicability; as interrogation is the formal equivalent of intellectual perplexity; as enumeration implies a sense of plenitude). The meaning of any ode depends not only on its transmutations of elemental images, but also on its registers of diction and the formally conveyed meaning of its governing figure.

And, finally, the meaning of an ode by Keats depends on what is conveyed by its architectonics, what I call in this book its shape. Stillinger postulates, as I have said, a single "up-down" shape for all the odes; his graph represents a peak coming somewhere between a low beginning and a low end. In a variant on this form, Sperry speaks of the "parabola-shape" of the odes. I think, in contrast to this simple model, that each ode has a different shape; and if there is any single part of this book that I feel confident about, it is the discussions of the structures of the odes and of their appropriateness to the matter of each ode and to its view of art. These discussions lead to the end point of the book: Keats's powerful discovery, in the ode *To Autumn*, of a form of structural polyphony, in which several structural forms — each one autonomous, each one pregnant with meaning, each one continued for the full length of the ode — overlap in a palimpsest of effects. Valéry draws the distinction between this supreme achievement and a simpler kind of shape:

> In lyrical poetry, to be sure, we find numerous examples of a development suggesting a simple figure, a perceptible curve. But the types are always very elementary.
> When I speak of composition, I have in mind poems in which an attempt is made to equal the masterly complexity of music by introducing "harmonic" relationships, symmetries, contrasts, correspondences, etc., between their parts.[9]

All of these structural shapes, like all figures, convey formal meaning. We are accustomed, perhaps, to shapes of visionary flight and homeward return of the sort mentioned by Stillinger and Sperry; we are equally familiar with shapes that decline from morning to night, or youth to age. But such shapes are only the most elementary ones, as Valéry says; and there are many others deserving of notice, as I hope to show. In calling attention, then, to Keats's transmutations of imagery, purposeful sequence of subjects, alterations of diction, and inventions of structural shapes, I hope I will have enlarged our knowledge of Keats's poetic means. And in order not to treat everything at once, I have usually, in the chapters that follow, outlined first the importance of the subject of the given ode to Keats, its place in the sequence, and its structural shape and constitutive trope; only then do I go back to consider more minutely the use of language and local effects of syntax or proportion.

But finally, of course, in treating the odes as a sequence (interpolating a brief chapter on Moneta's face as the transition without which the passage from the goddess Melancholy to the goddess Autumn cannot be seen clearly), I wish to reflect on their human meaning and what they can tell us about Keats's view of our human predicament and his own predicament as an artist. The complexity of Keats's reflective and constructive acts is now generally admitted; but that complexity has not yet been entirely seen, locally, in the phrases of the odes. The generally received readings of the odes are of course generally true, more or less: we all know now, thanks to a long tradition of criticism, the outlines of Keats's concerns. But I think we have not yet fully seen Keats's views on art; and there I hope to correct some misperceptions of the two central odes, *Nightingale* and *Urn*, which I see as meditations, respectively, on the nonrepresentational art of music and the representational art of sculpture. I believe the odes contain Keats's controlled experiments with sensation: he suppressed all senses in *Psyche*, he reserved one sense each (suppressing all others) for *Nightingale* and *Urn*, he allowed the "lower senses" to enter in *Melancholy*, and he reintegrated the complex of sensation in *Autumn*. I suggest as well that all the objects of veneration in the odes are female divinities (Leon Waldoff has been treating the same assertion from a psychoanalytical perspective),[10] and that the passage from the youthful "demon Poesy" to the reaper Autumn is an important one in Keats's conceptual progress.

The readings offered here are entirely interdependent. The ones that most dispute the common readings are those on *Nightingale*, *Urn*, and *Autumn* (though of course they necessarily comment on many features remarked by others). The polemic impulse from which this book began arose when I read Allen Tate's judgment that the ode *To Autumn* "is a very nearly perfect piece of style but it has little to say."[11] I thought *To Autumn* said everything there was to say. It was clear to me then that my understanding of how a poem "says" was different from Tate's. His understanding was propositional; he liked the *Ode to a Nightingale* because it "at least tries

to say everything that poetry can say." Tate did not entirely trust
Keats's "pictorial" nature (as he called it).

But it was clear to me that *To Autumn* "said" things by means of
what I then thought of as collocation—what Keats called (when he
praised it in Milton) "stationing." Somewhat later I came to see
that the autumn ode "said" things also by the activities of its imagery, by its overlapping structures, and by its exquisite explorations of suggestive diction. My entire effort here may be taken as an
argument against Tate's way of seeing *To Autumn*. Paraphrase of
the ode's content remains bald without consideration of its means.
But these means can be determined only contextually (and no poem
in the Keats canon has more contexts than this ode). We can only
know what the presence of fruit, for instance, signifies in the
autumn ode when we realize how absolutely Keats had forbidden
the presence of anything but flowers in the first four odes, and how
great a step he had taken in the submission to reality in introducing,
in the *Ode on Melancholy*, Joy's grape, which is nonetheless permitted to burst gratifyingly on the palate; the fruit in *Autumn*,
however, ascetically remains unconsumed, though crushed out of
its former being. Similarly, we only know what "seeking abroad"
means in the autumn ode when we recall how, until that moment,
Keats had perpetually sheltered himself in bowers or sanctuaries.
The admitting of fruit, on the one hand, and the resolve to enter
the open fields of the reaped furrow, on the other, thus become
heroic compositional choices, representing respectively the moral
admission of ineluctable sacrificial process and the generous adop-
tion of the whole world—not a sequestered portion of it—as the
territory of growth and art.

These are only instances chosen at random. Ideally, the reader of
this book will have, by the last chapter, a sense garnered from
previous chapters of the burden borne by every word in the final
ode. The deliberateness of Keats's compositional work in this ode,
and his serenely powerful orchestration of all his means, bring to a
classic perfection his sustained engagement with the genre of the
ode, in a great crystallization of culture and language. His appren-
ticeship to the form, as revealed in the sequence of the odes, bore a
fruit beyond what even he himself could have hoped.

I

Stirring Shades and Baffled Beams: The *Ode on Indolence*

This ardent listlessness.

Endymion, I, 825

How happy is such a 'voyage of conception,' what delicious diligent Indolence! A doze upon a Sofa does not hinder it, and a nap upon Clover engenders ethereal finger-pointings.

Letters, I, 231

In this state of effeminacy the fibres of the brain are relaxed in common with the rest of the body, and to such a happy degree that pleasure has no show of enticement and pain no unbearable frown. Neither Poetry, nor Ambition, nor Love have any alertness of countenance as they pass by me: they seem rather like three figures on a greek vase—a Man and two women—whom no one but myself could distinguish in their disguisement. This is the only happiness; and is a rare instance of advantage in the body overpowering the Mind.

Letters, II, 78–79: 19 March 1819

By John Keats.

One morn before me were three figures seen,
  With bowed necks, and joined hands, side-faced;
And one behind the other stepp'd serene,
In placid sandals, and in white robes graced.
       — *Ode on Indolence*, 1-4

Ode on Indolence

"They toil not, neither do they spin."

One morn before me were three figures seen,
  With bowed necks, and joined hands, side-faced;
And one behind the other stepp'd serene,
  In placid sandals, and in white robes graced:
They pass'd, like figures on a marble urn,
  When shifted round to see the other side;
    They came again; as when the urn once more
Is shifted round, the first seen shades return;
  And they were strange to me, as may betide
    With vases, to one deep in Phidian lore.

How is it, shadows, that I knew ye not?
  How came ye muffled in so hush a masque?
Was it a silent deep-disguised plot
  To steal away, and leave without a task
My idle days? Ripe was the drowsy hour;
  The blissful cloud of summer-indolence
    Benumb'd my eyes; my pulse grew less and less;
Pain had no sting, and pleasure's wreath no flower.
  O, why did ye not melt, and leave my sense
    Unhaunted quite of all but—nothingness?

A third time pass'd they by, and, passing, turn'd
  Each one the face a moment whiles to me;
Then faded, and to follow them I burn'd
  And ached for wings, because I knew the three:
The first was a fair maid, and Love her name;
  The second was Ambition, pale of cheek,
    And ever watchful with fatigued eye;
The last, whom I love more, the more of blame
  Is heap'd upon her, maiden most unmeek,—
    I knew to be my demon Poesy.

They faded, and, forsooth! I wanted wings:
  O folly! What is Love? and where is it?
And for that poor Ambition—it springs
  From a man's little heart's short fever-fit;
For Poesy!—no,—she has not a joy,—
  At least for me,—so sweet as drowsy noons,
    And evenings steep'd in honied indolence;
O, for an age so shelter'd from annoy,
  That I may never know how change the moons,
    Or hear the voice of busy common-sense!

A third time came they by:—alas! wherefore?
  My sleep had been embroider'd with dim dreams;
My soul had been a lawn besprinkled o'er
  With flowers, and stirring shades, and baffled beams:
The morn was clouded, but no shower fell,
  Though in her lids hung the sweet tears of May;
    The open casement press'd a new-leaved vine,
  Let in the budding warmth and throstle's lay;
O shadows! 'twas a time to bid farewell!
    Upon your skirts had fallen no tears of mine.

So, ye three ghosts, adieu! Ye cannot raise
  My head cool-bedded in the flowery grass;
For I would not be dieted with praise,
  A pet-lamb in a sentimental farce!
Fade softly from my eyes, and be once more
  In masque-like figures on the dreamy urn;
    Farewell! I yet have visions for the night,
And for the day faint visions there is store;
    Vanish, ye phantoms, from my idle spright,
  Into the clouds, and never more return![1]

THE *Ode on Indolence*, which Keats left unpublished, is, as Blackstone says, the seminal poem for the other great odes.[2] Though it was written down as late as May, perhaps just before the *Ode on a Grecian Urn*, since they share the same stanza (used afterward for the *Ode on Melancholy*), the experience which gave rise to it is related in March, in the 19 March section of Keats's journal-letter of 14 February–3 May 1819. The letter contains the imagery of the ode in little:

> This morning I am in a sort of temper indolent and supremely careless: I long after a stanza or two of Thompson's Castle of indolence . . . Neither Poetry, nor Ambition, nor Love have any alertness of countenance as they pass by me: they seem rather like three figures on a greek vase—a Man and two women—whom no one but myself could distinguish in their disguisement.
> (*Letters*, II, 78–79)

Keats later in the spring so reimagines himself into his March experience that he relives it among "the sweet tears of May"; nevertheless, the core of the ode remains his lassitude in March, his unwillingness to be roused out of his mysterious indolence by the three motives—Love, Ambition, and Poetry—which pass before him in Greek disguise.[3]

The uneasy structure of *Indolence* enabled Charles Brown, copying probably from loose sheets, to propose an incorrect sequence for its stanzas, which he subsequently corrected; but only a poem peculiarly static could have offered the possibility of such a mistake. In fact, the poem seems to make no apparent progress at all; as it begins, Keats is indolent; as it ends, he is indolent; the visit of the disturbing figures seems to have left him unchanged, an embryonic poet refusing to be born, nestled in the womb of preconscious existence.

The *Ode on Indolence*, however, offers two conflicting structural shapes to our inspection: the first, attributable to the speaker, might properly be called by the Yeatsian name of vacillation; the second, a stronger shape of steady recurrence, attributable to the figures, counters the first. Though the ode does record a vacillation of Keatsian mood, ranging from languor to yearning, from self-reproach to self-indulgence (reinforced, as we shall see later, by its language), the stronger shape in the poem is the shape of recurrent return, as the three sculptural allegorical figures again and again intrude upon the varying Keatsian dream. In some ways the poem never recovers — never wishes to recover — from its sight of that spacious and unhurried Greek procession which entirely subdues the poet to its plastic grace:

> One morn before me were three figures seen,
>   With bowed necks, and joined hands, side-faced;
> And one behind the other stepp'd serene,
>   In placid sandals, and in white robes graced:
> They pass'd, like figures on a marble urn,
>   When shifted round to see the other side;
>   They came again; as when the urn once more
> Is shifted round, the first seen shades return;
>   And they were strange to me, as may betide
>   With vases, to one deep in Phidian lore.

Everything in the opening stanza reinforces the persistence and power of these art-figures, who so resemble the three Graces. They come not alone but companioned; their hands are joined in a unity of self-presentation; their movements are done in unison; they are dressed identically; at first sight they even seem identical as to sex. The theme of return is insisted on: "One behind the other *stepped* . . . / They *passed* . . . / They *came again*; as when . . . *once more* / . . . the *first* seen shades *return*." The poem continues to repeat this magic hovering of appearance and return in several rhetorical ways — by addressing the figures; by repeating their returns; by enumerating them (once in presence, once in absence) as Love, Ambition, and Poesy; by twice bidding them farewell; by entreating them to fade; by adjuring them to vanish. The whole poem is constructed upon their steady reappearances; as I have said, they make it, structurally speaking, a poem of recurrence.

Though Keats's attitude toward these presences changes with his changing epithets for them (they are to him first "figures," then "shadows," next "ghosts," and finally "phantoms"), they remain the same steady Greek forms, becoming, as they finally reveal their countenances to Keats, creations like Wallace Stevens' hidalgo on the stair, "a hatching that stared and demanded an answering look." Though begged by the poet to return to their places on the urn, though commanded to vanish into the clouds, they show no inclination to disappear or to discontinue their haunting of the indolent visionary.

Keats here deliberately presents himself, as he does in *Psyche*, *Nightingale*, and *Urn*, as a poet. In this ode he speaks of his demon Poesy; in the others he refers to his "tuneless numbers," his "mused rhyme," and more generally in the *Urn* to "our rhyme." In *Indolence* the conflict between the claims of Poesy (accompanied by its motive, Ambition, and its subject, Love) and Keats's almost physical need for "indolence" seems insoluble. The figures, in their determination, are unpreventable and ungovernable, and cause recurrent agitation by each of their comings; and yet the claims of "indolence" are indisputable, and stubbornly reassert themselves against every reappearance of the Greek figures.

It is with the wisdom of hindsight—because we have read *Nightingale* and *Urn*—that we can see this conflict between form and indolence as if it were a battle between the two later odes. "Indolence" speaks with the tranced voice of the *Ode to a Nightingale*; the Greek figures, in their mute glance, evoke the language of the *Urn*; the one is the voice of the bower, the other the voice of the artifact. There is, of course, a third voice in *Indolence*—the voice which, awakened out of the bower and repudiating Greek gravity, speaks in the worldly-wise tones we associate with portions of *Lamia*:

> O folly! What is Love? and where is it?
> And for that poor Ambition—it springs
> From a man's little heart's short fever-fit.

We hear this affectedly cynical voice once more in *Nightingale*: "The fancy cannot cheat so well / As she is fam'd to do, deceiving elf." Keats rejected these defensive tones as unworthy in the later odes, *Urn* and *Autumn*; there, bitterness and regret, the emotions underlying those cynical expressions, are allowed their proper undeflected voice, in the remarks on human passion and its aftermath in the one, and in the nostalgia for the songs of spring in the other.

In *Indolence*, then, Keats tries the superposition of one structural shape on another; over the vacillating shape of the various resistances and yieldings of indolence to form, he places the steady recurrent shape of the rhythmic return of the Greek figures. Harold Bloom says very well that the three figures resembling the Graces are in fact Keats's Fates; we may therefore name the two rhythms as the rhythm of Fate superimposed on that of will. Each persists throughout the poem; but, as I have said, the inexplicable, prior, and beautiful appearance, at the opening of the poem, of the rhythm of Fate—for all the rebelliousness subsequently mustered against it—makes that rhythm in reality the eventual victor, or rather a victor whose eventual victory we find ourselves envisaging as the poem ends.

And yet—also with the wisdom of hindsight—we know that Keats had reason to prolong his state full of "visions for the night, / And for the day faint visions" (he changed the latter phrase to "waking dream" in *Nightingale*). It was during these waking trances and embowered sleeps that his powerful assimilations and creations first took on body and form. His hour of rendezvous with the urn has not yet come, he senses, and he wards it off, profitably, from March to May. The gestating indolence he insists on refuses any subjection to time; he is suspended in dream, as the sweet tears of May (later to fall in a weeping shower in *Melancholy*) remain suspended in cloud in the sky. The season does not advance; he does not stir. The silent but urgent imperatives for change—Ambition, Love, and Poesy—challenge his immobility: his defensive impulse will be, in subsequent poems, to immobilize them in return, placing immobile Love in the center of his *Ode to Psyche*, and immobile Love and Poesy at the center of the *Urn*.

In this ode, then, we see the unwilling fancy of the artist facing at once its mental and emotional stimuli and its eventual sculptural artifact. The sculptural figures long to take on life, but are banished—back to the dreamy urn or up to the clouds, it scarcely matters—for the time being. The three spirits, almost indistinguishable each from the other, represent the principal *dramatis personae* of *Endymion* replicated in outline: the ambitious youth flanked by two maidens, one Love, the other Poesy, must recall to us Endymion placed between the Indian Maid and Cynthia. (Keats's letter had referred to the figures as "a Man and two women": in the ode Love and Poesy are clearly female, while Ambition is presumably male.) In short, the Fates here are Keats's doubling of his own dilemma of vocation already debated in *Endymion*, and the poem represents a dialogue of the embryonic, unformed, languorous, dreaming poetic self with its later envisaged incarnation in accomplished form.

Keats will never again incarnate form, or figures to be venerated, as an allegorical trinity. Ambition occurs, but incorporated into the speaker's own natural self, in *The Fall of Hyperion*; Love and Poesy are coupled as Cupid and Psyche in the *Ode to Psyche*, which follows in inspiration the *Ode on Indolence*. The two sculptural figures in *Psyche* are no longer allegorical representations of the poet's faculties for love and poesy, but rather have taken on separate mythological existence, an existence which for Cupid lapses somewhat at the end (where the poet seems to prepare to substitute himself for the god) but which is allowed throughout to Psyche. As a pagan goddess, Psyche preexisted, in the realm of mythology, her poet, and does not depend on him for her essence, as do the Love, Ambition, and Poesy of *Indolence*. Keats's wish for an object of worship external to himself dictates several of his other later objects, henceforth single ones, of veneration—a bird, an urn, a season. Such choices, which go beyond an interest solely in an allegorical psychology of creation or in a mythological reading of existence, point, as I hope to show later, to Keats's interest in artifact, audience, and medium.

But in the *Ode on Indolence*, the speaker is the indolent, inward-turned Keats still in his pastoral chrysalis, projecting onto an urn-*Doppelgänger* his internalized ambition, love, and poesy. The urn-double is unaffected by the expostulations of the protesting speaker:

its figures return ever the same, ever poised, rhythmic, imperturbable, pregnant with meaning, placid, serene. In the top of sovereignty, these figures envisage all circumstance and remain unchanged under Keats's flurry of salutation, query, repudiation, and satire; their single gesture, a reproachful one, is to turn their profiles full-face and force his acknowledgment of their acquaintance. And yet, in spite of the placidity of their circling, the figures are in themselves not entirely placid; pale-cheeked Ambition betrays the fatigue of long vigils (a link forward to Autumn's patient watching), and the demon Poesy is "most unmeek." One might say that, like a poem, they manifest recurrence of rhythm while encompassing interior agitation. In this dialogue of Keats's mind with itself, suffering finds no vent in action.

The poem turns on the visual pun between "idle" and "indolence." In the severe judgment of the expectant figures, Keats may be said to have an "idle spright"; in his own defensive judgment, he is merely steeped in summer "indolence." He wonders, seeing himself as a lily of the field, whether the emphasis of the figures on a "task" is not merely the Philistine advice of "busy common-sense." Conversely, in an apprehensive twinge of self-reproach, he even suspects them of deliberately muffling themselves up so that they might abandon him to his self-indulgence; he imagines them stealing away with hushed steps so as—in their fancied plot—to leave his "idle" days without a task to occupy them.

The preliminary passings of the figures allow such speculation. When the spirits seem not to be noticing him, Keats is piqued; when they *do* notice him, he feels—after a moment of wild yearning after them—that they have torn him from his obscurely necessary reverie. As we notice now the underlying shape—what I have called the shape of vacillation underlying the shape of figure-recurrence— the first thing we realize is that the language of Keats's indolence takes two forms, as he rebukes the soliciting figures: we may call these forms of language, for convenience, the *Nightingale*-form and the *Psyche*-form. The first speaks in terms of a swoon, a numbness, and an insensibility; it sounds like a conflation of the opening drowsy numbness of the nightingale ode with its subsequent blind sinking toward death:

Ripe was the drowsy hour;
The blissful cloud of summer-indolence
Benumb'd my eyes; my pulse grew less and less;
Pain had no sting, and pleasure's wreath no flower.
O, why did ye not melt, and leave my sense
Unhaunted quite of all but—nothingness?

In this mood, Keats praises "drowsy noons, / And evenings steep'd in honied indolence."

If this first exploration of indolence borrows the language of death, the second, in *Psyche*-language, borrows that of birth. The sleep, no longer one of oblivion, is instead one of rich dreams, growing flowers, a chiaroscuro of light and shade, all that "information (primitive sense)," as Keats called it in his last letter (*Letters* II, 360), taking place in a landscape of incipient emotion, open casements, new-leaved vines, budding warmth, and a singing thrush. The language of the open casement and the budding warmth is the language of *Psyche*, just as Keats's self-stationing, his head "cool-bedded in the flowery grass," resembles his stationing of Cupid and Psyche, "couched side by side / In deepest grass . . . / 'Mid hush'd, cool-rooted flowers." The happy casement in *Psyche*, open to let the warm Love in, will eventually become in *Nightingale* the magic casements framing no human figures, and opening on things perilous and forlorn; but here, in *Indolence*, casements are still inviting, opening to press a leafy vine—the vine not yet, as it will be later, loaded and blessed with fruit, but rather full of pure potentiality. The first, benumbed, variety of indolence is principally sketched from thoughts of death, insensibility, and dissolution; but the second, creative, indolence draws its imagery from thoughts of birth, humidity, emergence, and illumination. The second indolence is briefly anticipated in the opening adjectives of the first—"ripe" was the drowsy hour, "blissful" was the cloud; but then numbness and blankness supervene, and it is only later that the budding creative indolence is explored.

There are, in short, two indolent Keatses and one ambitious one in this poem. The first indolent one wishes to obliterate sensation and the senses, removing at one gesture both the sting of pain (and even the sting of death, whence he draws the phrase "pain's sting," we might guess, given the ode's biblical epigraph) and the flower of pleasure. But the second indolent Keats is overbrimmed with inner and outer sensations of the most exquisite sort, mixing the apprehension of May's tears with the luxuriating in flowers, budding warmth, light and shade, and the poetry of birdsong. The third Keats—the ambitious lover and aspiring poet—disturbs the repose of both his indolent selves, distracting the one from oblivion and the other from sensation and reverie. Each "indolent" objection to the admonitory figures is fully and satisfyingly voiced; but we see that the linked figures, beautiful as they are, have not yet found for themselves a language equal to the "indolent" poetry of sheathed sensation that in a single breath ensconces delicious feeling and embroidered dreams:

> My sleep had been embroider'd with dim dreams;
> My soul had been a lawn besprinkled o'er
>   With flowers, and stirring shades, and baffled beams:
> The morn was clouded, but no shower fell,
>   Though in her lids hung the sweet tears of May;
>   The open casement press'd a new-leaved vine,
>   Let in the budding warmth and throstle's lay.

Keats speaks so easily here of the fertile soul, its dreamy sleep and its germinating ground, intimate with such completions and interminglings, that the separate, austere, discarnate urn-figures can scarcely seem an intimate part of that soul or of its contents.

The "moral" argument of the ode pretends to see poetic ambition as a temptation toward praise, love as a temptation to sentimentality: "I would not be dieted with praise, / A pet-lamb in a sentimental farce!" But the weakness of the satiric writing betrays Keats's inability to dismiss the true and justified sense of his own genius, and the intensity of his own passionate temperament. What was preventing his acquiescence in the demands of the figures was—though he could scarcely have known it in March—the incompleteness of those early dreams (including this dream of a rather unimaginatively decorated urn) which would yield, in a few weeks, the great odes.

If we recapitulate Keats's state of feeling in March (assuming that the ode is a reconstruction of his mind at the time), we find that his most powerful feelings were those of rapturous sensations both mental and physical, which took the form of sensing things beginning and about to happen—flowers budding, shades stirring, sunbeams seeking a path, tears about to fall, opening windows, bare vines growing green, warmth, birdsong, the vague shapes of night visions and waking dreams in daytime. These feelings are combated by an unwillingness to feel such new stirrings, a wish to sink into insensibility (prompted, we might suppose, by the illness of Tom Keats and his death a few months earlier on 1 December).[4] Keats is also tempted to repudiate as worthless all his dearest desires—for fame, for love, for poetry; and yet he feels a steady and unyielding pursuit of his attention by his poetic genius, which will not be denied no matter how often he refuses its solicitations and banishes it (together with all stirrings of ambition and love) from his presence. He senses his poetic genius as another self, moving in mysterious and separate recurrences quite without reference to earthly time, displaying always a dignity and serenity of purpose, and emerging somehow from the noblest examples of creation he had seen, the Phidian marbles. He feels irrepressibly his own vocation as artificer, worker in a medium, one whose destined creations have come from their matrix (here, from an as yet unrealized "dreamy" urn) to rebuke their creator for not yet having created them. They bear, for that reason, overtones of the haunting ghost of old Hamlet rebuking his son for not yet having entered upon action.

In spite of the beauty of the rich language of open casements, cloud-tears, dreams, a bird's "lay," and vegetative growth—a garden of Adonis for the odes later conceived—the single most memorable moment in *Indolence* comes, surprisingly, in the poet's penitent "How is it, shadows, that I knew ye not?" The pang of that self-address (since the qualities Keats "knew not" were his own) is the kernel of feeling from which the whole ode originates, representing the pain of the accusatory encounter which is the subject of the ode, and the pain that the poet feels at his own ignorance in the encounter. He did not know his own soul, not when it appeared before him in that strange trio conjoining a processional rhythm with maiden fairness, fatigued eye, pallid cheek, and demonic fancy. Not to know one's own soul is for Keats the most mortal of lapses; he cannot believe that he has not recognized himself in this objectified vision. It becomes clear in the course of the ode that he has not known the shadows because he did not wish to know them, and this refusal had been prompted on the one hand by an exhausted shrinking from all further experience, painful and pleasurable alike, and on the other by an inchoate, if deeply felt, need for a longer time of budding and ripening. The hint of deathliness in the three figures, as they are evoked by the successively more disembodied names of shadows, ghosts, and phantoms, points to the degree to which sensual life must be sacrificed in being mediated into art-figuration; but Keats is not yet willing to explore his instinct for the inseparability of creation and sacrifice.

If we turn to look more closely at the language of the ode, we see that it uneasily adopts at least four modes of speech: narration of a past event to a presumed reader ("One morn before me were three figures seen"); recollection of the past event in a dreamy self-reverie ("Ripe was the drowsy hour"); an address (in the present tense) to the figures seen in the past ("How *is* it, shadows, that I *knew* ye not?"); and agitated worldly interpolation, occurring in the latter half of the poem only ("O folly! What is Love? and where is it?"). There is a marked unsettling of consciousness as Keats passes from one form of speech to the other. It may be most visible in the affected Byronic dismissal of Love and Ambition, but it is no less disturbing, if better managed, in the transitions from narration to recollection, from recollection to direct address, and so on. The poem exhibits Keats's problems in composition, problems occasioned by a wish to be fair, at one and the same time, to all sides of his nature and his art. Once he has decided on the visionary *donnée* of the poem, he feels compelled to explain his ghostly procession to those not so privileged, thus generating the heavy-handed narration of the ode, so much more swiftly accomplished in its original allegorical and nonvisionary form in the journal-letter. In the letter he feels no obligation to claim any status as seer or sage; but to authenticate in the poem both his vision and his original bafflement, he feels it necessary to establish his *bona fides* as an interpreter of

Greek figures (he is learned, he tells his reader, in statues, but has not yet progressed beyond "Phidian" lore to an expertise with vase conventions). All this narration and explanation is incurred for the benefit of a putative listener to Keats's flowery tale, since Keats would not need to tell himself again how many times the figures passed, or why he did not recognize the iconography of vase decoration, or what his credentials in interpretation might be.

Quite another motive from the explanatory one lies behind the powerful and sensual recreation of the drowsy hour, the most successful "writing"—in the limited sense of "intense, magical, and profound use of language"—in the poem. It will be my aim in these chapters to insist on a larger sense of "writing" in Keats—a sense which will include the grander issues of poetic conceptualization and architectonics as well as "magical" language—but every reader's first response to Keats (and many readers' final response) rests on judgments of his success or failure at the level of intensity or adequacy of language at any given instant, and on that alone. At any given instant, however, besides finding the *mot juste*, Keats is also deciding on a means of conceptualization (as, here, he has decided for three figures, which change conceptually from figures to phantoms, and from profiled figures to full-face figures); and at any given instant, he is also deciding how to continue, delay, or complete the structure of his poem (here, by the device of successive apparitions). The invention of appropriate language, in short, is only one of many inventions. Two others, invention of concept and invention of structure, are equally important in the odes, even if they have so far, by comparison to "writing" *tout court*, been comparatively neglected in criticism.

Since the most adequate language Keats finds in *Indolence* is the language for private re-creation of the scene of indolence (the language of private memory and reverie, not directed to an audience), I take it as axiomatic that the kernel of the poem, as a crystallization of accomplished feeling, lies in these passages. This does not prevent the competing kernel—a crystallization, in the figures, of a will for future accomplishment—from claiming entire emotional authenticity as well; but it is an authenticity for which a style has yet to be found. The restless stirrings of the will for accomplishment motivate all modes of speech here except the re-creative indolent one. But it is to that re-creative one, with its two facets of deathliness and ripening, that I wish now to turn.

The note of re-creation enters with the blended richness of two Keatsian themes—growth and sleep—in "Ripe was the drowsy hour," a line apparently promising both fruit and dream-visions. But we are balked of both as the first facet of indolence is momen-tarily turned to us—the apparent death of the senses, as they sink into an unconsciousness of almost all stimuli, "unhaunted quite of all but nothingness." It is, as we know, the vision of the three figures which prevents the poet's senses from that absolute annihila-tion. Keats's language for the negation of sense in sleep is fatally contaminated here with the luxuriousness of sense: it is far from the withered sedge and from places where no birds sing. Something very rich in his indolence is struggling for expression behind these negations. If his eyes are benumbed, it is by a *blissful* cloud; his pulse lessens by *growing* (even if by growing less and less); the two inter-polated "no's" can scarcely obliterate the main nouns clustered in "pain . . . sting . . . pleasure's wreath . . . flower"; and the sweet and joyful steeping of evenings in honeyed indolence cannot be thought to represent a "nothingness."

In passing to the second, more openly creative facet of indolence, the activities of the "soul" when we are laid asleep in body, Keats borrows from *Tintern Abbey* a Wordsworthian division of body and soul which will not, in the long run, prove congenial to him. The philosophical Wordsworthian language for what happens when we are laid asleep in body and become a living soul is an impossible idiom for Keats; his soul, in its activities, is indistinguishable from his senses. The promise in "Ripe was the drowsy hour" now becomes fulfilled in dream, blossom, and song, in the most ac-complished lines of the ode. In this fifth stanza, the "dim dreams" of the indolent soul borrow their language proleptically from the "dreamy urn"; the "stirring shades" within the soul's garden are named almost cunningly from "the first seen shades" of the urn-figures; the "besprinkled . . . flowers" arise from the repudiated "flower" of pleasure's wreath; the "clouded" morn in the awakened, if dreaming, soul is born from the "blissful cloud" of summer indolence numbing the eyes of sense; and, in the most evident parallel of all, the "tears of May" gather above those unshed "tears of mine," as the poet calls them, which he would refuse to have shed at the adieu of the figures (or so he boasts), had they consented to retreat, and leave him undisturbed.

The invasion, then, of the diction of the deep soul-dream by the diction of externality (whether of the external figures or the surrounding landscape) is proof that the soul-dream cannot remain sheltered from the world of time (the changing of the moons) and human "annoy" (pain and pleasure alike). "The voice of busy common-sense" (which we may call a denigration of the voice of mind in its pragmatic mood) Keats will not here dignify by conceptualizing it into a figure. But he does conceptualize the three other figures of "annoy"—Love, Ambition, and Poesy—and the problems of conceptualization provoke equal problems of diction.

In the journal-letter, the figures are psychological motives, externalized because at the moment they are being rejected, or defended against; and their allegorization comes in a simile of appeal and detachment at once; the motives are contemplated but they are inert, having no "alertness of countenance," and seeming "like three figures on a greek vase." The externality and lifelessness of the motives do not survive their poetic reification into visionary forms: though they begin in placidity and serenity, they quickly arrive at disquieting, if disguised, intent; and one, the "demon Poesy," takes on an "unmeek" power rather like that of Lamia, who seemed "some demon's mistress, or the demon's self" (*Lamia*, 1, 56). The changing vocatives to the figures, and the uncertainty of conceptualization, suggest that Keats was not entirely master of the evolution of the poem.

Keats's suspicion of the figures yields the first tentative conceptualization of their function. Have they muffled themselves to steal away from him unrecognized, and leave him unmanned, without a task? Are they plotters against him, disguising their deep and silent plotting? Beholding one's own former energizing motives while refusing to acknowledge their present claim is the experience described in the journal-letter: Keats's change of nonacknowledgment to nonrecognition compels an ascription of intent to the reified motives which is not, in terms of the fiction of the poem, entirely coherent, since Keats seems both to desire and to repudiate a task in one breath. As I have said earlier, it is the conflict of "idleness" (as both the voice of busy common-sense and the voice of the figures, if they had one, would seem to call it) and "indolence" (as the voice of creative patience would call it) which is in question; but the melodramatic and theatrical diction of muffled shadows engaged in a deep-disguisèd plot, while it may be summoned up by those memories of Shakespeare, particularly *Hamlet*, which lie behind several of the odes, is a diction wholly unsuitable as a mode of address to urn-figures, and it vanishes leaving not a trace behind.

The reproachful "haunting" which seems the main intent of the figures links them, for Keats, with the ghost of Hamlet's father, with his purposeful remanifesting of himself to his indolent son; the figures are therefore invoked in purgatorial epithets suitable to revenants or shades. On the other hand, they are also life-figures, secular motives from the world of pain and pleasure, and to describe them Keats borrows, in an explanatory fashion connected with his narration to a common reader, diction from the common stock of emblematic moral iconography, to which he will again resort in the *Ode to a Nightingale*. Love the "fair maid" and Ambition "pale of cheek, / And ever watchful with fatigued eye" belong to the same static frieze of commonplaces on which we can see palsy shaking "a few, sad, last gray hairs," and men sitting and hearing each other groan. These fixed emblems evoke in every case Keats's feeblest diction precisely because they are representative of fixed and received ideas. He cannot bring himself to resort to one of these emblems for Poesy, at least not here in the ode. In the letter, Poetry had been as inert as Ambition or Love; but here Poesy takes on incremental life; the more blame is heaped on her, the more Keats loves her, a process mimicked by the phrase "more, the more . . . , most" incorporated into the stanza.

Keats first conceptualized the figures as graceful unknown visitors, next as theatrical muffled plotters, next as reproachful revenants, and next as moral emblems of duty or desire; his last conceptualization of them, and in the event his governing one, is as deities. The figures become the gods who preside over the ode, refusing to be dismissed by the speaker, for all his adjurations to them to fade and vanish. Protests are in vain; Keats might say of them, as Yeats does of his Magi:

> Now as at all times I can see in the mind's eye,
> In their stiff, painted clothes, the pale unsatisfied ones
> Appear and disappear.

One of Keats's difficulties with the conceptualization of his un-satisfied ones is that they represent such different internalized objects of the self. Love represents the erotic object, Ambition the social object, and Poesy the creative object: these figures are at once self-projections (Keats as lover, as fame-seeker, and as poet) and internalized objects. Ambition belongs at least in part to the world of busy common-sense and sentimental farce; Love, Keats fears, belongs especially to the world where change the moons; and Poesy, he suspects, belongs to a world more demonic than pastoral. But besides being self-projections (Love and Poesy, by convention "unmanly," must be projected as female beloved and female Muse) and internalized objects, these figures are, in the Keatsian sense, "presiders," as Shakespeare was to Keats a presider. Their elevated state dictates Keats's elevated language of address, different from the conversational narration ("One morn before me") or the affectedly colloquial language of expostulation ("and, forsooth! I wanted wings") or the dreamy language of sensual luxury in spiritual germination (evoked by the "lawn besprinkled o'er / With flowers"). The elevated diction does not preclude intimacy ("How is it, shadows, that I knew ye not?"), accusation ("O, why did ye not melt?"), or defiance ("Ye cannot raise / My head cool-bedded in the flowery grass"). But each time Keats moves into direct address to the deities (away from description, recollection, or social expostulation), the temperature of the poem rises in what we may call odal fire, a very different temperature from the incubating vernal warmth of the re-creative stanzas. By reducing the number of persons addressed and by keeping direct address throughout, Keats made the later odes more coherent than *Indolence*, with its three addressees only intermittently addressed.

In its passages from first-person narration to second-person address and back again, *Indolence* is unique among the odes, as *Melancholy* is unique in never addressing its presiding deity, but rather being a second-person address to the poet's own self. In the other odes, the deity — whether soul-goddess (*Psyche*), artist (*Nightingale*), art-object (*Urn*), or season (*Autumn*) — is unfailingly the object of address. In fact, Keats's largest single aesthetic decision in writing the greater odes was to place them squarely in the poetic tradition of invocation and prayer, where he had placed the first of his ambitious odes, the hymn to Pan in the first book of *Endymion*. (The later ode sung by the Indian Maid to Sorrow, in Book IV, mixes narration and invocation, and includes, in its incorporated vision of a Bacchic procession, interrogations of attendant damsels and satyrs prefiguring the interrogation of the figures on the urn.) The second firm aesthetic decision Keats made in the later odes was to speak in *propria persona* — not through a dramatic character like the Indian Maid, not in the choral unison of worshipers as in the hymn to Pan, but in his own troubled and aspiring single voice. Even when he mentions "other woe than ours" or "breathing human passion," the voice that utters those words is not the voice of a chorus or of humanity in general but that of a single speaker. Keats's third great decision, having adopted his single speaker, was to minimize the role of that speaker in successive odes until, from the visible single poet in *Indolence*, *Psyche*, and *Nightingale*, he has become the self-effacing and anonymous speaker, not specified as a poet, of *Autumn*.

The Byronic language of irony, which, as I have said, appears briefly in *Indolence*, is motivated no less by Keats's defensive guilt at the approach of the figures than by his own leap of the heart as he wishes to follow them: "I burn'd / And ached for wings." The motive of self-distrust rarely yields good poetry in Keats, and will fade from the odes, but this instance of it heralds the later outbursts against the cheating Fancy, the cold Pastoral, and the inaccessible Melancholy (in the canceled first stanza of that ode). All of these testify to the hostile energies released (after an attempt at idealization, invocation, or transcendence) by the journey homeward to habitual self. Until the motive of these necessary journeys homeward can be incorporated into the motive of idealization itself (and this does not happen until the close of *Melancholy*), the intemperate diction of disillusion must, if Keats is to remain truthful to his own emotions, confront the ecstatic or worshipful or in any case invocational diction provoked by the divine or idealized object.

We can see, in the concluding stanza of *Indolence*, all of Keats's previously established modes of speech jostling each other in an uncomfortable medley—the invocational ("So, ye three ghosts, adieu!"), the indolent re-creative ("my head cool-bedded in the flowery grass"), the ironic and hostile ("A pet-lamb in a sentimental farce!"), the descriptive-narrative ("masque-like figures on the dreamy urn"), the deprecatory language critical of sensation ("my idle spright"), and the language for the as yet discarnate stirrings of the will ("I yet have visions"). Eventually his boast that "for the day faint visions there is store" will be abundantly manifest in *Autumn*, her "store" anything but faint; but for the moment the claim is asserted only, its fruit invisible.

I cannot forbear to add a note on sentence rhythm, because Keats is quickened into different syntactic rhythms by his different languages. The stately pentameter passage of the first quatrain of the ode is somewhat dulled in the rather pedestrian repetitions of the following four lines; a new note of beauty is not discovered until the re-creative series of clauses is ushered in with the medial trochaic inversion "Ripe was the drowsy hour," and a waywardness of phrasal rhythm (which I reproduce here) begins to please the ear:

> Ripe was the drowsy hour;
> The blissful cloud of summer-indolence benumb'd my eyes;
> My pulse grew less and less;
> Pain had no sting, and pleasure's wreath no flower.

Though this is not an exquisite progression, the last line being too sententiously phrased for the state of soul it wishes to express, there is a kinetic deployment of rhythm which turns the pentameter away from stateliness and into a pulse of breathing irregularity. A religious formality resumes with "A third time pass'd they by," and then rhythmic inventiveness flags in the entirely too programmatic enumeration of the allegorical figures, with one line given to Love, two to Ambition, and predictably three to Poesy, a pattern repeated in the subsequent repudiation of the figures, which again reserves one line for the refusal of Love, two for Ambition, and three for Poesy. Rhythmic inventiveness recurs only in the second scene of re-creation, after which Keats resorts to a rhythm more or less confined to simple pentameter, in which syntax is accommodated to metrical form.

The diction of re-creation, in which Keats, after his exercises in *Endymion*, is already wholly accomplished, is a sensual diction (even if it is used, as it is here, to describe a spiritual state in which the senses themselves are benumbed and the pulse is lessened). Its elements include, as in so many other passages we shall encounter, drowsiness, ripeness, honey, dreams, a chiaroscuro (here of "stirring shades, and baffled beams"), flowers, grass, moisture, clouds, a personified time (which can be a month or season, here May with her "sweet tears" and morn with her "lids" in which raindrops hang as tears), an open casement, leaves, buds, warmth, and birdsong. This moist, sensual complex exists in conjunction (sometimes in competition) with a complex associated with idealization; some of its elements include stone (here an urn; elsewhere an altar or steps), figuration (here the urn-shades), dance, masque, or procession (here the joined hands and the serene pace), wings (as here, Keats would need wings to follow the figures), and architectural enclosure. Clouds, as the source of natural moisture and the realm of divine habitation, are common to both clusters of imagery; and dreams or visions seem, though springing from the one realm of indolence, to engender the other, that of idealization. All of these images will recur, and be amplified, and reduced, and reaffirmed, and criticized, in the later odes.

Keats searches in *Indolence* for a proper mode of self-cognition. The speaking "I" wishes, for the moment, to know itself solely as a being still in gestation, one whose senses have been laid to sleep and whose soul is an indolent lawn full of restless glimmers, dreamy budding, warmth, and overheard song. It does not wish to know itself in its erotic role as lover, its social role as seeker for fame, or its creative role as poet. It arduously repudiates the possibility that it may incarnate itself in an artifact. These questions of self-definition—in roles passive, active, erotic, social, and creative—will persist through the odes. *Indolence* is too timid even to take credit for its own visions: the figures come not by being summoned but rather appear inconclusively veiled in the passive: "One morn before me *were* three figures *seen* . . . / They pass'd, like figures on a marble urn, / When *shifted* round . . . / They came again; as when the urn once more / *Is shifted* round." *Indolence*'s dual projection of the Keatsian self—into drowsy vegetative nature and into stern Greek figures—will also recur in the odes, as tension, as problem, and ultimately as solution.

We are left, in the end, with the two rhythms of the poem. One of them, the recurrent processional stateliness (as, in the manner of a charm, three figures come three times), is the rhythm of an embodied art and a compelling Fate. It is counterpointed, no less intensely, by the other, fitful, rhythm of refusal—now refusing in a lethargic lessened pulse, now in a rather uneasy cynicism, now in a ripeness of sensation and faint vision. In spite of his putative indolence, the poet is forcefully drawn into a relation with the allegorical figures, abruptly and briefly in the first, disturbed, address, posing the profound question of self-cognition—"How is it, shadows, that I knew ye not?"—and, again in a more prolonged way, in the repeated farewells which close the poem:

> O shadows! 'twas a time to bid farewell! . . .
>
> So, ye three ghosts, adieu! . . .
>
> Fade softly from my eyes . . .
>
> Farewell! I yet have visions . . .
>
> Vanish, ye phantoms . . .

These farewells and adieux place the poet in the position of an impotent magus or a would-be Prospero summoning and dismissing spirits.[5] We see that these spirits will not be dismissed, that Keats has raised himself, in his dispute with them, from indolence. He begins to command his spiritual world even in attempting to refuse it; though he has not yet conceptualized its demands (which he will later call Beauty and Truth), he has conceptualized its aims (to love, to be ambitious for greatness, to be a poet). He remains, for the moment, the artist shrinking from embodying his faint vegetative visions in anything resembling an artifact, refusing even the purely mental cultivation of Fancy (in which he will take such active pleasure in *Psyche*). In making the constitutive rhetorical figure of *Indolence* that of dialectic, or dispute, Keats proposes an art of inconclusiveness: the rhetorical shape of the poem is that of a stalemate—nothing, neither way. The budding warmth of spiritual sensuality refuses to the end the cold pastoral of art; but the very insistence of the pressure toward figuration makes the shape of dispute seem a disingenuous one. The language, too, offers an unresolved conflict between the deathly and the lifelike; one scarcely knows whether the figures are more or less alive than the throstle. What is clear is that the budding natural warmth of this ode does not at all yet see its way clear to becoming an aesthetic warmth, in "the way some pictures look warm," which will so mercifully enable the composition of *To Autumn*. Keats, like his later bees, hopes in this poem that warm days will never cease; but the figures—silent, gentle, but persistent—have come to tell him otherwise.

II

Tuneless Numbers:
The *Ode to Psyche*

Till in the bosom of a leafy world
We rest in silence, like two gems upcurl'd
In the recesses of a pearly shell.

   Sleep and Poetry, 119–121

As she was wont, th' imagination
Into most lovely labyrinths will be gone.

   Sleep and Poetry, 265–266

So felt he, who first told, how Psyche went
On the smooth wind to realms of wonderment;
What Psyche felt, and Love, when their full lips
First touch'd.

   I stood tip-toe upon a little hill, 141–144

Of fair-hair'd Milton's eloquent distress
   And all his love for gentle Lycid drown'd.

   Keen, fitful gusts are whisp'ring here and there, 11–12

God of warm pulses, and dishevell'd hair
And panting bosoms bare!
Dear unseen light in darkness!

   Endymion, III, 984–986

They lay calm-breathing on the bedded grass;
 Their arms embraced, and their pinions too;
 Their lips touch'd not, but had not bade adieu.
   —*Ode to Psyche*, 15–17

Ode to Psyche

O Goddess! hear these tuneless numbers, wrung
   By sweet enforcement and remembrance dear,
And pardon that thy secrets should be sung
   Even into thine own soft-conched ear:
Surely I dreamt to-day, or did I see
   The winged Psyche with awaken'd eyes?
I wander'd in a forest thoughtlessly,
   And, on the sudden, fainting with surprise,
Saw two fair creatures, couched side by side
   In deepest grass, beneath the whisp'ring roof
   Of leaves and trembled blossoms, where there ran
      A brooklet, scarce espied:
'Mid hush'd, cool-rooted flowers, fragrant-eyed,
   Blue, silver-white, and budded Tyrian,
They lay calm-breathing on the bedded grass;
   Their arms embraced, and their pinions too;
   Their lips touch'd not, but had not bade adieu,
As if disjoined by soft-handed slumber,
And ready still past kisses to outnumber
   At tender eye-dawn of aurorean love:
      The winged boy I knew;
   But who wast thou, O happy, happy dove?
      His Psyche true!

O latest born and loveliest vision far
   Of all Olympus' faded hierarchy!
Fairer than Phoebe's sapphire-region'd star,
   Or Vesper, amorous glow-worm of the sky;
Fairer than these, though temple thou hast none,
   Nor altar heap'd with flowers;
Nor virgin-choir to make delicious moan
     Upon the midnight hours;

No voice, no lute, no pipe, no incense sweet
　From chain-swung censer teeming;
No shrine, no grove, no oracle, no heat
　Of pale-mouth'd prophet dreaming.

O brightest! though too late for antique vows,
　Too, too late for the fond believing lyre,
When holy were the haunted forest boughs,
　Holy the air, the water, and the fire;
Yet even in these days so far retir'd
　From happy pieties, thy lucent fans,
　Fluttering among the faint Olympians,
I see, and sing, by my own eyes inspired.
So let me be thy choir, and make a moan
　　Upon the midnight hours;
Thy voice, thy lute, thy pipe, thy incense sweet
　From swinged censer teeming;
Thy shrine, thy grove, thy oracle, thy heat
　Of pale-mouth'd prophet dreaming.

Yes, I will be thy priest, and build a fane
　In some untrodden region of my mind,
Where branched thoughts, new grown with pleasant pain,
　Instead of pines shall murmur in the wind:
Far, far around shall those dark-cluster'd trees
　Fledge the wild-ridged mountains steep by steep;
And there by zephyrs, streams, and birds, and bees,
　The moss-lain Dryads shall be lull'd to sleep;
And in the midst of this wide quietness
A rosy sanctuary will I dress
With the wreath'd trellis of a working brain,
　With buds, and bells, and stars without a name,
With all the gardener Fancy e'er could feign,
　Who breeding flowers, will never breed the same:
And there shall be for thee all soft delight
　That shadowy thought can win,
A bright torch, and a casement ope at night,
　To let the warm Love in![1]

THE total shape of the *Ode on Indolence* is, as I have said, a dialectical one of advance and refusal, advance and refusal, advance and refusal—the shape of a stalemate. At the moment represented by the ode, both the reverie of gestating vision and the regressive choice of preconscious insensibility are being jealously protected from the claims of the heart, of fame, and even of art itself. To think of constructing anything at all—a love affair, a place in the world of ambition, a poem—threatens the slumbering embryonic self. Keats finally remains obdurate, the dreamer of the dim dream, the viewer of the faint vision. But the strain evident in the disparate and parallel languages of *Indolence*, as well as in the inherent instability of the condition of spiritual stalemate, predicts a tipping of the balance: as we know, it tips away from immobility toward love and art.

The odes that follow *Indolence* investigate creativity by taking up various attitudes toward the senses, almost as though the odes were invented as a series of controlled experiments in the suppression or permission of sense-experience. Keats's deliberate interest in sense-response has usually been cited as proof of his love of luxury or his minute apprehension of sensual fluctuation. It has not been generally realized that Keats's search for "intensity" led him as much to a deliberate limiting of sense-variety as to a broadening of sensation, and led him as well to a search for an "intensity" of intellect that would rival the intensity of sense. In fact, the intensity to be found in the mind attracted Keats at least as much as, if not more than, the apparently easier intensity of sense; and the lapse of intensity following sexual climax seems to have been only an instance, for Keats, of a curious failure intrinsic to physical sensation itself. He described this eventual ennui of the senses at length in *Fancy*, contrasting it there with the associative powers of mental Fancy, which is able to assemble hybrid seasons and hybrid mistresses that combine all beauties and can never fade. Imaginative intellectual ecstasy seemed to Keats, at this point (*Fancy* was composed a few months before the odes), a more promising source of sustained intensity than physical sensation, and the second of the odes, the *Ode to Psyche*, is in this respect the most "puritanical" of the group in its intent (if not in its effect). It aims, whatever its sensual metaphors (and these will demand their own recognition later), at a complete, exclusive, and lasting annihilation of the senses in favor of the brain. The locus of reality in the ode passes from the world of myth to the world of mind, and the firm four-part structure emphasizes the wish to reproduce earlier sensual and cultic reality in a later interiorized form. The implicit boast of *Psyche* is that the "working brain" can produce a flawless virtual object, indistinguishable from the "real" object in the mythological or historical world. "O for a life of Thoughts," says this ode, "instead of Sensations!"

In *Psyche* Keats emerges from the chrysalis of indolence, permits his soul to become a winged spirit, and takes the smallest possible step toward the construction of a work of art. He concedes that he will shape his reverie toward some end (that reverie which had remained floating and inchoate in *Indolence*), but decides that it will prescind from the bodily senses, and will remain an internal making, as in *Fancy*, contained entirely within his own mind. The shape of the *Ode to Psyche* is, in its essence, the shape of that initial constructive act, and so is a very simple one. It is a reduplication-shape; we might compare it to the shape made by a Rorschach blot. Everything that appears on the left must reappear, in mirror image, on the right; or, in terms of the aesthetic of the ode, whatever has existed in "life" must be, and can be, restored in art.

The notion of art which underlies Keats's continual use of the trope of reduplication in the ode is a strictly mimetic one. The internal world of the artist's brain can attain by the agency of Fancy—so the trope implies—a point-for-point correspondence with the external worlds of history, mythology, and the senses. The task of the poet is defined in excessively simple terms: he is, in this instance, first to sketch the full presence of Psyche and her cult as they existed in the pagan past—that is, to show the locus of loss—and then to create by his art a new ritual and a new environment 'for the restored divinity.[2] Of course Psyche is incomplete without her other half, the god Cupid. Dissatisfied with the thinness of his allegorical and emblematic urn-figures in *Indolence*, and economically reducing his figures from three to two, Keats writes a hymn to the goddess traditionally representing the soul, but the soul under one aspect—the soul in love.³ Each of the subsequent odes worships a single divinity; each, like Psyche, is female; after Psyche, all are unpartnered.

In the view of the *Ode to Psyche*, a pursuit of the most minute verisimilitude becomes the task of art, since divinity will not grace art with her presence if she lacks an exact interior re-creation of her former sensual and cultic world. In the fiction of this ode, art does not objectify the natural world in an external medium such as music or sculpture or even language. In the ode, Keats's art is the insubstantial one of Fancy, the inner activity of the working brain, not even, as yet, the art of poetry embodied in words. The àrt in *Psyche* is the pre-art of purposeful, constructive, and scenic or architectural imaginings, not the art of writing; and the entire locus of this art is a mental domain, within the artist's brain, where Fancy, engaging in a perpetual rivalry with nature, remains forever in a competitive (but apparently victorious) relation to an external world.

In brief, in the *Ode to Psyche* Keats defines art as the purposeful imaginative and conceptualizing activity of the artist—entirely internal, fertile, competitive with nature, and successful insofar as it mimics nature, myth, and history with a painstaking spiritual verisimilitude. It is art without artifact. The artist is both worshiper of a divinity and its possessor: the possession is envisaged here in mental, if erotic, terms, terms of invitation and entreaty rather than of domination or mastery.

The shape of the poem pairs the opening tableau of the mythological Cupid and Psyche embowered in the forest with the closing envisaged tableau of the unpartnered Psyche awaiting Cupid in the bower of the artist's brain; and, in the center, it juxtaposes the absent historical cult of Psyche with her imagined mental cult. I believe that the later odes demonstrate how unsatisfactory, on further reflection, Keats found this reduplicative mirror-image conception of art—art as a wholly internalized, mimetic, imaginative activity.

The ode declares, by its words and by its shape, that the creation of art requires the complete replacement of all memory and sense-experience by an entire duplication of the external world within the artist's brain (a process we have seen, in its undirected and simply pastoral sense, in *Indolence*, where the soul had itself become a lawn of flowers, complete with weather, light, and shade). *Psyche* asserts that by the constructive activity of the mind we can assert a victory, complete and permanent, over loss:[4]

> And there shall be for thee all soft delight
>   That shadowy thought can win,
> A bright torch, and a casement ope at night,
>   To let the warm Love in!

The reparatory plot of the poem — the restoration of the proper cult and bower of Psyche — necessitates its mirror-shape, in which the second imaginative half of the poem reduplicates the first nostalgic portion, the replication in diction being most exact at the center of the poem. Psyche, because a late-born goddess, has, says Keats, no

> virgin choir to make delicious moan
>   Upon the midnight hours;
> No voice, no lute, no pipe, no incense sweet
>   From chain-swung censer teeming;
> No shrine, no grove, no oracle, no heat
>   Of pale-mouth'd prophet dreaming.

Keats will heal, one by one, with exact restitution, each of these lacks:

> So let me be thy choir, and make a moan
>   Upon the midnight hours;
> Thy voice, thy lute, thy pipe, thy incense sweet
>   From swinged censer teeming;
> Thy shrine, thy grove, thy oracle, thy heat
>   Of pale-mouth'd prophet dreaming.

> Yes, I will be thy priest.

This nearly exact repetition (within a relatively short poem) of identical words, the earlier ones describing precise lacks, the later precise reparations, is adapted from Wordsworth's reparatory technique of repetition in his *Ode: Intimations of Immortality*.[5] This strategy, unobtrusive in Wordsworth, is here verbally insisted on by Keats, so that the curative and restorative intent of this structure cannot be overlooked. At "So let me be thy choir," the *Ode to Psyche* folds over upon itself and by repetition of diction intends to heal its wounds of loss.

What is the wound that is being healed? It is, in Keats's view, a wound to poetry itself, inflicted by Christianity. Because Christianity banished the pagan divinities, good and bad alike, the body of poetry inherited from the ancient world was, by Christian poets, mutilated. It was in Milton's Nativity Ode that Keats found the amplest description of the banishing of the pagan gods, and he borrows his vocabulary for *Psyche* from Milton's equivocal and beautiful account of the effect of the nativity of Jesus on pagan religions. I quote Milton's ode, italicizing Keats's borrowings for *Psyche*:

> The *oracles* are dumb,
> No *voice* or hideous hum
> Runs thro' the arched *roof* in words deceiving.
> Apollo from his *shrine*
> Can no more divine,
> With hollow shriek the *steep* of Delphos leaving.
> No *nightly* trance, or breathed spell
> *Inspires* the *pale-eyed priest* from the *prophetic* cell.

> The lonely *mountains* o'er
> And the resounding shore,
> A *voice* of weeping heard and loud lament;
> From *haunted* spring, and dale
> Edg'd with poplar *pale*,
> The parting genius is with sighing sent;
> With *flow'r*-inwoven tresses torn
> The Nymphs in twilight shade of tangled thickets mourn.

> In consecrated earth,
> And on the *holy* hearth,

The Lars, and lemures *moan* with *midnight* plaint;
   In urns, and *altars* round,
   A drear and dying sound
Affrights the Flamens at their service quaint . . .

   Peor and Baälim
   Forsake their *temples* dim; . . .
   And mooned Ashtaroth,
   Heav'n's queen and mother both,
Now sits not girt with tapers' *holy* shine.

All of Keats's Miltonic words in *Psyche* are drawn from Milton's banishing of the gentler and more civilized pagan divinities; none is drawn from Milton's subsequent stanzas on the defeat of the more "brutish" gods.[6] It is not to Keats's purpose here to suggest the darker side of the pagan pantheon. For him, the classical world (even in its latest manifestation, Psyche) represented a repository of truth-giving mythology, and not, as it did for Milton, "error" or "fable." Therefore Keats's description of Psyche echoes the superlatives of Spenser's *Hymn to Heavenly Beauty*:

These thus in faire each other farre excelling,
As to the Highest they approach more near,
Yet is that Highest farre beyond all telling,
Fairer than all the rest which there appear.

Psyche, says Keats (recalling as well Shakespeare's glow-worm), is the

   latest born and loveliest vision far
   Of all Olympus' faded hierarchy!
Fairer than Phoebe's sapphire-region'd star,
   Or Vesper, amorous glow-worm of the sky;
Fairer than these.

Keats's ode, then, is a hymn to pagan heavenly beauty which, in despite of Milton's ritual banishing, he will restore to sovereignty and will duly worship, thereby replenishing an impoverished poetic world where imagination lacks proper deities to worship.[7] The goddess who has captured his veneration is Psyche, the soul in love, and the problem the poet sets himself is to find a spell powerful enough to conjure Psyche back into existence.

In one sense, of course, Psyche exists eternally, forever entwined with Cupid, in the realm of mythic forms.[8] Keats must find a liturgical language suitable for her eternal mythical being, and then a language seductive enough to woo her into an allegorical being, within his mind. Everyone has noticed the revelatory change in language which takes place in the poem: the first two stanzas are written, as one critic put it, in "early Keats," while the last stanza exhibits in part the language of "late Keats."[9] In this ode, the early language of erotic experience disputes the later language of aesthetic experience, as Psyche is embowered first with her lover Cupid in the forest of myth, but lastly with her poet-priest in his internalized shrine. Cupid and Psyche, though drawn, as Keats said in his letter sending the poem to his brother, from Apuleius, are described in terms Keats had gleaned from Lemprière. Keats's decision to take up this material at this time, material which he had long known, is explained in part by his evolving notion of the world as a vale of soul-making, unfolded in the same letter as the poem. But Cupid and Psyche remind us too of Love and Poesy in the *Ode on Indolence*, though they have exchanged sexes, with Love now a masculine Cupid, Poesy a Muse called Psyche. Ambition (which vanishes entirely from the later odes) is here still present in the vow, with something of a boast in it: "Yes, I will be thy priest." The motives of Love, Poesy, and Ambition are still intertwined, but Keats has decided to modify allegory as a way of exemplifying them, and has turned to mythology instead—not entirely seriously, as he had in *Endymion*, but in a more playful and self-conscious way: "I am more orthodox than to let a hethen Goddess be so neglected" (*Letters*, II, 106).

Keats's perplexity on the subject of mythology arose from his severe notion of what it was to tell the truth. Though he had (as *I stood tip-toe* reveals) adopted Wordsworth's theory in *The Excursion* about the allegorical source of mythology—that it originated from an attempt to adorn natural sights with the charm of story (a narcissus drooping over a pool, the moon alone in the sky) — Keats had expressed, as early as *Sleep and Poetry*, a suspicion that the proper subject of poetry was not only "the realm . . . / Of Flora, and old Pan" (101–102; that is, the realm of allegorized natural beauty like that of the narcissus or the moon), but also human life. In the realm of Flora he could read allegorically "a lovely tale of human life" (110), but he would have to bid those joys farewell, in leaving them for "a nobler life, / Where I may find the agonies, the strife / Of human hearts" (123–125). It is not clear to Keats whether he can write about those agonies in mythological terms at all. One of his reproaches of the Augustan poets seems to be their neglect of nature and mythology at once; and yet, when in *Sleep and Poetry* he begins to enumerate his own possible subjects, he does not come to mythology until he enters, in memory, the house of Leigh Hunt, and recalls looking with him at a portfolio including a picture of Bacchus and Ariadne. After that, there follows a confusion of subjects — nature, mythology, past poets, ancient heroes, and modern revolutionaries, not excepting the allegorical figure of "Sleep, quiet with his poppy coronet." In turning in a "modern" and "worldly" way to the tale of Cupid and Psyche, a topic already the subject for sophisticated, even decadent, interpretation, both in literature and in the fine arts, Keats hoped, we may surmise, to enjoy the benefits of mythology without seeming to engage in a false archaism. His struggle with mythological material was not, as we shall see in the subsequent odes, to be so easily resolved, if only because he connected it so strongly with the pictorial and sensuous representational arts, rather than with thought and truth.

Keats's first sophisticating of mythology is evident in his assumption that it exists not so much in the pagan past as in an eternal region where, by purifying himself of skeptical modernity of thought (the dull brain that perplexes and retards), he may once again find himself. There is a formal liturgical beginning to this ode (to which I shall return), but its beginning in narrative time retells Keats's penetration to that eternal region, as, by wandering "thoughtlessly" in a pastoral realm, he comes as spectator upon two wingèd creatures:

> Their arms embraced, and their pinions too;
> Their lips touch'd not, but had not bade adieu,
> As if disjoined by soft-handed slumber,
> And ready still past kisses to outnumber
> At tender eye-dawn of aurorean love.

We recognize this couple—this "happy, happy dove" and her "wingèd boy"—as sentimental adumbrations of the youth and maiden on the Grecian urn, warm in their "more happy love! more happy, happy love!" shaded by their happy, happy boughs which cannot "ever bid the spring adieu." However, by the time Keats writes the *Urn*, though he is still using the *Psyche* language of double happiness and no need to bid adieu, he has recognized that the blissful stasis can only precede consummation, not, as in the more innocent *Psyche*, outlast it. (By "recognize" of course, I mean, "realize in language and structure"—there was no time in which Keats did not recognize these plain truths in life.)

To present erotic desire unlessened by recent consummation, as Keats does here in the figures of Cupid and Psyche, is to imagine an eroticism without any share in the human cycle of desire and satiation. (Mythology thus becomes here the world of heart's desire, which puts into question its capacity as a literary vehicle for the agonies of human hearts.) The symbolic landscape in which Cupid and Psyche lie avoids the passionate and unequilibrated; the flowers are hushed, their roots are cool, they are even cool-colored: "blue, silver-white, and budded syrian" (corrected from the blushing eroticism of "freckle-pink")—though no one knows what Keats intended "syrian" to convey. (His publishers changed it to "Tyrian.") The lovers themselves lie calm-breathing. In short, the divine couple are the pure idealization of an eternal erotic desire for unsated and recurrent sexual experience with the same partner.[10] In this fantasy, love and beauty are served, but truth of human experience is not.

The poet-spectator, having had a vision of the eternal Psyche, decides, against Milton's proscription of pagan gods, to restore her cult, and to that end addresses her liturgically with the words which formally open the ode. He hails her in terms deliberately borrowed from *Lycidas* (as indeed the flower-catalogue of Psyche's forest bower is also partially so borrowed): just as "bitter constraint, and sad occasion dear" compel the uncouth swain, so Keats's "tuneless numbers" are wrung by "sweet enforcement and remembrance dear," in piety and pity for the banished goddess. Keats's numbers must be "tuneless" (that is, silent, offering no audible tones) because the audible lyre of the ancients has fallen into disuse, but also because his own song will be only a silent inward one, an unheard melody. Keats's only audience, in the internal theater of his working brain, is Psyche herself, the soul, bereft of all other devotees. Keats's pious memory of her existence, and his sense of obligation in re-creating, however late, her cult, explain his "remembrance dear" and "sweet enforcement" to this piety. Yet the echo of *Lycidas* also tells us that this poem is, like its Miltonic predecessor, an elegy for a vanished presence.

The restoration of the forgotten Psyche is the real subject of the poet's endeavor, and two forms of re-creation are attempted in the ode. In the first, which opens the ode, the beloved divinity is represented as existing eternally in a world accessible by dream or vision when the conscious mind is suppressed, a world exterior to the poetic self. Had she been only within, the poet's vision of her could with propriety only be called a dream; but if she were without, he could genuinely affirm that he had seen her with awakened eyes. (Once again, I interrupt to say that I do not mean that Keats, in life, is uncertain whether or not he had had a dream or seen a vision. The diction of dream and waking is for Keats a way of making truth-claims; when he wishes to insist that poetry has something to offer us which is more than fanciful entertainment, he turns, as in his description of Adam's dream, to the metaphor of awakening and finding it truth.) The early rhetorical question in this ode—"Surely I dreamt to-day, or did I see / The winged Psyche with awaken'd eyes?"—is clearly, as I will conclude later, meant to be answered, "With awakened eyes." This, then, is the first restoration, a pastoral, "thoughtless" waking vision; the second is the restoration by consciously inward architectural reduplication, where Psyche will lie not in the forest grass but in the shrine of the working brain. The first restoration requires of the poet a mythological doubling of the self as a visible Cupid; in the second, the poet in his own person becomes the allegorical Love. In the drama of these parallel experiments—the poet in the first so passive, a thoughtless, wandering spectator, in the other so active, a creator with a working brain—lies the interest of the ode, and the proof of its evolution out of *Indolence*. The meaning of divinity changes in the two restorations: in the first, divinity is conceived of as an idealized presence revealed in a past vision; in the second, divinity is conceived of as a presence which the poet must actively invoke, and create a repository for; and the intent of the poem in its latter part is consequently couched in the future tense of hope and will. The earlier part sees revelation as casual and easy:

> So did he feel, who pull'd the boughs aside,
> That we might look into a forest wide,
> To catch a glimpse of Fauns and Dryades.

That had been Keats's earlier description, in *I stood tip-toe* (151–153), of the poet's activity, in his writing motivated by "the fair paradise of Nature's light" (126). Such a poet, Keats continues, would have been the one who wrote the tale of Cupid and Psyche, writing of them as if they were fauns and dryads, inhabitants of an unallegorized natural paradise, their tale one of charming adventure, happily ended (147–150):

> The silver lamp,—the ravishment,—the wonder—
> The darkness,—loneliness,—the fearful thunder;
> Their woes gone by, and both to heaven upflown,
> To bow for gratitude before Jove's throne.

But this facile parting of forest boughs to show us a tale of love lost and won is no longer Keats's idea of art, nor of the use to which it can put mythology. Poetry is no longer entertaining tale-telling, or even seeing; it is active doing, the poet's human work, here seen, however, as a private task rather than as a service to society.

The *Ode to Psyche* intends a wresting away of Psyche from the past, and a seduction of her into the present. Though Keats's first tones to the goddess are those of elegiac religious observance ("O Goddess! hear these tuneless numbers"), he ends with wooing:

> And there shall be for thee all soft delight
>   That shadowy thought can win,
> A bright torch, and a casement ope at night,
>   To let the warm Love in!

Though Psyche is originally said to lack a cult and prayers, what she is offered in the last stanza is a landscape and a chamber for love, all in the theater of the mind (which will become eventually Moneta's hollow skull).

The elements of erotic bower and sacred temple, which will fatefully lose their unison in *The Fall of Hyperion*, are still peacefully conjoined in the *Ode to Psyche.* The poet promises a "rosy sanctuary" (an erotic version of the *Urn*'s "green altar"), dressed "with the wreath'd trellis of a working brain, / With buds, and bells, and stars without a name," in a landscape where "the moss-lain Dryads" sleep: there Psyche will find a fane that will be a bower for her and Cupid. These materials — wreath, trellis, bells, and moss in an architectural setting — are also found (as Bloom early noted, in *The Visionary Company*, p. 394) in the beautiful "arbour" with its roof and doorway, placed near the opening of *The Fall of Hyperion* (25–29):

> I saw an arbour with a drooping roof
> Of trellis vines, and bells, and larger blooms
> Like floral-censers swinging light in air;
> Before its wreathed doorway, on a mound
> Of moss, was spread a feast of summer fruits.

But on closer view the feast is seen to be over, and the arbor is littered with empty shells and half-bare grape stalks. When the poet consumes some of the remaining feast and drinks a draught of "transparent juice, / Sipp'd by the wander'd bee" (the nectar, we may suppose, of the gods), he sinks into a swoon, mastered by "the

domineering potion." When he awakes, he finds the landscape
changed (60–62):

> The mossy mound and arbour were no more;
> I look'd around upon the carved sides
> Of an old sanctuary with roof august.

In this fairy-tale substitution, the "drooping roof" of the trellised
arbor has become the "roof august" of a sanctuary no longer rosy,
like that of Psyche, but carved, as the later Keats fully accepts the
separation of nature and art. Keats's symbols in the epic imply his
grand theme: that while the first, youthful, perception of the world
is erotic, the second, adult, one is sacrificial. As he wrote to
Reynolds after completing, so far as we can judge, all the odes but
Autumn, "I have of late been moulting: not for fresh feathers &
wings: they are gone, and in their stead I hope to have a pair of patient sublunary legs" (*Letters*, II, 128). In *Indolence*, Keats had ached,
within his chrysalis, for wings; in *Psyche*, both Cupid and Psyche
are winged creatures though not yet shown in flight; in *Nightingale*,
Keats at last wills to fly, if not on actual wings, then on the
viewless wings of Poesy. The erotic dream died only with difficulty;
in *Psyche* Keats is still in the realm of wings and arbors, not steps
and sanctuaries.

But though in *Psyche* bower and sanctuary are still one, a strain is
evident in the fabric of writing. The ode attains its greatest writing
not in its description of the rosy sanctuary-bower at the close, but
in the slightly earlier description of the landscape surrounding that
fane, the landscape of the as yet untrodden region of the mind that
lies beyond the Chamber of Maiden Thought. Keats had been in
what he called "the infant or thoughtless Chamber" when the ode
began, as he wandered in the forest "thoughtlessly." When the
working brain enters, he is no longer thoughtless: we are, he says,
"at length imperceptibly impelled by the awakening of the thinking
principle—within us" into the second Chamber, that of Maiden
Thought, and it is there that the working brain operates, as it does
through most of *Psyche*, "intoxicated with the light and the atmosphere, see[ing] nothing but pleasant wonders." That realm is

still pastoral, but beyond it lie the "precipices" which show "untrodden green," as Keats had said in his sonnet to Homer (Bate mentions the analogy in *John Keats*, p. 493): those steeps and cliffs are not barren, but green with a new, if more alpine, verdure. As one breathes in the atmosphere of the Chamber of Maiden Thought, Keats adds, in the famous letter I have been quoting (*Letters*, I, 280–281), that "among the effects this breathing is father of is that tremendous one of sharpening one's vision into the heart and nature of Man—of convincing ones nerves that the World is full of Misery and Heartbreak, Pain, Sickness and oppression—whereby This Chamber of Maiden Thought becomes gradually darken'd and at the same time on all sides of it many doors are set open—but all dark—all leading to dark passages." Keats had written this passage a year before writing the *Ode to Psyche*, and we sense a positive effort, at the close of the ode, to stave off the encroaching dark passages:

> Yes, I will be thy priest, and build a fane
> In some untrodden region of my mind,
> Where branched thoughts, new grown with pleasant pain,
> Instead of pines shall murmur in the wind:
> Far, far around shall those dark-cluster'd trees
> Fledge the wild-ridged mountains steep by steep.

So the passage begins, opening into untrodden heights, and acceding to both the pain and the pleasure of thought as work which *Indolence*, refusing pain's sting and pleasure's wreath alike, had forbidden. But, as we recall, the rosy sanctuary finally seems to lie within a cultivated garden, "with buds, and bells, and stars without a name, / With all the gardener Fancy e'er could feign." It is not, however, the "gardener" Fancy who created the wild-ridgèd mountains and the dark-clustered trees: they are the creations rather of unconfined imagination, and they represent the sublime, as the garden represents the beautiful. Many parallels in sublimity have been cited for these lines, parallels from Milton and Shakespeare especially, but their effect in the poem—given their Miltonic origins in the setting of Paradise (*Paradise Lost*, IV) and in the mountains and steep of the Nativity Ode—resembles the effect in Wordsworth's Immortality Ode of corresponding lines:

> The cataracts blow their trumpets from the steep;
> I hear the echoes from the mountains throng;
> The winds come to me from the fields of sleep.

The winds, the mountains, and the steep form a characteristic Wordsworthian configuration of the sublime. The new dark-clustered thoughts this region will require will, Keats knows, give him pain, even though a pain which, because it calls up new creations, is compounded with pleasure. The new domain seems limitless: "*Far, far around* shall those dark-cluster'd trees / Fledge the wild-ridged mountains *steep by steep*." The far-reaching and arduous sublimity of soul here envisaged is not maintained; the poem returns to the delicate, the beautiful, and the sensuous. It is hardly accidental that Keats should appropriate to himself, in a poem about two winged creatures, new pinions of his own by using the word "fledge" of his mountain-thoughts;[11] but the pinions, and the hope of steeps and mountains, show that Keats's notion of the pursuit of sublimity here flies on eagle wings. The patient sublunary legs are still to come.

The earthly paradise described in the last stanza of the ode is entirely nonseasonal, nonagricultural, and nonbucolic (there are no crops, no flocks); it is a paradise within the working brain. Keats uses the paradisal index—the "there" or *là-bas* or *dahin* of that "other country"—but he has abandoned the dream of a passively received revelatory vision with which he began. The chance sight of Cupid and Psyche is not one simply recoverable by a glimpse through forest boughs. Yet his new, allegorical, later paradise reduplicates the earlier, mythological one. There are, in the interior world, sleeping Dryads lain on moss, just as the sleeping Cupid and Psyche had been couched in grass; there are dark-clustered trees where there had been a forest; there is a murmur of pines where there had been a whispering roof of leaves, streams where there had been a brooklet, stars to replace Phoebe's sapphire-regioned star, mental flowers where there had been mythological ones, soft delight where there had been soft-handed slumber, wide quietness where there had been calm breathing, a bright torch to substitute for the aurorean light, and a "warm Love" in place of the wingèd boy. In all of these ways, the internalized closing scene of the poem is a copy, in its imagery, of the opening forest scene, just as the second of the two central Miltonic stanzas of the ode is a copy, in its catalogue of reparation, of the first, with its catalogue of loss. The imperative of reduplication is as clear in the matching of bowers as in the matching of cultic pieties. However, what is missing in the tableau of the last stanza is of course crucial: we miss the figural center of the opening tableau, the "two fair creatures" embracing. "Let me prepare toward thee," Keats might be saying at the end of the poem, as he lavishes all his profusion of imagery on the prospective interior world to be inhabited by Psyche. But she is not yet visible there, nor is Cupid: the close of the poem is an entreaty and a promise, as Keats writes the archetypal poem of an absent center.

If the *Ode to Psyche* were simply a restitution of what Milton's Nativity Ode had extirpated from English poetry, it would end with its restitutive fourth stanza of restored cultic practice. Milton's ode is far grander, in poetic success, than Keats's; but even in this novice effort Keats sees that what is life to Milton is death to him. It is not enough to restore Psyche's cult with a twin stanza written in Milton's religious vocabulary; Keats must reinvent Psyche's cult in his own language, the vocabulary of the luxuriant eroticism of his initial vision.[12] Milton's pagan deities, as they are seen in the Nativity Ode, are in no way erotic: even those who might have been are not so presented—Ashtaroth sits alone as heaven's queen and mother, and Thammuz is dead. Psyche's restoration, for Keats, must be not only the restoration of her cult—voice, lute, pipe, incense, shrine, grove, oracle, and prophet—but also the restoration of her atmosphere and presence. Milton's austere language permits itself nostalgia but no more; Keats, as Psyche's worshiper, requires the radiance of present conjuration. The radiant eroticizing of the interior landscape of the mind, as it is decked and adorned and decorated, is Keats's chief intent, as he makes himself a mind seductive to Psyche. When Psyche will have been won, and Love will have entered, the initial tableau will have been reproduced entire—but this last tableau will be a wholly mental one, in which the mind has been furnished by Fancy for the amorous soul, and Love is a welcome guest. Keats's characteristic erotic adjectives—soft, bright, warm, rosy—together with the activity of Fancy, his presiding *genius loci*, engaged in perpetual breeding of flowers, transform the mind from a place conventionally reserved for philosophical thought to a place where all possible thoughts and fancies (conceived after the manner of the poem *Fancy*) are eroticized by the goddess's imagined arrival. Worship, work, and embrace will be one in the mind-garden, in which the more literal Miltonic cult of swinging censers and moaning choir gives way to a new cult of tuneless numbers, in which Psyche's priest becomes himself her lyricist, her bower, and her Cupid.

Nonetheless, in spite of this amorous and sensual redefinition of religion and of the functions of the creative mind, the deepest energies of the *Ode to Psyche* lie in two nonamorous places—in the sublime, uncultivated periphery, lying outside the bower, of new-grown thoughts, and in the bold claim not for amorousness but for independent divining power, outstripping the soft dimness of dreaming: "I see, and sing, by my own eyes inspired."[13] These high and solitary sublimities—almost sequestered in this poem of amorous contact and decorative luxuriance—predict the more solitary Keats of *Urn, Autumn,* and *The Fall of Hyperion.* And it must be remembered that the cost of the bower in *Psyche* is the total yielding up of the temporally bound senses for a wholly spiritual world, the consequent singing of numbers that must be tuneless (since they are embodied in no outward melody), and the absence of all audience for this song except one's own soul. These sacrifices of sense for mind, of melody for tunelessness, and of audience for a putative, though scarcely realized, solipsism, coexist uneasily with Keats's sensually opulent style in the ode, a nonascetic style developed for the happier embraces, both spiritual and physical, of *Endymion.* The tension between the amorous mythological style and the desolate sacrificial implications of *Psyche* will not be solved conceptually until Keats writes the *Ode on Melancholy,* and not solved stylistically until he writes the ode *To Autumn.* But in the internalizing of divinity, Keats has already advanced, conceptually, beyond *Endymion*'s awkward doubling of the Indian Maid and Cynthia and beyond *Indolence*'s three self-projections. The wholly internalized Psyche—one's own soul as interior paramour, as Stevens would call it—is one solution (but by no means a finally satisfactory one for Keats) to the question of the proper representation of divinity in art; and the internalized atemporal and nonagricultural bower is a solution (but again, for Keats, not an eventually satisfying one) to the problem of the modern representation of the *locus amoenus*, or beautiful place.

Keats wished (as he says in his famous journal-letter immediately contemporary with the odes) to sketch this world as a "vale of Soulmaking," "a system of Salvation which does not affront our reason and humanity":

> It is pretty generally suspected that the chr[i]stian scheme has been coppied from the ancient persian and greek Philosophers. Why may they not have made this simple thing even more simple for common apprehension by introducing Mediators and Personages in the same manner as in the hethen mythology abstractions are personified—
> (*Letters*, II, 103)

Abstractions, Mediators, and Personages are the means of making moral truths "simple for common apprehension." Keats's own mythological and allegorical personages, whether Psyche or Moneta or Autumn, represent his groping after a method he thought common to all "systems of salvation," and therefore true in a way beyond fancifulness. If Psyche, a "happy, happy dove," seems to us understandably insufficient as a personage aiding in salvation, she is nonetheless proof of the immense if circumscribed faith Keats placed, at this time, in the active soul emerged from its chrysalis, in the strength of love in the soul, and in the imaginative force of the mind in finding constructive forms.

The *Ode to Psyche* was of course inspired at least in part by the presence of Fanny Brawne next door in Wentworth Place, and Keats may not at first have been aware, as his ode took on its final dimensions, of the social, moral, and aesthetic restrictiveness of its wholly internalized, timeless, and tuneless cult. Psyche, his only audience for his tuneless numbers, both is and is not a mythological being, both is and is not an allegorical form. The ode does not solve the equivocal nature of her being, just as it does not solve the rela-

tion between beautiful Fancy and truthful Thought — the one concentrated in a small garden-fane full of happy spontaneity of erotic
invention, the other mysteriously far-ranging, sublime, and connected with pain as with eagle-aspiration. Cupid and Psyche
together make up the actual joint divinity of the poem, and they
stand for a unity of being through spiritualized eroticism, for flesh
and soul in one couple — at the beginning not quite fused but not
quite separate, at the end both invisible in darkness. It is a divinity
Keats will forsake: all his subsequent divinities in the odes, as I have
said, are unpartnered females — the light-winged Dryad-nightingale,
the unravished bride-Urn, veiled Melancholy, and the goddess
Autumn.[14] *Psyche*'s exact reduplicative pairing of the outside world
(whether of myth or of cult) with the inside world (of mind or
Fancy) enacts the erotic pairing of the sensual Cupid with the
spiritual Psyche celebrated in the matter of the ode. This is Keats's
most hopeful ode, and yet his narrowest one. The willed pairing of
flesh and soul in a perpetual and immortal embrace, the studied
equivalence of the flowery bower of Nature and the architectural
bower of Fancy, the total reconstitution of past religion in the
present — the perfect "fit" of these competing realities is the dream
embodied in the reduplicative shape of the *Ode to Psyche*. In the col-
lapse of Keats's hopes for a spiritual art exactly mimetic of the sensual vision there collapsed as well the erotic joint divinity, the
happy coexistence of Fancy with Thought, the notion of art as
idyllic verisimilitude, the concept of aesthetic activity as a purely interior working, the valuing of decorative, atemporal Beauty over
austere, evolving Truth, and the pure idealization of the immortal
soul rescued, by the agency of the poet, from the attrition of time.

Psyche originally thought to find its distinctive language in the
realm of religion mediated through Milton — as though the clear
religion of heaven, as Keats wished to announce it, could borrow its
diction from the religions of the past, Christian and pagan alike.
Keats's wish, expressed in the letter I have quoted, to find
something to substitute for Christianity explains his first notion of
a deity's appropriate "numbers" as vows, voiced in piety, and
culminating in a sanctuary. He will not cease to struggle for a
religious diction appropriate to his purposes, as *The Fall of Hyperion*

testifies. But in mute confrontation with the religious language in *Psyche* there stand two other languages—that of pastoral eroticism and that of pastoral allegory, the first in the opening description of the forest bower, the second in the closing description of the cerebral fane. Each of these is contaminated, so to speak, by traces of the diction of religion; the diction of religion is contaminated, in its turn, by traces of them. The latter case is more quickly made: *Psyche* is a vision, as a devotee might say, of a religious goddess, but she is addressed in the diction of physical love. She is the "loveliest" of visions, "fairer," in this lover's comparison, than Venus or Vesper, that "amorous glow-worm of the sky"; her choir is a virgin one making delicious moan (a detail not borrowed from Milton, but inserted by Keats), and her pale-mouthed prophet dreams in a fever of heat. She is brightest or bloomiest, and possessed of "lucent" fans (the adjective later repossessed for Fanny Brawne's "warm, white, lucent, million-pleasured breast"). The religious, Miltonic edge is softened, warmed, coaxed into pastoral bloom. But that very bloom and heat is itself chilled or chastened by the religious use to which it is to be assimilated, into the formality of "O Goddess" and the austerity of "tuneless numbers." With the introduction of Psyche's "soft-conchèd ear" the earliest lines begin their modulation into sensuality, and yet a restraint put on sexual warmth causes the introduction into the forest embrace of the clear note of the brooklet, the cool note of the roots, and the denial of rosiness to the flowers. The suspension of the lovers' lips checks the double embrace of arms and pinions (the latter the warmest, and most boyish, imagining in the poem—"Their arms embraced, *and their pinions too*," a dream of an embrace doubled beyond merely human powers). The "trembled blossoms" and "tender eye-dawn" bear out the fragile and near virginal nature of this aurorean love; Keats is uneasy, given his purportedly religious aims, about the extent of the erotic that he can allow into his devotions.

The governing question of the opening of the ode—"Who wast thou, O happy, happy dove?"—is, strictly speaking, epistemological rather than devotional, and springs, I think, from the opening of *Indolence* (already conceived even if not yet written down): "How is it, shadows, that I knew ye not?" Keats had asked that question in self-reproach, and then had exclaimed, in self-release, after seeing the three figures full-face, "I knew the three." To know them is also, as Keats admits in wishing to banish them, to know "how change the moons." In *Psyche*, "the winged boy I knew," says Keats, but Psyche is at first strange, as the urn-figures in *Indolence* had been; she, like them, is eventually recognized.[15] Keats here raises the question of what he knows when he knows these personages, and though he briefly considers that his glimpse might have been a dream, he decides, as I have said, that he saw them with awakened eyes: I "saw" two fair creatures, he announces, and later adds, "I see, and sing, by my own eyes inspired"; Psyche is the loveliest seen thing, the loveliest "vision." There is no further mention of dreaming, after Keats's first wondering question; everything else in the text supports those "awaken'd eyes" in their seeing. Seeing, and knowing who it is that one sees, and seeing truly, not in dream, is the first condition of Keats's clear religion, the opened eyes precluding any surrender to the drowsiness Keats strove to maintain in *Indolence*. For all the resemblance between *Indolence* and *Psyche* in what we might call their use of the diction of bedded grass, it is, we must recall, Keats who drowses, in *Indolence*, amid stirring shades and baffled beams, his head cool-bedded in the flowery grass; but in *Psyche* it is the sleeping lovers who lie calm-breathing on the bedded grass, and Keats has become the clear-sighted observer with awakened eyes. Therefore, "not seeled, but with open eyes" (Herbert), Keats sees his own former bower; like Ribh at the tomb of Baile and Aillinn, he has eyes by "solitary prayer / Made aquiline," which see what they could not have seen when he drowsed in indolence. Keats as yet scarcely realizes whither his newly aquiline gaze will lead. Eventually, as we know, it will disclose to him, behind a parted veil, Moneta's face. But for the moment Keats yearningly believes that he can, while lifting his own head from the grass, maintain a heavenly couple there in his place. The diction appropriate to their eroticism grows the chaster for his separated gaze, but it preserves enough warmth for knowledge and passion alike to be entertained in the hospitality of the poem.

The curb Keats has put on erotic fever in this passage is clear when we glance back to the passage on Cupid and Psyche in *I stood tip-toe* (143–146):

> What Psyche felt, and Love, when their full lips
> First touch'd; what amorous, and fondling nips
> They gave each other's cheeks; with all their sighs,
> And how they kist each other's tremulous eyes.

The balance of warm and cool is, in the ode, delicately kept in all the "stationing" of the first long stanza—the couple, though side by side, are nonetheless calm; embraced, they are disjoined; not bidding adieu, they are nevertheless not touching; they lie ready for a dawn that has not yet broken. The imagery of erotic pastoral is cooled not only by Keats's detached seeing and knowing but also by his deliberately "tuneless" singing.

Keats's diction for the embracing couple here is far more secure than his diction with respect to himself. Though he begins in high seriousness, the Byronic irony fitfully evident in *Indolence* has its say here too, though shrunken to the brief double condescending to the "fond believing lyre" and to "these days so far retir'd / From happy pieties." This tone, never a successful one in Keats, marks an instability in his enterprise, and a doubt of the very possibility of ode-writing. How believing is his own lyre in this hymn; how remote can he be, in truth, from his own skeptical epoch? The irony in his joking tone about the neglected goddess in the letter to George does not survive very well its translation into verse. And of all the language in the poem, the language of religious cult, borrowed from Milton, is most derivative, and least Keatsian.

The last diction invented in the poem is the diction for Psyche's fane. It is at once the best and the feeblest in the poem, showing, as I have said earlier, the strain under which Keats is working. The feebleness is seen in two places: in the random enumerative arabesque of "zephyrs, streams, and birds, and bees, / . . . buds, and bells, and stars without a name,"[16] and in the unselective amassing of Keatsian erotic words—rosy, soft, delight, bright, warm. But the diction of Psyche's fane also possesses a strength; the fane is Keats's first portrait of himself as artificer, as he becomes for the first time not the youth in love, the ambitious man, or even the votary of the demon Poesy (as he was in *Indolence*) but a maker of an object, here the goddess's sanctuary. Emerged from his embryonic indolence, Keats is born into work; but his indecision about a proper diction for creativity disturbs him here. The diction of "the gardener Fancy" is still the diction of pastoral eroticism, that of "breeding"; and it issues (as in *Fancy*) in buds and flowerlike "stars" and "bells." These Spenserian breedings take place in the realm of the Dryads, amid moss and streams and birds and bees, where lulling sleep is (as it was in *Indolence*) the governing mode of being. In conflict with this soft, mythic pastoral is the Shakespearean and Miltonic strenuousness of the fane's mountain landscape; and yet the sublime landscape is itself vegetative, "grown" from that pain and pleasure which, though two separate things when refused in *Indolence*, grow to one paradoxical single thing, "pleasant pain," when admitted to the precincts of mind. The phrase is of course a blemish on the poem; but like so many of Keats's blemishes it stands for an intellectual insight for which he has not yet found the proper style in poetic language. Keats, at this moment, can only note, baldly, that pleasure and pain have some intimate connection; the answerable style for painful pleasure and pleasant pain is yet to be found.

The diction of the fane is, as I have said, allegorical, as the original diction of Psyche's bower is not (being mythological, and narrative). Keats had thought of following the line "Who breeding flowers, will never breed the same" with the line "So bower'd Goddess will I worship thee," but he deleted it, realizing that his goddess was no longer in a bower but in a fane, that bower language is not fane language, that nature is not architectural artifact. Catching himself up short, he put in the open casement, that casement which in *Indolence* had so meltingly brought the man-made and the natural into conjunction, as "the open casement press'd a new-leaved vine." Here, the open casement will serve, so the poem hopes, to admit warm Love, the human form divine, instead of the natural bloom. But the landscape has perceptibly, in the thought-burdened allegorical moment, darkened from the erotic one presented mythologically; the new forest region, unlike the original one, is unknown, as yet untrodden; there are branches rather than buds or blossoms; they cluster darkly; mountains loom, wild-ridged; instead of feathery pinions there is a sterner fledge of trees; zephyrs are replaced by wind. The darkness persists into the indeterminacy of "shadowy thought" at the end, as Keats undertakes at one and the same time the burden of allegorical writing and the architectural objectification of self in artifact, an artifact which remains as yet internalized in thought, but which has been effectively freed of its creator and endowed with architectural presence and topographical depth.

The *Ode to a Nightingale*, which we next approach, marks a fresh approach to all the questions raised by the odes preceding it. In it Keats takes a step beyond the creative reverie of *Indolence*, beyond even the first creative interior constructions of mental Fancy in *Psyche*, and envisages the artist's necessary embrace of a medium — in this case music, the art of Apollo. He thus takes up, in choosing music, the idea of an art which of its nature precludes mimesis and verisimilitude, an abstract art appealing only to the sensation of the ear, an art devoted, perforce, to a beauty to which truth is irrelevant. He will, pursuing his symbol of the artist as musician, adopt a more ironic view of aesthetic experience, one in which a remote composer-singer, indifferent to and unconscious of any audience, pours forth a song to a listener who is physically so passive, being pure ear, as almost to approach the condition of insentience. In *Nightingale* the immortal world of art, far from being an exact reduplication of the world of life, as in *Psyche*, is in fact in all ways its opposite. In *Psyche*, the embracing sculptural frieze-figures are no longer allegories of the poet's desire for ambition, love, and poesy, but rather have taken on a separate, objectified existence of their own. This existence lapses somewhat at the end, where the poet seems to prepare to become Cupid, but Psyche retains her independence. As a pagan goddess, she preexisted her poet, and does not depend on him for her essence, as the Love, Ambition, and Poesy of *Indolence* do. Keats's attraction toward a presence less contingent than his own selfhood dictates several of his other objects of worship — a bird, an urn, a season. In the later odes, after *Psyche*, he goes beyond an interest only in the psychology of inner reparatory creation into an interest in artifact, medium, audience, and the intrinsic will-to-annihilation in art itself. But in one aspect, *Nightingale* represents a regression from *Psyche*. Though the composer-singer-bird is not "indolent," neither does she have a "working" brain; her art is one of happy spontaneity, coming as naturally as leaves to a tree. Keats still hopes that art need not be "work" intellectually planned. But the working brain will not be absent forever; art as work reappears with the *Urn*.

III

Wild Warblings from the
Aeolian Lyre:
The *Ode to a Nightingale*

On things for which no wording can be found,
Deeper and deeper sinking, until drowned
Beyond the reach of music.

    Endymion, IV, 961–963

Where the nightingale doth sing
Not a senseless, tranced thing,
But divine melodious truth;
Philosophic numbers smooth;
Tales and golden histories
Of heaven and its mysteries.

    Bards of passion and of mirth, 17–22

Softly the breezes from the forest came . . .
Clear was the song from Philomel's far bower;
Grateful the incense from the lime-tree flower . . .
Lovely the moon in ether, all alone.

    Calidore, 152, 154–155, 157

As though a tongueless nightingale should swell
Her throat in vain, and die, heart-stifled, in her dell.

    The Eve of St. Agnes, 206–207

Faint fare-thee-wells, and sigh-shrilled adieus!
    Endymion, I, 690

71

A haunting music, sole perhaps and lone
Supportress of the faery-roof.

Lamia, II, 122–123

Melodies sung into the world's ear.

The Fall of Hyperion, 188

Fair world, adieu!
Thy dales, and hills, are fading from my view:
Swiftly I mount, upon wide spreading pinions.

To My Brother George, 103–105

Gone and past
Are cloudy phantasms. Caverns lone, farewel!
And air of visions, and the monstrous swell
Of visionary seas! No, never more
Shall airy voices cheat me to the shore
Of tangled wonder, breathless and aghast.

Endymion, IV, 650–655

Wild warblings from the Aeolian lyre
Enchantment softly breathe, and tremblingly expire.

Ode to Apollo, 34–35

My ear is open like a greedy shark,
    To catch the tunings of a voice divine.

Woman! when I behold thee flippant, vain, 27–28

Fled is that music.
— *Ode to a Nightingale,* 80

Ode to a Nightingale

My heart aches, and a drowsy numbness pains
  My sense, as though of hemlock I had drunk,
Or emptied some dull opiate to the drains
  One minute past, and Lethe-wards had sunk:
'Tis not through envy of thy happy lot,
  But being too happy in thine happiness, —
    That thou, light-winged Dryad of the trees,
      In some melodious plot
  Of beechen green, and shadows numberless,
    Singest of summer in full-throated ease.

O, for a draught of vintage! that hath been
  Cool'd a long age in the deep-delved earth,
Tasting of Flora and the country green,
  Dance, and Provençal song, and sunburnt mirth!
O for a beaker full of the warm South,
  Full of the true, the blushful Hippocrene,
    With beaded bubbles winking at the brim,
      And purple-stained mouth;
  That I might drink, and leave the world unseen,
    And with thee fade away into the forest dim:

Fade far away, dissolve, and quite forget
  What thou among the leaves hast never known,
The weariness, the fever, and the fret
  Here, where men sit and hear each other groan;
Where palsy shakes a few, sad, last gray hairs,
  Where youth grows pale, and spectre-thin, and dies;
    Where but to think is to be full of sorrow
      And leaden-eyed despairs,
  Where Beauty cannot keep her lustrous eyes,
    Or new Love pine at them beyond to-morrow.

Away! away! for I will fly to thee,
   Not charioted by Bacchus and his pards,
But on the viewless wings of Poesy,
   Though the dull brain perplexes and retards:
Already with thee! tender is the night,
   And haply the Queen-Moon is on her throne,
      Cluster'd around by all her starry Fays;
         But here there is no light,
   Save what from heaven is with the breezes blown
      Through verdurous glooms and winding mossy ways.

I cannot see what flowers are at my feet,
   Nor what soft incense hangs upon the boughs,
But, in embalmed darkness, guess each sweet
   Wherewith the seasonable month endows
The grass, the thicket, and the fruit-tree wild;
   White hawthorn, and the pastoral eglantine;
      Fast fading violets cover'd up in leaves;
         And mid-May's eldest child,
   The coming musk-rose, full of dewy wine,
      The murmurous haunt of flies on summer eves.

Darkling I listen; and, for many a time
   I have been half in love with easeful Death,
Call'd him soft names in many a mused rhyme,
   To take into the air my quiet breath;
Now more than ever seems it rich to die,
   To cease upon the midnight with no pain,
      While thou art pouring forth thy soul abroad
         In such an ecstasy!
   Still wouldst thou sing, and I have ears in vain—
      To thy high requiem become a sod.

Thou wast not born for death, immortal Bird!
   No hungry generations tread thee down;
The voice I hear this passing night was heard
   In ancient days by emperor and clown:

Perhaps the self-same song that found a path
    Through the sad heart of Ruth, when, sick for home,
        She stood in tears amid the alien corn;
            The same that oft-times hath
        Charm'd magic casements, opening on the foam
        Of perilous seas, in faery lands forlorn.

Forlorn! the very word is like a bell
    To toll me back from thee to my sole self!
Adieu! the fancy cannot cheat so well
    As she is fam'd to do, deceiving elf.
Adieu! adieu! thy plaintive anthem fades
    Past the near meadows, over the still stream,
        Up the hill-side; and now 'tis buried deep
            In the next valley-glades:
        Was it a vision, or a waking dream?
        Fled is that music:—Do I wake or sleep?[1]

*I*N THE *Ode to a Nightingale*, Keats continues his inquiries into the nature of art, both in the mind and in the various media available to the mind. The reflection on the medium of music embodied in this ode distinguishes it from its predecessors. In *Indolence*, Keats had acknowledged a wish to create art, but had refused in favor of reverie within nature. In *Psyche*, his mind was roused to art, but to an art of interior gardening and architecture which changed the unplanned, besprinkled lawn of Indolence into Fancy's garden surrounding an architectural fane. In *Psyche*, Keats still conceived of art as exclusively mental, expressed in no visible or audible artifact, and directed to no audience except Psyche, the poet's own soul.

Keats's firm sense that his own medium was words (he refers to himself as a poet in the first four odes) made him wish to inquire into other art media, notably music and graphic (or plastic) representation. These two fine arts were popularly allied to poetry, the first by the metaphor of the lyre of Apollo, the second by the axiom *Ut pictura poesis*.[2] Keats's persistent invocation of the figure of Apollo as musician, on the one hand, and his frequenting of Haydon's studio, on the other, ensured his continued reflection on the capacities of the two media parallel to his own, a reflection prompted by admiration and envy alike. It is no accident that both the *Ode to a Nightingale* and the *Ode on a Grecian Urn* were first published in *Annals of the Fine Arts*, a journal whose readers would have taken *Nightingale* to be a poem on the art of music, and *Urn* to be a poem on bas-relief sculpture.[3]

It has commonly been thought that the nightingale's song represented to Keats the music of nature, to be contrasted with human art, whether verbal or musical. But most commentators have also felt, paradoxically, that Keats identifies himself as poet with the nightingale, and, by analogy with the human arts of Fancy, sees the nightingale's song as a delusive enchantment. We know that Keats at first passionately wished to conceive of art as an activity lying wholly within the natural order, not at all opposed to it, and so chose a "natural" song as his symbol for human music. "If Poetry" (he wrote in 1818 while under the spell of this wish) "comes not as naturally as the Leaves to a tree" (or, we might substitute, "as song to a bird") "it had better not come at all" (*Letters*, I, 238–239). If I dwell especially on Keats's use of birdsong to represent the artistic medium of musical melody, it is because that symbolic intent in the ode generates, I believe, the countermeditation on the plastic arts which issues in the *Ode on a Grecian Urn*.

In choosing music as its artifact, the *Ode to a Nightingale* decides for beauty alone, without truth-content. The representational function of both literature and the visual arts precludes their being taken as "pure" examples of aesthetic being. Questions of ideational content and of social or moral value arise perhaps inevitably in criticism of literature, painting, sculpture, and even dance; but such questions become very nearly unintelligible when posed with respect to instrumental music.[4] Vocal music is another matter, of course; but the interesting thing about the song of Keats's nightingale is that it is vocal without verbal content, a pure vocalise. Though such music was ideal for Keats's end in view—the isolation of a pure principle of expressive beauty—the symbol was one which had already aroused in him a certain dissatisfaction. Keats thought, in conventional terms, that music existed to warm the heart luxuriously, or to offer madness or delight, as the "rich notes" were fitted by the instrumentalist "to each sensation": it was an art solely of sensation, not of thought:

> But many days have past since last my heart
> Was warmed luxuriously by divine Mozart;
> By Arne delighted, or by Handel madden'd;
> Or by the song of Erin pierc'd and sadden'd:
> What time you were before the music sitting,
> And the rich notes to each sensation fitting.

These lines from the early epistle *To Charles Cowden Clarke* suggest that it was only when words (as in "the song of Erin") accompanied the music that Keats ascribed a referential meaning to the notes; otherwise the notes existed to transmit sensation alone. Even Apollo's music is without truth-content: though Keats sometimes speaks of "Apollo's song," the word "song" in this usage seems simply to mean "music." Nowhere in Keats is Apollo shown singing words to his music; the music he produces is always instrumental music, and is described as ravishing the ear, rather than containing any specifiable import. As late as *Hyperion*, Apollo's music stimulates feeling while remaining itself inscrutably without meaning (II, 279–289):

> My sense was fill'd
> With that new blissful golden melody.
> A living death was in each gush of sounds,
> Each family of rapturous hurried notes,
> That fell, one after one, yet all at once,
> Like pearl beads dropping sudden from their string:
> And then another, then another strain,
> Each like a dove leaving its olive perch,
> With music wing'd instead of silent plumes,
> To hover round my head, and make me sick
> Of joy and grief at once.

In a letter, now lost, to Reynolds written on 31 January 1818, Keats had included a poem addressed to Apollo (*God of the meridian*) puzzling over the relations between soul and body, art and sense, vision and thought. The poem (which we know from Woodhouse's transcript of it) conceives at one point of the soul, inspired by Apollo, as a creature in flight, while the body is "earthward pressed":

> Aye, when the soul is fled
> Too high above our head,
> Affrighted do we gaze
> After its airy maze.

The soul, fled too high to be seen by the body pressed to earth, loses itself, as a lark might, in an airy maze of sunshine (since the soul "is flown" to the "bowers" of Apollo, "god of the meridian"). These details will remind us of the *Ode to a Nightingale*, which nonetheless changes the occasion of the soul's flight from a sunlit idyll to a darkened nocturne. At the close of the poem to Apollo, Keats senses some tempering that is lacking in the soul's headlong flight, and he prays:

> O let me, let me share
> With the hot lyre and thee
> The staid philosophy.

It is a prayer that the *Ode to a Nightingale* cannot quite make, but which Keats cannot forget.

Almost a year later, Keats returned to the question of meaning in music. In the "rondeau" beginning "Bards of passion and of mirth," he represents the heaven of poetry as a place

> Where the nightingale doth sing
> Not a senseless, tranced thing,
> But divine melodious truth;
> Philosophic numbers smooth;
> Tales and golden histories
> Of heaven and its mysteries.

Yeats will of course give his golden bird those tales and histories and philosophical prophecies to utter, as it sings "Of what is past, or passing, or to come." But Keats's earthly nightingale possesses no divine truth or staid philosophy; it is only a "senseless, tranced thing." It may confer benefits, but it intends none. Like Love, it blesses the world unknowingly, as Keats had said in *Endymion*: Love blesses the world

> As does the nightingale, upperched high,
> And cloister'd among cool and bunched leaves—
> She sings but to her love, nor e'er conceives
> How tiptoe Night holds back her dark-grey hood.
>   (*Endymion*, 1, 828–831)

In choosing to press Fancy outward, into a medium, away from the dim dreams of *Indolence* and the purely mental architectonics of

Psyche, Keats changes his view of art: he brings it into nature, into a relation with an audience, and into the power of the senses. The *Ode to a Nightingale* takes art to be the projection of beauty and sensation into an external medium — here, that of heard melody, numbers not tuneless but audible, not timeless but changing in time, and consequently vanishing. Keats has deliberately chosen in this ode to forgo gradually in his role as protagonist all immediate sensory experience except that of hearing: that is, in this experiment he represents himself eventually as pure ear, pure audience, alone. In this almost perfect aesthetic separation from "habitual self," he explores what one version of the aesthetic response can be. The ode is remarkable by the fineness and profundity of Keats's meditation on listening.

But the nightingale as natural poet represents, for Keats, another aspect of himself, a model for the human poet; and the nightingale is a voice of pure self-expression. Keats inherited a controversy over the sex of the nightingale and the import of its music: was it female or male; and was it "most melancholy," as Milton thought, or was it rather "full of love and Joyance," as Coleridge insisted (and as *Endymion* implies)? Coleridge's conversation poem *The Nightingale* is one long argument against the pathetic fallacy, arguing that "in nature there is nothing melancholy," that the nightingale is "merry," and that it is only we who have "made all gentle sounds tell back the tale of [our] own sorrow." Keats's ode (borrowing from Coleridge several details of language) follows Coleridge's injunction to the poet that he should refuse to be coerced away from natural perception by the inherited mythological legend of Philomela's sorrow; instead he should "stretch his limbs . . . in mossy forest-dell" and "surrender his whole spirit" to nonrepresentational sensation — "the influxes / Of shapes and sounds and shifting elements." In this way, by echoing the true joyous sound that he actually hears, he will gain poetic authenticity from nature, and "his fame should share in Nature's immortality." Because the nightingale among the leaves has never known the sorrows of the world, Keats, obeying Coleridge, thinks that he too must sequester himself from the woes of the world, and, suppressing other senses in favor of hearing, listen raptly to the nightingale.

Keats does not entirely follow Coleridge (who had talked of

nightingales during their one meeting). Coleridge's nightingale (because Coleridge refuses the representational and legendary link with Philomela) is defiantly male, warbling

> his delicious notes
> As he were fearful that an April night
> Would be too short for him to utter forth
> His love-chant, and disburthen his full soul
> Of all its music.

Keats's bird is faintly female (it is briefly a Dryad, and is later linked with the female Fancy who "cannot cheat so well as she is fam'd to do"), but the poet's identification with the bird is so strong, and Keats's rejection of the legend of Philomela so conclusive, that we feel the bird to be sexless, no more than a "wandering voice" to which the poet attends. "Hearing" is here a synecdoche for aesthetic receptivity attuned to one wholly beautiful expressive form. How can the aesthetic experience in music be entered? How can it be sustained? What does it offer us? How do we cooperate with it? What are our feelings when it ends? What is our final judgment on it? These and other questions are at issue in the poem, which nevertheless seeks to suppress questions for a time in its effort to maintain pure aesthetic responsiveness. Such questions will find their fullest expression in *The Fall of Hyperion*, but they are one of the chief motives for the ode, which found its anguished theme at Tom Keats's deathbed, as Keats put art (and its helplessness in the practical realm) to the test of a deathbed vigil: "This morning Poetry has conquered—I have relapsed into those abstractions which are my only life—I feel escaped from a new strange and threatening sorrow.—And I am thankful for it" (*Letters*, 1, 370).

The *Ode to a Nightingale*, in attempting an escape from threatening sorrow by a deliberate averting of the eyes from human suffering, and, formally speaking, by its flight from representation, is a poem of wish and will, where Keats's "yearning and fondness . . . for the Beautiful" (*Letters*, 1, 388) are forced into assertion. It suppresses questioning till, at the end, it is forced to; its tone, when it becomes hectic, can spoil the singing of the nightingale. Keats's ambition, his genius, and his intensity of infeeling all demanded that he join the nightingale in passionate, living expressiveness; but his guilt as a survivor of his brother's death and his sense of the pain of the world pressed him toward silence and suicide.[5] The conflict causes what Jones calls the antiphonal structure of this ode (p. 225 and *passim*). In fact, not one but several thematic structures are observable in the poem.

The most evident thematic structure is the repeated antithesis between the earthbound poet and the free bird; another is the antiphonal voicing of what Jones names "ripeness" and "withering," a structure of thought equally present in the *Urn*. But if we are intent on distinguishing the odes from each other, we must ask more particularly how *Nightingale* is composed, looking less at its polarities of theme than at its extension in time. Though both *Indolence* and *Psyche* had intellectually recognized the intensity of poetic creation (*Indolence* by its figure of the "demon Poesy," a "maiden most unmeek," and *Psyche* by mentioning the pain mixed with pleasure in approaching the untrodden regions of the mind), the *Ode to a Nightingale* is the first of the odes to represent structurally the penalty incurred by the poet if he externalizes or consummates that interior intensity. The cessation of the nightingale's music is Keats's first metaphor in the odes for that disillusion which follows the physical embodiment of Fancy in act and artifact.

The entry into intensity in the ode is followed eventually, as we know, by an ultimate disappointment. But criticism has been content, on the whole, to regard the rest of this longest of the odes — its middle, so to speak — as rather a random succession of impressions, a drift of mind. In its absence of conclusiveness and its abandonment to reverie, the poem appeals to readers who prize it as the most personal, the most apparently spontaneous, the most immediately beautiful, and the most confessional of Keats's odes. I believe that the "events" of the ode, as it unfolds in time, have more logic, however, than is usually granted them, and that they are best seen in relation to Keats's pursuit of the idea of music as a nonrepresentational art.

The entry into intensity in the ode is symbolized by a descent, which I take to be away from the "higher" mind and toward the "lower region" of the senses. Though Keats's declared intent is by a "flight" to join the bird, the retirement into the forest grove is logically a horizontal motion; and the suggestions of Lethe and hemlock, and the continued elevation of the nightingale above the poet, make the poet's progress one that goes downward to darkness. The suggestions of elements of the grave in the poet's bower add to the notion of descent, and at the point of deepest descent Keats writes the greatest stanza of the ode:

> I cannot see what flowers are at my feet,
>   Nor what soft incense hangs upon the boughs,
> But, in embalmed darkness, guess each sweet
>   Wherewith the seasonable month endows
> The grass, the thicket, and the fruit-tree wild;
>   White hawthorn, and the pastoral eglantine;
>   Fast fading violets cover'd up in leaves;
>   And mid-May's eldest child,
>   The coming musk-rose, full of dewy wine,
> The murmurous haunt of flies on summer eves.

This is Keats's greatest bower, the heir of many earlier ones. The poet's position in embalmèd darkness, with flowers at his feet, makes him seem a tomb-effigy, one who could say, with Lorenzo in *Isabella* (298–301),

> Red whortle-berries droop above my head,
>   And a large flint-stone weighs upon my feet;
>   Around me beeches and high chestnuts shed
>   Their leaves and prickly nuts.

To deck his bower, Keats turns not to nature but to art: the violets and musk-roses and eglantine are borrowed from Titania's bower in *A Midsummer Night's Dream*, described by Oberon (as this bower is described by Keats) from memory, not sight.[6] The "verdurous glooms and winding mossy ways" of the bower are like those of the entrance slope to Hades; the darkness, fragrantly "embalmed," is not without deathly overtones; and the fast-fading violets (time cannot be evaded even in the conceiving of the bower) are covered up in leaves. To listen to music, with all one's other senses laid asleep (the next line, where even the soft incense is forgotten, is "Darkling I listen"), is, for Keats, very nearly to be dead. The focusing power of aesthetic experience, its concentration in the enrapturing of a single sense, entails the temporary "death" of the other sense faculties.

In every Keatsian bower there is a rendezvous. The tryst in this bower should be with the Nightingale, since the entire yearning of the poem is apparently directed toward her; she is a female principle, she is identified here with the Fancy (also, in this poem, female), and she represents ecstasy. But as we know, this underworld tryst is with Death, invoked with Keats's characteristic erotic adjectives, "soft" and "rich":

> Darkling I listen; and, for many a time
>   I have been half in love with easeful Death,
> Call'd him soft names in many a mused rhyme,
>   To take into the air my quiet breath;
> Now more than ever seems it rich to die,
>   To cease upon the midnight with no pain.

Keats's language in the bower of Death is borrowed from Hamlet's suicidal soliloquy: "To die, to sleep"; "To die, to cease." Other echoes of *Hamlet* all point to the tragic intent and tragic origin of this ode:[7] Hamlet's "weary, stale, unprofitable world" recurs via *The Excursion*, as Keats's "weariness, the fever and the fret"; Hamlet's wish that his flesh might "melt, / Thaw, and resolve itself into a dew" reappears in Keats's wish to "fade far away, dissolve, and quite forget"; as the Ghost in *Hamlet* "fades," so Keats wishes to "fade away" and so the nightingale's anthem "fades"; and we hear the echo of the Ghost's "Adieu, Adieu, Adieu" in Keats's "Adieu! . . . / Adieu! adieu!"[8] Whatever the beauty of Keats's bower, it must be interpreted in a tragic sense. But the bird's music is not tragic; it is rather Keats's feeling of pain that colors the music, as he listens darkling.

The vulnerability of the bower to time—at least to the cyclical rhythms of the vegetative cycle of fading violets and coming roses—

prevents its offering any real escape from that world "where youth grows pale, and spectre-thin, and dies." The bower seems at first to be a refuge because it contains no human society—only the nearly discarnate poet, his ordinary consciousness suspended in the act of listening, and the nearly disembodied bird, represented by a stream of sound. The act of listening, by annihilating touch and sight and even, at last, the sense of smell, removes us from human woe temporarily by making our physical state corpselike; but it is a momentary "death" that we die in aesthetic attention, not a real one.

Keats's chief intellectual demonstration in this ode is that of the compulsive image-making of the entranced imagination. The listener in darkness, offered pure natural music without human ideational content, fills both bower and song with fancies of his own. These fancies compose in fact the substance of the ode. There are, at beginning and end, brief projective attempts to characterize the song of the bird (initially as happy, full-throated, melodious, ecstatic, later as a requiem and an anthem): otherwise, the successive fancies which are allowed to arise match the bird's song only momentarily (only the first, the fantasy of the vintage, could be said, for instance, to be happy or ecstatic). The hope of a sustained melodiousness attended to without perplexing thought becomes in the poem more wish than fact.

The characteristic Keatsian movement from inception through intensity to desolation occurs in *Nightingale, Urn, Melancholy,* and *Autumn,* in different ways.[9] The pattern is sometimes referred to in sexual terms (for example, by Jones, who calls it a "metasexual orgasm," p. 241), but its commoner critical names use terms of intensity followed by a perception of transience, mortality, evanescence, and so on, and are usually negative namings. In *Nightingale,* though all these sadder names of disappointment and forlornness are applicable, I should rather call this Keatsian rhythm by a positive name, and term it a wish for completion. "Completion" is a Keatsian word (I take it from the *Hymn to Pan*) and I use it because the odd result of the desolations in *Nightingale* and elsewhere is that we feel, in those pained awakenings from Fancy, Keats's most solid poetic strength, a strength which eventually affirms not a vanishing but a discovery. He himself will not discover this strength in *Night-*

ingale but only in the later odes.[10] The pursuit of a fancy to its completion is, for the purposes of this ode, Keats's working concept of
aesthetic experience; he found its model in Shakespeare's sonnets,
where he admired the "intensity of working out conceits" which
caused the sonnets to be "full of fine things said unintentionally"
(*Letters*, I, 188).

Keats seems to intend, in *Nightingale*, that each conceit to which
he turns should be "worked out," forced to bear the entire weight
of completion. Each single object of attention must be fully described, and must exhaust its own significance. In loading every
image-rift with ore in this way, he risks both excess of description
and obscuring of structural lines. However, with each successive
stanzaic experiment, he seems to learn more and more about what
can be done with the trope of reiteration, which is his principal
trope in this ode. It is of course a static trope: it bends its scrutiny
to one thing, and says over and over what that one thing is, or
what it is like, or how much it can be said to contain. By its exploratory tarrying on one concept at a time — what can be said of wine,
what is the dark bower like, what is the relation of audience to
nightingale — we can distinguish a poem using the trope of reiteration from one employing the ongoing trope of enumeration, the
trope of lists, of numerical plenitude.

The first element of significance that Keats treats in a reiterative
way is wine, and in his scherzo on the draught of vintage, the conceit of wine is made to contain within itself several regions: the cool
vault of the deep-delvèd earth (linked with the melodious plot, the
shadows numberless, and the subsequent images of grave and
burial); the realm of song (related to that of the nightingale); of
sunburnt mirth and Flora (parallel to the bird's projected theme of
summer); of Hippocrene (the realm of art); of winking bubbles and
purple-stained mouth (a synecdoche for Bacchus, as Blackstone saw,
recalling "young Bacchus' eye-wink" in *Endymion*, IV, 267); and of
intoxication and loss of consciousness (allied with the drowsy
numbness of the opening of the ode). Though it is true that the sequence about wine follows Keats's usual rhythm of expansion and
sinking, the impression left by the stanza (on us as on Byron) is one
of feverish and insistent self-manipulation. Wine is to be everything

at once—a refreshing cool draught, a warmth, an incitement to thoughts of sunburnt mirth, an inspiration to song, a bacchic intoxicant, an opiate. The older poets, says Keats, erred in thinking of the Muses' spring as water; the true Hippocrene, the authentic drink of inspiration, is claret. This forced exuberance is finally distasteful to Keats himself, here in the ode as in the later lines to Fanny: "Shall I gulp wine? No, that is vulgarism" (*What can I do to drive away*, 24). Nonetheless, Keats will try, again and again, to cram significance of every sort into each subsequent conceit as he did into his fleeting, and rapidly rejected, wish for wine. The trope of reiteration is almost forced upon him by the very vacancy of the bird's song; unable to describe it, Keats lavishes description on everything else.

The sketch on wine is followed, after the feeble reiterative variations on "fade," by the largely allegorical sketch of the miseries of the world. This sketch falls into a confused generic mixture, as the stanza presents first a hyperbolic generalization about the world as a place where "men sit and hear each other groan," and next offers us a fixed Spenserian stationed figure, palsy, who "shakes a few, sad, last gray hairs"; he is followed by a small Spenserian masque of mutability, extended over time, in which "youth grows pale, and spectre-thin, and dies."[11] Up to this point in the ode, Keats has represented the unhappiness of the human world in terms of groans, palsy, age, disease, weariness, fever, and fret—all inflictions, afflictions, imposed on man by life's progress. But when Keats, always intelligent, presses on to consider human unhappiness more deeply, he abandons this vocabulary of temporal dooms, contingencies, accidents, and ills. Going to the heart of things, he says that in this world "but to think is to be full of sorrow." The admission that consciousness itself is the essential source of human grief is Keats's most truthful statement in this stanza, and leads to the fundamental choice, on which the ode turns, between unhappy consciousness and the unconsciousness of death. But Keats averts his gaze rapidly from this disabling glimpse of the necessary conjunction of thought and sorrow, and returns to two more causes of ordinary unhappiness—the dulling of Beauty's luster, and the brevity of Love's fidelity. The two sculptural frieze-figures—Beauty, lustrous-eyed, and Love pining in adoration—would remind us of Psyche and

Cupid, except for the authorial comment about the impermanence of their bloom and constancy. Keats's rejection of the joint divinity worshiped in *Psyche*, eternally fixed in loveliness and fidelity, foretells his eventual emphasis of the sacrificial over the erotic.

The uneasiness of Keats's poetry in rendering this frieze of human suffering is evident. Keats does not know whether he should station a group of emblematic figures—palsy, Love, Beauty, youth—in eternal self-characterizing postures (as he does with palsy), whether he should allow his allegorical characters movement in time (as he does with youth), or, finally, whether he should simply prophesy their evanescence (as he does with Beauty and Love). He sees two alternatives to allegorical writing: he could be realistic and mimetic, as he is at the opening of the stanza, and show us men groaning and listening to groans; or he could dispense with all his *dramatis personae*, mimetic and allegorical alike, and say, in his own voice, in the propositional mode, that but to think is to be full of sorrow. He chooses to have it all—realistic puppets; emblems static and emblems moving to prophetic doom; and tragic propositions.

Sometimes the villain in this stanza is the physical unhappiness of early doom, sometimes it is the metaphysical unhappiness of the thought of transience, sometimes it is simply consciousness itself. There is no particular order to the stanza's reiteration of the conceit of evils; even at the cost of diffuseness and contradiction, Keats is bent on completeness (even on a surfeit) of causes of unhappiness. Just as in the stanza on wine, he here decides that in reiteration lies intensity. While enumeration (the dominating figure of *To Autumn*) is the cornucopia trope of exterior plenitude—whether good things or evil ones—reiteration (by which I mean not adding more things but rather exploring the parts of one thing, whether wine or "the world") is the trope of inner intensity; it is only by a pressing reiteration that Keats feels he can convey either the benefits available from wine or the griefs imposed by life. As in the case of the earlier stanza on wine, the tone becomes high-pitched in this stanza of reiterated suffering. In the nature of things, there is no reason for reiteration ever to cease, since any topic is infinitely subdivisible—Keats could have added further items to his praise of wine, or to his denigration of the world, without materially affecting the poem. It is for this reason that the passages on wine and suffering strike us as less than compelling in their architectonics: however descriptively beautiful (the praise of wine) or however true (the catalogue of human suffering), they do not exhibit that structural necessity which would prevent our thinking them infinitely extensible.[12] The later passages on the bower and on the nightingale's audiences exhibit (as I hope to show) a structure which constrains them to finish when they finish: we cannot imagine Keats adding on further details after he has arrived at the flies on the musk-rose or the faery lands forlorn.

The first well-managed completion and reiteration of the poem comes in the bower scene, that self-interment at the center of the poem. After his two early rejections — of the wine which induces a false ecstasy, and of the world which cannot sustain happiness — the poet approaches, in the bower, the center of being that is offered by the poem. It is, as I have said, the center offered by the conjunction of the wings of "Poesy" (yet to be defined) on Keats's part, and song, on the part of the nightingale. It is the center empowered by that "greeting of the spirit" here represented by hearing; to melody we bring only our ears. "Poesy" seems to mean here a state of pure sensation, comparable to the ecstasy afforded the senses by wine, which has been dismissed not because it is not a boon to sensation, but because the wings of Poesy are more efficacious as sensation than wine can ever be. Poesy, in this ode, is a name for the empathic flight of the Fancy rather than for composition in "numbers"; Keats is harking back to his *Psyche*-conception of poesy as an internalized activity, but here, though internal in the listening poet, it is actualized in the "tuneful numbers" of the singing bird.

Though Keats's bower has sometimes been thought to represent nature, it can represent nature only as it exists in the repository of memory and art. Nothing here can be seen or identified; in this tender night, only inference and guess are possible. Classical presences — the Moon and her starry Fays, remembered from Milton's Nativity Ode — are excluded, not by dismissal as belonging to the embittering world of those quasi-human beings palsy, youth, Beauty, and Love, but by being put gently by. They belong to the larger mythological world, celebrated in *Psyche*, which can include the visual; the mythological must be refused in this poetic world so purely restricted to a fragrant blind hearing:

> Haply the Queen-Moon is on her throne,
>   Cluster'd around by all her starry Fays:
>   But here there is no light—

or almost no light. The faint beams which blow with the breezes serve only to define the glooms of the encompassing bower. The brief glance back to sight and touch in the verdurous glooms and mossy ways is preparatory to the true underworld venture of the poem. Nonetheless, by invoking—even if to dismiss—the Moon, the stars, and the blown light dispersed in gloom and mossy labyrinth, Keats adds an imaginative completeness to his bower. It exists, he tells us, in a continuum with light, the heavens, and mythological presences—in short, with Milton's domain—but Keats wishes in this poem to turn his attention to the restricted center of all art-circles, a pure close conjunction of medium and audience, and so here forgoes both visual panorama and classical legend.

Finally, the poet is within the bower, and begins his greatest, and yet most unaffected, list of completions. "The simple flowers of our spring," as he called them from his sickbed,[13] are, in this place, wholly indistinguishable from the art-flowers of *Lycidas* and of Shakespeare's fairy land.[14] The "seasonable" month of May, endowing all her child-vegetation with different sweets, is the predecessor to the maternal Autumn loading and blessing the vines with the vegetation of her season. Both govern realms where inexorable times and seasons obtain; in this ode Keats forsakes all hope for the timeless mythological bower of *Psyche*. Like his seasonable month, Keats touches with his unseeing but unerring vision each beauty in turn. His first task is to define the boundaries of his darkened space—and those boundaries give the trope of reiteration, as we see it in the bower, that structural firmness it had earlier lacked. First, Keats points low to the flowers at his feet and high to the soft incense on the boughs above. Next he creates a gradually ascending enclosure, planting, so to speak, first the grass, then the thicket, then the overhanging fruit tree. He then redescends to shrubs, haw-thorn and eglantine, and ends, where he began, with flowers—the violets and musk-rose. This quiet mastery of spatial contours, learned from Milton, establishes the garden enclosure here, as later, in the ode *To Autumn*, Keats will establish the boundaries of his cottage farm. Within his bower, Keats adds a second structural firmness, conjoining time with space. He balances the fading violets with the coming musk-rose, and the participles "fading" and "com-ing" draw the bower into the realm of the "passing" night where the bird is "pouring" forth a song. This is not the earthly paradise of simultaneous flowering and fruit-bearing that we seem to see in-itially in the autumn ode; but it resembles a paradise, though a changing one, since as the violets fade the musk-rose comes into bloom (a passage not allowed to the flowers of *Psyche*). The dewy wine of the musk-rose replaces, with a sweeter sensation, the wine of Bacchus forgone earlier in the poem. Nothing seems lost. Every-thing is rich, tender, soft, embalmèd, dewy, and sweet. But when the musk-rose is blown, what then? The summer celebrated by the bird's song is strangely invaded as the full-blown rose becomes "the murmurous haunt of flies."[15] The flies are the link to Keats's admis-sion of a tryst with Death, announced in the next stanza, and they spell the end of the paradisal illusion of the bower, a conceit dear to Keats from *Endymion* on. At the same time, the flies make the bower complete. Keats excludes nothing from the bower, not even overripeness and carrion-presences, however delicately intimated, and his inclusion in the bower of the winged insects and temporal decay marks an intellectual and psychic advance over the fanciful suspension of the season in *Indolence* and the purely floral and un-fading (because purely mental) bower in *Psyche*.

"Darkling I listen," Keats reminds us—but we have forgotten him as listener, since the blind space of the bower has been actively substituting for the bird, as its objective correlative. The motion of the bower stanza, as it sketches its upper and lower boundaries and then pauses exquisitely on the sparely named and untroubled beauty of its grass, thicket, and trees before allowing the violets to fade and the musk-rose to open its cup, is managed with absolute sureness and order, literary and psychological, culminating as the murmurousness of the flies modulates into Keats's own murmur to Death, calling him soft names in musèd rhyme. The bird's "melodious numbers" have been simply the void on which Keats has projected those internal images which must stand, in art, for the riches of human sense-receptivity. The pure world of sound—from which all representational sights, all allegorized human beings, and all visual mythological presences have been banished—is itself so close to the world of death that one could with ease slip over the threshold from the bower to the realm of Lethe. The poem has descended deeper and deeper into a narrowing consciousness (with a corresponding intensity of the sensual ear), and must here choose annihilation or a return to life.

The intensity of sense-perception which accompanies aesthetic concentration is evident in the exquisite precision with which Keats "guesses" his sensuous surroundings and all their sweets. What becomes evident in the new quantitative discriminations of the following stanza, with its multiple distinctions (Keats has been *half* in love with Death for *many a* time, has addressed him in *many a* musèd rhyme; it seems rich to die, now *more than ever*), is that the poetic flight has begun to weaken, and the sensual is being invaded by memory and judgment. We witness the entrance of the philosophic mind, able to characterize the quality of its own breath even as it breathes. The awakening of the philosophic mind marks the end of the aesthetic trance; just as Keats comes near to abandoning himself altogether to death or trance—he scarcely knows one from the other—he remembers Hamlet's and Claudio's speculations on death, and in an analogue to Claudio's fear that he will "become a kneaded clod" (*Measure for Measure*, III.I.120)[16] he summons up the thought of himself "become a sod," and ends the embowered trance. At the moment of near acquiescence in dissolution, Keats chooses life, and thought.

The means Keats employs by which to put this choice of life to himself offers yet another instance of the trope of reiteration—this time a list of putative audiences for the bird's song. Though this list, it would seem, might be infinitely extended, since the bird has sung in all ages and to all audiences, there is in fact a structure to the list. We recall that in his decision to leave the world behind,

Keats had banished human beings from his poem; at that point, consciousness had seemed the grimmest cause of sorrow. Now, at this later point, the obliteration of consciousness in death seems a worse evil. Death, even if postponed, cannot be avoided; in Keats's bitter view, each hungry generation tramples its forebears underfoot, and Tom's fate was only, however premature, the common one. In the nightingale's song there are only notes, there is no tale of death; since the nightingale, for the purposes of the ode, *is* its song, it is exempt from death or the consciousness of death, and goes on singing unconscious of the obliterations of time. In an attempt to repudiate the terrible vision of the nightingale eternally singing above the carnage of generations, Keats rejects his earlier flight from human presence, and reintroduces human beings to his poem, imagining himself, in his function as the nightingale's present audience, linked to a brotherhood of other listeners in other ages. At first Keats sees in the nightingale's song a democratic diffusion: the song is audible to all alike, whether emperor or rustic (culture, as Arnold said, seeks to do away with classes). Next the audience becomes any soul which, like Keats's own, stands in need of consolation, and the song, for a moment given purpose in a pathetic fallacy of providential intent, is said to find a path into the hearts of those who, like Ruth, are sick for home, standing in tears in alien stubble-fields. I recapitulate: in the first of these reiterations of audience, art is for everyone; in the second, art, it is promised, will find a path into the being of those whose woe needs solace. Or—a chilling hypothesis following on these two humane ones— art is for no one. Keats takes his list of auditors to its beautiful and empty conclusion: art, in the last reiteration of audience, richly fills its own land, a land with nobody in it. The last listeners to the bird are those unpeopled magic casements,[17] in their land forlorn of all human inhabitants, opening onto a perilous sea harboring no vessel.

If we now stop to reflect on the large formal shape of the *Ode to a Nightingale*, we can say that it is one of entrance and exit, of entrancement and disillusion, one long, unbroken trajectory, beginning with a repudiation of both the human world and of Bacchic intoxication, continuing with a descent into a disembodied but intense listening in a dark bower, and ending in a reentry into the world as soon as consciousness reawakens and trance is broken, a breach initiated by the memory of earlier literary invocations of Death and symbolized by the departing flight of the nightingale. The Fancy, so constructively mentally active as the gardener in *Psyche*, is here accused as the deceitfully inhuman agent of a Spenserian faery-delusion, its charming open of casements alliterating with its cheating.

Keats attempts in the *Ode to a Nightingale* a view of the aesthetic act more complex than the one he had postulated in *Psyche*, where the act had been considered only from the point of view of the constructing artist. Now he also includes the audience and the artifact, in his trio of bird, listener, and song. Art, in this ode, has no conceptual or moral content. Ravishingly beautiful and entirely natural, it is a stream of invention, pure sound, in no way mimetic, on which we as listeners project our own feelings of ecstasy or grief. Art utters itself unconscious of any audience, pouring its soul abroad in pure self-expressiveness. Though its audience may be consoled by it, it is indifferent to that audience, singing as raptly to a clown as to an emperor, as beautifully to empty rooms and lands forlorn as to a Ruth in tears. It is available to us only in a moment of sensual trance in which we suspend intelligence and consciousness of our suffering human lot. Its immortality ranks it among Keats's divinities, but unlike Psyche it needs no cult, being wholly self-sufficient. Between its solipsistic immortal world and our social and mortal one there can be no commerce except by the viewless wings of sensation in Poesy-Fancy, which cannot bear us long aloft. A certain concession appears at the end of the ode, in which a putative truth-value is hoped for in calling the ear-experience a "vision," and hoping that one saw it, as one saw *Psyche*, with awakened eyes. Yet the other conclusion—that it was a trancèd daydream from which one has awakened to sober reality—finds more powerful support in the constitutive shape of the poem: its drugged entrance and its aversion from the spectacle of suffering, its central dark obliteration of consciousness, its reliance on the sensual ear, its banishing of the brain, its journey homeward to habitual self, and its blighted exit from sensation and beauty into thought and selfhood.

Keats was not satisfied with the postulate of this ode—that lyric art, of which the model is natural music, is self-expressive, a vehicle of sensation, nonmimetic, deceptive, uttered to no particular ear, and beautiful without respect to truth or verisimilitude. He was not satisfied, either, with the trope of intensity, reiteration, as his chief rhetorical resource. Nor was he satisfied to think of the divinity of art as a being immortal, unchanging, and indifferent to social function, lodged in an inaccessible realm. Finally, he was unwilling to attribute to art a function fundamentally deceitful with respect to its audience. In attempting a truer view of art, he will virtually rewrite the whole of *Nightingale* in *Urn*.

So far I have been speaking of the themes and rhetorical conduct of the Nightingale ode. It is difficult to turn to its language: it is so very familiar, and so hallowed by long association with Keats in the public mind, that it is almost impossible to see it freshly. The ode has been loved for its language more than for its structure or for originality of thought, and to express a preference for any other ode over *Nightingale* is to arouse the dismay of many readers, who invariably mention "the language" of the poem as the motive for their attachment to it. The ode does require all of Keats's richness of language in order, so to speak, to stay afloat; its language—uneven at the beginning and end where Keats must find a way in and out of trance—finds a luxurious stability at its center.

Keats had been, in *Endymion*, a visual poet, imagining scenes of encounter, stationing figures in processions, and giving his gardener Fancy free rein to produce a sumptuous and varied landscape. The imaginative scheme for *Nightingale* forbade, as it turned out, that central visual exercise of his powers, since the poem was to take place in the dark, with a poet-speaker who had become, after the best poetic fashion, a blind seer, listening to a Muse, a fellow artist in music. A convincing language of blindness had to be found, and Keats's triumph in finding it has made the ode memorable. But he had also to find language for the fading and obliteration of the sense of sight, as well as for the regaining of it, and these necessities taxed his invention in a different way. The ode shows signs of improvisation, notably in its passage from a sunlit day to a midnight scene (with no apparent allowance for the passage of time) and in its gradual change of reference to the song of the bird, as it passes from a happy, natural ecstasy to a sad art-composition referred to variously as a requiem and an anthem. The poem seems composed as an exercise upon itself, since each stanza generates a problem of expression or position which the next is designed to solve. Consequently the only practical way of discussing its language is to take it up in the sequence in which it occurs.

In choosing present-tense narration ("My heart aches") combined with invocation ("thou, light-winged Dryad") as his rhetorical framework, Keats is adapting the mixed frame, of narration and address, that he had used for *Indolence* and *Psyche*; but in *Indolence* the narration of procession, since it was written in the past tense, took on remoteness and dreaminess by comparison to the vexed remarks to the Figures, voiced in the actual present-tense moment of the poem. But in *Nightingale* the present-tense narration brings the ode into the configuration of what we tend to call confessional poetry; this alone is enough to account for the pressing appeal of the ode to many readers. "My heart aches . . . I will fly to thee . . . Darkling I listen . . . I have been half in love with easeful Death . . . Do I wake or sleep?"—the first person utterance is the strand by which a reader finds his way through the labyrinth of the poem. In *Psyche* the speaker had confined his own function to that of visionary and prophet; his private feelings were not of importance, his ritual function took precedence. In *Indolence* the speaker had allowed himself one moment of confessional description—"and to follow them I burn'd / And ached for wings"—but on the whole that ode repudiated private outcry in favor of numbness and drowsiness. The awakened ache of personal feeling in *Nightingale* is the stronger for the reticences of the previous odes; every reader feels in the abrupt opening "My heart aches" the impossibility of the poet's any longer keeping silence.

It is the contradiction implicit in the first stanza that generates the rest of the ode—the contradiction between a drowsy numbness which attempts to blot out the happy song of the bird and the intense empathy which wishes to participate in the bird's happiness. This is the contrast of heartache and joy, of silent pain and full-throated ease of utterance. The *donnée* of *Nightingale*—a recumbent poet, a soliciting Presence—thus resembles that of *Indolence*, but instead of sinking back to indolence or idleness on the grass, Keats here chooses the other option—to take wings himself and follow the fading voice. (Had he followed the Presences in *Indolence* on those wings he ached for, he would have found himself with them in spirit on their dreamy urn—as, later, he did.) He chooses to follow the voice, to "fade away" with it into its proper sphere, a sphere conceived of at first as a "melodious plot / Of beechen green," next as a "forest dim," and finally as the entire world— imperial, rustic, pastoral, and imaginative—of the nightingale's reach, whether it finds a path to emperor, rustic, Ruth, or faery land. The nightingale is created first as a mythological visual ob- ject—a "light-winged Dryad of the trees"—and the wine which seems a possible route to the nightingale is also in part mytholog- ically and visually created: we are offered not only a Bacchic beaker full of "beaded bubbles winking at the brim, / And purple-stained mouth," but also a frieze representing "Flora and the country green, / Dance, and Provençal song, and sunburnt mirth."[18] The frieze is intended to convey, by visual means, the taste of the wine; and Keats continues to rely on the sense of sight (before sacrificing it for good) in his next frieze, the scene of human suffering:

> Here, where men sit and hear each other groan;
> Where palsy shakes a few, sad, last gray hairs,
> Where youth grows pale, and spectre-thin, and dies;
> Where but to think is to be full of sorrow
> And leaden-eyed despairs,
> Where Beauty cannot keep her lustrous eyes,
> Or new Love pine at them beyond to-morrow.

The oddity of the last two items in this frieze is that they are *not* visible; they are the negation of a desired frieze which would show Beauty, ever lustrous-eyed, and Love, ever pining—the frieze Keats will later create on the urn. The odd emphasis on the luster of the eyes as that which Beauty will lose, and the eyes as that feature at which love pines (echoed later in *Melancholy*), is caused, I think, by the irruption into the allegorical frieze of the two nonfigural lines preceding the figures of Beauty and Love: "Where but to think is to be full of sorrow / And leaden-eyed despairs." Those leaden eyes belong to the drowsiness with which the poem began and to that forgoing of sight to which the poem is tending as it proposes to leave the world "unseen." When we call to mind the emphasis of the odes on seeing as the chief means to knowledge—the three Figures seen, and eventually known, in *Indolence*; the winged Psyche seen and known with awakened eyes in *Psyche*; the urn saying of its visually perceived self that it is all we know on earth and all we need to know; the emphasis in *Melancholy* on the goddess's being seen only by the initiate—we realize that Keats is here disavowing knowledge along with sight, wishing, as he leaves the world "unseen," to forget what the bird among the leaves has never "known." The nightingale's song is linked, by way of *Indolence*, to the throstle's lay; what the thrush had said to Keats, in February of the previous year, was to fret not after knowledge. The thrush had, in its utterance, linked together darkness, the repudiation of knowledge, song, wakefulness and sleep, and an evening that listens—all ingredients Keats later repossessed for use in *Nightingale*:

> O thou, whose only book has been the light
> Of supreme darkness which thou feddest on
> Night after night, when Phoebus was away,
> To thee the spring shall be a tripple morn.
> O fret not after knowledge—I have none,
> And yet my song comes native with the warmth;
> O fret not after knowledge—I have none,
> And yet the evening listens. He who saddens
> At thought of idleness cannot be idle,
> And he's awake who thinks himself asleep.
> (*O thou whose face hath felt the winter's wind*, 5–14)

In March 1819 Keats had written to Haydon promising to be "dumb" and not write unless his knowledge or experience should make him run over. He said playfully, in a *Psyche*-mode, that he knew "the satisfaction of having great conceptions without the toil of sonnetteering. I will not spoil my love of gloom by writing an ode to darkness" (*Letters*, II, 43). And yet a year later he found himself compelled to write that ode—to gloom, darkness, and repudiation of the brain's conceptual knowledge. "Embowered from the light, / Enshaded in forgetfulness divine," he could, in the "still midnight," close his willing eyes not in sleep (as in the *Sonnet to Sleep* contemporary with the Nightingale ode) but rather in the act of listening, having grown "all ear" in his role as audience to the nightingale's melody. He could himself no longer, in his leaden-eyed despair, keep the luster of his own eyes awake. The nightingale, in a verb of visual vanishing, "fades" into the dim forest; Keats in desire "fades away" with it; the violets "fade," the plaintive anthem "fades"; the diminution of the visual in listening is maintained throughout in this one word, borrowed I think from the ghost in *Hamlet* who faded on the crowing of the cock (and self-borrowed from *Indolence* as well). After the first three stanzas of the poem, vision is repeatedly denied; the wings of Poesy are "viewless" or invisible;[19] the Moon may perhaps be on her throne, but "here there is no light" (except what faintly and temporarily permits the glooms to be called "verdurous"), and Keats "cannot see" the flowers, but in "darkness" can only "guess" their nature. Finally, it is midnight, and the poet listens "darkling," with no light or perfume left, hearing only "the voice I hear this passing night." This superb descent into absolute darkness and restriction to the one sense of hearing alone governs one strand of diction in the ode, whereby seeing is abolished, though with many lingerings and regrets. Keats is sorry to leave behind the Bacchic frieze and Floral pageantry of wine, dance, and song; but the pastoral frieze-figures of intoxication are paired so formally in the poem with the frieze-figures of palsy and spectral thinness that we realize that in order to forget human decline we must be willing to forget human exuberance as well.

The next regret that Keats feels is that he must, in leaving behind light and the knowledge it represents, leave behind "the beautiful mythology of Greece." He had been willing to forswear it in *Indolence* as he adjured the Figures to return to their dreamy urn, or to vanish into the clouds; but he had promised, in the *Ode to Psyche*, to restore, at least in an internalized way, the pagan mythology that Milton had banished as a source of truth from English poetry. By recalling the Nativity Ode once more in the Queen Moon and her starry Fays,[20] Keats admits that he must forfeit as well, for the descent into the dark, the world of Greek sculptural myth. In the "soft incense" of the bower we have the last faint, sensual echo of the legendary cult of Psyche, with its "incense sweet"; with the vanishing of the incense and the guessed-at flowers we come to the last purity of the reciprocity of ear and song, where no longer is anything seen, or remembered, nothing diffuses an odor on the night, no wine is dewy to the taste, nothing is touched. When, at the end of the stanza beginning "Darkling I listen," Keats abolishes the ear as well, at least in thought — "and I have ears in vain" — the bodily annihilation is complete, and Keats becomes the "sod" which his soul-as-besprinkled-lawn (*Indolence*) must become, once deprived of all light and its corollary conceptual and legendary knowledge. (The repossession of all the senses in the autumn ode — including the cultic incense in the fume of Demeter's poppies — is one of Keats's greatest hymns to life and consciousness, measured, as we must measure it, against the Nightingale ode.)

It is a mark of Keats's intensity of linguistic gift that the language of the absence of the visual is itself so sensually luxurious. The night is "tender," Keats is "half in love" with a Death so "easeful" as to be related to the "ease" of the nightingale's song; he has called Death "soft" names, and it seems "rich" to die while the nightingale pours forth not its song but its soul, in ecstasy. But the mention of love and richness and ease would not convince were the words not drawing on their bower-correlative established in the preceding stanza through the spontaneous vegetative beauty of flower and fruit, and through the seasonable rich providence of Maia, the May goddess, about to give birth to her eldest child, whom she will see full-blown and changed to the haunt of flies in later, summer evenings. The "soft" incense of the one stanza guarantees the "soft" names of the next; "rich" in the simple worship of a single one of the May goddess's days, Keats can find it "rich" to die, to let his song "die away," as he had written the year before on May Day. Representation by the senses has now been forgone, and so have those things — mythological and natural alike — that cannot live except in sense-representation (but by sleight of hand they are, by being denied, made present in the poem). Keats has come, by the time he envisages himself as a sod, to the end of the senses. It is midnight; he is, in imagination, dead, and he has abandoned all hope of sense-projection upon the void of song.[21]

With imaginative self-annihilation complete, Keats cannot any longer speak of himself as a listener, but only of the immortally singing bird and other listeners in the past. The choice of listeners seems at first perplexing. The bird is a Dryad; the nightingale of poetry is conventionally a Greek bird; why are the listeners Shakespearean and biblical and Spenserian? We recall that in insisting on darkness and "naturalness" in his art-poem, Keats has had to leave behind classical mythology. He associated myth, as I have said, with the visual arts more than with literature; to leave the eye behind means to leave sculptural friezes behind. But also the gods belong to an "artificial" world, whereas this art of vocalise exists in the realm of nature, surrounded by the human world containing clowns and emperors and Ruth. It is obvious that something changes when Keats arrives at the magic casements, and I shall return to them; but even there, the separation from the classical continues. In pursuing his delineation of an art like the leaves of a tree, organic to the sensual body, Keats must forgo the allegorical nature of a classical and mythological art; the listeners, then, come not from the visual arts of painting or sculpture but from the world of literature. Keats looked to Gibbon or Shakespeare for the emperor, to Shakespeare certainly for the clown, to the Bible for Ruth, and to Spenserian literary romance for the magic casements. And with the gradual reduction of self, first to the one sense of hearing, and then to nothingness as that one sense imaginatively dies into a sod, Keats can only be thrown back on the nightingale-musician itself as the single remaining principle of continuity, a type of aesthetic immortality. (His own "I will die" gives rise to a Horatian "I will not *wholly* die" which is displaced onto the bird.)

In January 1819 Keats had described his poem *Bards of passion and of mirth* as a poem "on the double immortality of poets" (*Letters*, ii, 25); and it was in considering that double immortality that he placed the bards in a heaven where the nightingale is the official bard, singing tales and golden histories. The nightingale is there conceived of as a poet with narrative and historical content, therefore rightly called the singer of truth. In singing "divine melodious truth; / Philosophic numbers smooth," the heavenly nightingale wonderfully adds propositional or philosophical truth to its truth of tale or history. But art which is neither historical nor narrative nor philosophical nor propositional—the art of melody, as Keats now conceives it—has no "sense" and can be sung in a "trance" that prescinds from, in fact repudiates, that dull brain which perplexes and retards. It is as an artist that the nightingale can properly, like the ensphered bards, be called immortal.

The nightingale reaches the status of divinity as it is hailed as immortal, and the poem most fully becomes an ode, rather than an idyll, in these lines. In the tone of familiar address at the beginning, the poet had seemed to speak to the bird almost as to a companion, and the reciprocity of language (being too happy in its happiness) had suggested an equality of states. But by the penultimate stanza the distance has widened immensely between the bird and its almost annihilated devotee:

> *Thou* was not [as I was] born for death, immortal Bird!
> No hungry generations tread *thee* down [as they tread down
>   me and mine].[22]

Such a distance from his object of veneration is intolerable to Keats: as he invents surrogates for himself as listener to the music, those surrogates from literature (once the routine summoning of emperor and clown has been gotten over—though this programmatic democracy has its roots in his own class origins) reenact his own experience in the ode. Like Ruth, he has emerged into a strange land: his exile was to leave the mythological realm of Flora and old Pan, of spring and budding, and accede to the lapses of time—for him usually symbolized by the passage from budding to being full-blown, and from the season of flowers to the season of fruit or corn. "The very corn which is now so beautiful, as if it had only took to ripening yesterday, is for the market: So, why should I be delicate" (*Letters*, II, 129). The sad heart of Keats, sick for his proper home in leafy luxury, stood in tears amid the alien corn of his brother's reaping. To find the corn and its harvest-destiny not alien will be the task of the autumn ode; but in *Nightingale* the passage from being a bud to being gleaned for the market still seems unbearable; the poet, still a bud (or at most a flower) in his own self-conception (as we know from *Indolence*), feels premature and alien among the gathered sheaves. To say this is to make explicit what Keats touches with the lightest breath; but the allusion to Ruth cannot pass unexplained in the emotional economy of the poem. The poet has left potentiality behind and has entered process. He temporarily forgives the inhuman, temporal, and lapsing melody of art its immortality since it can find a way to the sad heart of Ruth, and solace it. But to leave natural process for art itself is actually to choose extinction. In making his last audience for the nightingale the empty and unpeopled magic casements, Keats creates the self-reflexive world of art and makes the scene on which the casement opens the scene of art's activity—"the foam / Of perilous seas, in faery lands forlorn." There is a tone of "that undiscovered country, from whose bourne / No traveller returns" about the faery lands forlorn and their perilous seas. It is as though Keats had been charmed away to the faery world, and found himself listening as the song hovered over the magic casements empty of human presence.[23] The "charm" of the song is now not an accidentally charitable one, as it had been when it found a path to the sad heart of Ruth; there it acted as Keats thought art should act, as a friend to man, soothing his cares and lifting his heart (*Sleep and Poesy*). Now the song is purely aesthetic, and savors of the Belle Dame sans Merci. The painful juxtaposition of the ever tangentially kindly function of art as man stands in the field of his eventual reaping, and the inhuman and immortal self-sufficiency of art in its own realm presses the penultimate stanza into its death-knell, tolling the annihilation of the conjunction between the entranced Keats and the entrancing music. The habitual sole self is resuscitated.

It may surprise us that the conjunction of self and bird is not figured in sexual terms. But the bird remains virginal (linked by her form as Dryad, her midnight appearance, and her "melodious plot" to the virgin choir in *Psyche* that makes "melodious moan," in the draft, "upon the midnight hours"). This suppression of sexuality (or rather its displacement onto the male figure of Death) allies the remote Nightingale to the chaster Muse of Milton, and to that unravished bride, the Urn. Keats will not attempt the integration of art and sexuality until *Melancholy*, and will not perfect it until the ode *To Autumn*.

With the dissolution of trance, Keats defensively reverts to the cynical tone he had earlier used in *Indolence*, and reproves this new short fever-fit of Fancy, linking her too (as Spenserian "elf ") to the faery lands forlorn. But the triple adieu, remembered (as I have said earlier) from *Hamlet*, brings with it in memory "Remember me"; and the lingering geographical delineation of the passage of the fading song ("past W, over X, up Y, and now buried deep in Z") ensures that it is preserved in the heart as it fades. The last word used about the nightingale's melody tells us what it had become for Keats—music. The words he uses of it are increasingly words appropriate to art-music—even more appropriate to art-music than to a bird's song: requiem, voice, song, anthem, music. In returning to his original visual *donnée* of drowsiness and sleep, dissolution and fading, to ask (in visual terms) whether his experience was a vision or a waking dream, whether he wakes or sleeps, Keats departs, for the sake of closure, from his examination of the limits and powers of wordless, abstract, and nonrepresentational music. He reverts, in short, from listening to seeing or not seeing, a motion he will recall, and reverse, in *Autumn*. In fact he has "seen" nothing of the nightingale; nothing has presented itself to him as a "vision" or, for that matter, as a dream with visual elements. On the contrary, everything in the ode has emphasized the lack of light, the lack of sight, the dimness, the dissolving of outline, the fading, the gloom, the closing of those eyes which had become leaden from sorrowing thought. The eyes are, as proverbial wisdom would have it, the windows of the soul, where thought is made visible. The brain, which, by interposing thought, perplexes and retards the trance of listening, is finally, with the disappearance of sight, lulled to unconsciousness. No propositional or historical "truths" are enunciated once Keats enters the tender night; instead, all is description and evocation, sensation and beauty. "Philosophical" proposition proper reenters the poem with the memory of previous suicidal fantasies, with the realization of self as sod, in the contrastive "Thou wast not born for death, immortal Bird!" and in the closing repudiation of Fancy; but in each case, the bird's song takes descriptive preeminence over those propositions, whether by charming casements or by fading slowly past the meadows. In the end, neither descriptive "song" nor propositional "truth" (of death, of cheating charm) is allowed the victory. Rather, the trope of interrogation — neither sensuous descriptive reiteration nor intellectual asserted proposition — is invoked for closure; and the vocabulary of physical state and music ("a vision . . . a dream . . . music . . . wake or sleep"), with its Shakespearean echoes, is finally preferred, for speculative purposes, to a vocabulary of philosophical derivation ("Was I deceived by illusion?"). The ode ends, then, as a poem inscribed to beauty rather than to truth, to sensation rather than to thought.

Of course Keats's conceptions of beauty, truth, sensation, and thought will change a great deal between this ode and *To Autumn*. The brave beginning of a faith in thought in *Psyche*, with its "branched thoughts, new grown with pleasant pain," is in *Nightingale* suspended, and the brain is denigrated as dull and retarding to poesy. Mythology as a source of truth, so confidently embraced in *Psyche*, is here eliminated in the persons of Bacchus and the Queen Moon and her Fays. A defensive repudiation of the world, begun in *Indolence* (even though the world there came beckoning in attractive, if demanding, forms), is here consolidated, and the world is made to seem horrible. Literature is still embraced, but it is not "the beautiful mythology of Greece" to which Keats looks; he looks instead to a more native literature, to Shakespeare and the English Bible and Spenser.

The absence of intentional structural form in the bird's song — it simply fades away to be continued elsewhere — means that the structural form we see in *Nightingale* cannot be truly mimetic of artsong, but rather of trance — mimetic, that is, of an internal reverie, comparable to that of *Indolence*, rather than of an internal construct (bower and shrine), as in *Psyche*. And since the language of the music reverie cannot be analytic, propositional, or interrogative, given the firm rejection of the perplexing and retarding brain, it must be synthetic, sensational, and illustrative. The reiterations of the ode are richly loaded, but until Keats informs them with intellectual structure (as he does through the categories of space and time in the bower, and through an argument of exile and estrangement in the evolving of successive "audiences") they offer only a static aesthetic injunction—to load each rift with ore. Loading rifts is a retarding aesthetic, and does not in itself contain a structural and intentional principle which can move a poem forward. Like a reiteration which can go on forever, this ode could go on forever— until Keats allows his mind back into the poem, or, to put it another way, until he allows the bird to fly away. Structure is sacrificed here to the language of rich converging illustration; and everything is said so many times (witness the extraordinary degree of anaphora and of parallelism of syntax) that the poem risks becoming obvious.

To one who reads backward from the *Ode on a Grecian Urn* to this ode, the poem seems like a desperate attempt to find in the music of a song without words the model of an art form where the evils of the world need not be represented, where an enchanting melody alone is required of the artist, where to rich sensations the musician (or poet) can fit rich explorings of his medium, and where, in the intensity of working out conceits, he can say fine things. The fact that the art of music need not, and cannot, represent life mimetically means that it is a "happy" art, and in one sense it offered a model of the sort of art for which Keats's talent was evidently fitted: "His art is happy," said Yeats of Keats, "but who knows his mind?" In fact Keats's mind was difficult for Keats himself to know. He knew he had no training in philosophical or propositional thinking; and he also knew that his mind was scenic and his art descriptive. And yet the obligations he felt to Wisdom, if he were to join the company of the bards, urged him to an art which could speak to mortals:

> Of their sorrows and delights;
> Of their passions and their spites;
> Of their glory and their shame;
> What doth strengthen and what maim.

> Thus ye teach us, every day,
> Wisdom, though fled far away.
> (*Bards of passion and of mirth*, 31–36)

So he addressed his bards; and while music might be said, conceivably, to speak to mortals of passions or delights, it could scarcely, Keats decided, instruct us in those ethical and philosophical truths called Wisdom. It seems inevitable that Keats should turn away from the realm of abstract melody to the realm of representational art, to see whether he could find a model for his own practice in those arts which represent in visible mimetic form the passions, ideals, and sufferings of men. To do so would mean to admit human beings and their lives into the representational field of the aesthetic object,[24] and to permit the perplexed brain its sovereign, if difficult, moment in aesthetic creation and response. A new effort toward representation would mean that all the questions suppressed (until the last moment) in the *Ode to a Nightingale* would have to be allowed. Interrogation, the trope *par excellence* of the questioning mind, would have to take precedence over *Psyche*'s reduplication (the mimetic trope of a historically predetermined reparation) and over reiteration (the intensifying trope of pure sensation). The abandon of abstract art for an art with ideational content would mean that truth would have to go hand in hand with beauty. And so Keats once more had recourse to the astonishing inventive powers of his genius and devised an urn — one never seen on land or sea, but invested more than any actual urn with the consecration and the poet's dream. The reintroduction of mortal human beings to his art meant that Keats could turn again to Greece, and could gratefully draw from its sculpture those images which had always been for him, far more than music, the repository of his idea of beauty. Keats will never again, after *Nightingale*, find it necessary to reject his deep allegiance to Greek forms. It is in part his wondering relief that those temporarily suppressed forms still exist to do him good that prompts the devout greeting of the spirit with which he will hail his urn:

> Thou still unravish'd bride of quietness,
> Thou foster-child of silence and slow time.

And it is because the dead artist of the urn represents a whole culture rather than simply a single soul (like a bird) that Keats can forsake the first-person and self-expressive voice, imitative of the bird's own voice, that he used in *Nightingale*, and can adopt not the ritualized cultic priest-voice of *Psyche* but the impersonal voice of the contemplative poet-spectator, gazing at a comprehensive frieze-in-the-round which fills with grateful visual forms both his sensual eye and his conceiving mind. Finally, in the ode to the urn, Keats abandons for good the idea of an effortless, purely spontaneous, and socially indifferent art. The artist's work, as we see it in the Hellenic urn, has a social purpose, and it is deliberate and arduous — the art of the sculptor's chisel, not the art of a singing bird.

Truth the Best Music:
The *Ode on a Grecian Urn*

I deem
Truth the best music in a first-born song.

Endymion, IV, 772–773

Not yet dead,
But in old marbles ever beautiful.

Endymion, I, 318–319

Silent as a consecrated urn.

Endymion, III, 32

The marble fairness of old Greece.

Fragment of Castle-builder, 61

A Question is the best beacon towards a little Speculation.

Letters, I, 175

Who are these coming to the sacrifice?
    To what green altar, O mysterious priest,
Lead'st thòu that heifer lowing at the skies,
    And all her silken flanks with garlands drest?
        —*Ode on a Grecian Urn*, 31–34

Ode on a Grecian Urn

Thou still unravish'd bride of quietness,
  Thou foster-child of silence and slow time,
Sylvan historian, who canst thus express
  A flowery tale more sweetly than our rhyme:
What leaf-fring'd legend haunts about thy shape
  Of deities or mortals, or of both,
    In Tempe or the dales of Arcady?
    What men or gods are these? What maidens loth?
What mad pursuit? What struggle to escape?
    What pipes and timbrels? What wild ecstasy?

Heard melodies are sweet, but those unheard
  Are sweeter: therefore, ye soft pipes, play on;
Not to the sensual ear, but, more endear'd,
  Pipe to the spirit ditties of no tone:
Fair youth, beneath the trees, thou canst not leave
  Thy song, nor ever can those trees be bare;
    Bold lover, never, never canst thou kiss,
Though winning near the goal—yet, do not grieve;
    She cannot fade, though thou hast not thy bliss,
  For ever wilt thou love, and she be fair!

Ah, happy, happy boughs! that cannot shed
  Your leaves, nor ever bid the spring adieu;
And, happy melodist, unwearied,
  For ever piping songs for ever new;
More happy love! more happy, happy love!
  For ever warm and still to be enjoy'd,
    For ever panting, and for ever young;
All breathing human passion far above,
    That leaves a heart high-sorrowful and cloy'd,
    A burning forehead, and a parching tongue.

Who are these coming to the sacrifice?
　To what green altar, O mysterious priest,
Lead'st thou that heifer lowing at the skies,
　And all her silken flanks with garlands drest?
What little town by river or sea shore,
　Or mountain-built with peaceful citadel,
　　Is emptied of this folk, this pious morn?
And, little town, thy streets for evermore
　Will silent be; and not a soul to tell
　　Why thou art desolate, can e'er return.

O Attic shape! Fair attitude! with brede
　Of marble men and maidens overwrought,
With forest branches and the trodden weed;
　Thou, silent form, dost tease us out of thought
As doth eternity: Cold Pastoral!
　When old age shall this generation waste,
　　Thou shalt remain, in midst of other woe
Than ours, a friend to man, to whom thou say'st,
"Beauty is truth, truth beauty," — that is all
　　Ye know on earth, and all ye need to know.[1]

WE MUST PRESUME, since Keats went on after writing the *Ode to a Nightingale* to write the *Ode on a Grecian Urn* (as near a twin to the earlier ode as one poem can be to another),[2] that his experiments in analyzing, distinguishing, and objectifying his thoughts and feelings about creation, expression, audience, sensation, thought, beauty, truth, and the fine arts were still in some way unsatisfactory to him. And yet he was not ready to examine "art" in some general way: abandoning nonrepresentational "natural" music as his metaphor, he took as metaphor another special case, the one (because of the Elgin marbles) most in the public eye, the case of sculpture.[3] He has, we realize, given in and joined his phantoms of *Indolence* on their urn; but in this new speculative enterprise he has somewhat changed the cast of characters, retaining Love and Poesy (as maiden and pipe player) but discarding Ambition, and adding new figures to which we shall come.

The *Ode on a Grecian Urn* squarely confronts the truth that art is not "natural," like leaves on a tree, but artificial. The sculptor must chisel the stone, a medium external to himself and recalcitrant. In restricting itself to one sense, the *Urn* resembles *Nightingale*, but in the *Urn* the sense is sight, not hearing. The *Urn* suppresses hearing, as the *Ode to a Nightingale* had suppressed sight (and as both suppress the "lower senses" of touch and taste). If *Nightingale* is an experiment in thinking about art in terms of pure, "natural," nonrepresentational music prolonged in time, the *Urn* is an experiment in thinking about art in terms of pure, "artificial," representational visuality extended in space (a space whose extension, in Keats's special case, rounds on itself—the urn is a self-limiting frieze). As we have seen, precisely because the nightingale's song is nonrepresentational it can ignore that world "where men sit and hear each other groan"; because it is nonconceptual or nonphilosophical it can avoid those sorrows and leaden-eyed despairs inseparable from thought. The *Ode to a Nightingale* can therefore bypass (until the questions which break its trance end the poem) the question of truth, and expatiate in its consideration of sensation and beauty, suggesting, by its darkness, that the more indistinct and dim and remote that beauty, the better. Beauty, in the form of the bird's song without words, stimulates the reverie of the musing Fancy, which endlessly projects itself on a perfect void—the essentially vacant, if transfixing, song of the nightingale.

All of this changes with the *Ode on a Grecian Urn*. Keats now proposes, with respect to art as he understands it and wishes to practice it, that art is a constructive and conscious shaping of a medium, and that what is created is representational, bearing some relation to "Truth." He proposes to examine this premise through a deliberately invented vehicle for understanding, a carved marble Hellenic urn.[4] Recognizable represented forms—male, female, and animal—appear on the urn (crowding to the borders of composition the leaves and grass so dear to decoratively breeding Fancy; the leaves are the nostalgic tribute to the earlier naive view of the artist as one who puts forth leaves as naturally as trees). The attitudes conferred by Keats on his represented forms are also clearly recognizable and unambiguous: they are attitudes of sexual pursuit and flight, of music-making and courtship, and of communal religious performance. Instinctive and civilized actions alike are represented: human beings—and perhaps even the gods themselves (though they are here indistinguishable from human beings)[5]—are the natural inhabitants of this medium. The forms, and the attitudes in which they are displayed, are beautiful—in the largest sense of that word (a sense Keats had imbibed from the Elgin marbles), a sense which includes the striking, the conflictual, and the memorable as well as the graceful and decorous. The urn seems in fact remarkably like life, framing as it does vivid moments of action or feeling.

This advance in Keats's conceiving of what art is like—an advance over the less complex (because instinctually expressive and nonrepresentational) postulate of the nightingale ode—requires a different response to the artifact. The actions represented on the urn excite in the beholder an empathy like that solicited in the listener by the *melos* of the nightingale, but they, unlike the birdsong, are allowed to provoke him to early questions. The constitutive trope of the *Urn* is interrogation, that trope of the perplexed mind.[6]

Three times the poet "enters" a scene on the urn; but, as I see the progress of the poem, he enters each successive scene with a different view, as spectator, of what the urn is and what it does. Each entrance can be represented conceptually as a different Keatsian hypothesis about what is offered us by aesthetic experience, each provoking a different conclusion on our part about propriety of response. Keats once again plays the part of "audience," as he had in *Nightingale*; but he has turned from listener to spectator (or so we at first believe — the terms were always problematic to him, since his own art of written poetry entails in its audience both a seeing and a listening). Keats has, by eliminating a live self-expressive artist (like the bird), turned his attention more profoundly to what an artifact, in and of itself, without first-person expressive or biographical context, may be said to convey. And by making his symbol not ambiguously "natural" (as was the "music" of the Dryad-bird) but unarguably man-made in a highly intellectual and conventionalized form, he can examine the question of the capacities and limits of an aesthetic medium far more exactly than he could in *Nightingale*.

Keats's first hypothesis about aesthetic experience, evoked by the orgiastic first scene on the urn, is that art tells us a story, a history, about some people who are not ourselves. The proper response to the urn in this instance is then to question it, to ask of it, "Who are these people, and what are they doing?" — the question of a believer in naive mimetic art, in art as illustration. It is the question Keats himself had asked in *Psyche* when he saw the embracing couple: "Who wast thou, O happy, happy dove?" It was the question that had irritated him when he could not at first solve the identities of the urn-figures in *Indolence*, since he had been acquainted with Phidian statues rather than with vases; the figures "were strange to me, as may betide / With vases, to one deep in Phidian lore." To ask "What men or gods are these?" is to suppose that there is a simple and satisfiable relation between beholder and art object, that the beholder can eventually know the "truth" of the leaf-fringed legend that haunts about the shape of the urn, determining its figurative decoration. In *Indolence*, Keats had eventually recognized that the figures which had been haunting some urn, and had departed from it to come and haunt him, were called (allegorically) Love, Ambition, and Poesy. They might have been called (mythologically) Venus, Cupid, and Psyche, or (historically) Achilles, Hector, and Helen; in any case, they had names. He had not at that time envisaged an art of visible but unspecifiable forms, forms deriving their interest neither from the emotions (allegorized), nor from mythology, nor from historical fact. All of Keats's early questions in the ode ("What men or gods are these? What maidens loth? / What mad pursuit? What struggle to escape?") could be given their "true" answers, he thinks, if only he knew the lost legend that the dead sculptor presumably had in mind, and here illustrated.

Keats's second hypothesis about aesthetic response is evoked by the second scene, which shows a piper accompanying a youth courting a maiden. This second hypothesis (prompted by his own use of allegorical frieze in *Indolence* and *Nightingale*) proposes that the urn represents not mythologically or historically identifiable figures acting out some known (if lost) legend, but rather what would nowadays be called a universal or archetypal "Truth"—in this instance, the truth of the unity of Love, Beauty, and Art, symbolized by the classic icon of a lover courting a maiden to music. The archetype is idealized—that is to say, it represents a human fantasy: that the lover will forever love, and the beloved be forever fair, and their courtship give rise to, and be accompanied by, an eternally refreshed art, "songs forever new." In this hypothesis, the urn is not representing other people, mythological or historical, but is allegorically representing ourselves and our feelings—except that it shows us ourselves and our actions "in a finer tone."[7] Our proper response to the urn is, under this hypothesis, to give up useless questions of what historical or mythological story it illustrates, rejoice in its extreme beauty, regret the discrepancy that exists between the fantasized and the real, and yet recognize the truth of our aspirations (here, toward a "happy" art accompanying constancy in love and perpetuity of beauty) represented in the actualized fantasy. Keats is now attempting to reverse his declaration in *Nightingale* that "Beauty cannot keep her lustrous eyes, / Or new Love pine at them beyond tomorrow." If not in life, at least in the truthful allegorical representation of our idealism, "For ever wilt thou love, and she be fair!"

The response stimulated by the second hypothesis—a response of sympathy with an idealized human state—is incompatible with the response solicited by the first hypothesis, that query about historical or legendary names and places. In the second response, the speaker is not exercised to discover originating legend or narrative, but naively once again enters wholly into the pictured scene, temporar- ·ily "forgetting" that he is contemplating a vase, and taking in the sculptured spectacle purely as life: "More happy love! more happy, happy love! . . . / For ever panting, and for ever young."

Keats, I believe, saw both of these naive responses (in which he shows his spectator of the vase fully participating) as in themselves alone not adequate to art. Art does not exist to offer historical truth alone, whether social or divine or sylvan; neither is it created primarily to offer the moral truth of accessible archetypal ideals. Consequently, in exhibiting each of these two responses, Keats does not permit the excitement generated by them to survive. The mind cannot rest in either hypothesis. In the first instance, the questions rise to a frenzy—"What pipes and timbrels? What wild ecstasy?" —but the frenzy toward specification is instantly quieted by a change of orchestration, as Keats allows the excited mind which posed the questions to abandon historical inquiry and try to begin, rationally, to consider the import of art. Keats turns to generaliza- tion and to philosophical diction, introducing a new movement, one of thought rather than empathy, as he meditates on the relative capacities of music, poetry, and the visual arts.

This new movement rejects the "heard melodies" so praised in the ode Keats had just completed on the nightingale (those melodies addressing the sensual ear) in favor of spatial and visual melodies which address the spirit. However, the criterion of aesthetic praiseworthiness here is still "sweetness" or *melos*. The bitterly truthful or the dissonant seem as yet to have no place in Keats's con- ception of this sculptural art, which is said to have "sweeter" melodies than music, and to express a "flowery" tale (like that em- bowered one of Cupid and Psyche, perhaps) "more sweetly" than Keats's own art of poetry could do.

This philosophical meditation on the superiority of spiritual to sensual melody interrupts the speaker's naive participation in the initial orgiastic scene; in the same way, a reflection on earthly passion and its putative inferiority to sculptured passion interrupts his second naive entry, this time an entry into the love on the urn. Once again, Keats draws a hierarchical comparison — not, now, one favoring visual art over sensual music or "our" rhyme, but rather one favoring the love on the urn over our "breathing human passion" far below it. To recapitulate: neither the naive factual questioning nor the naive thoughtless empathy is allowed to continue undisturbed: one is checked by a debate on the relative sweetness of music, rhyme, and sculpture, the other by a bitter intellectual recollection of the realities of human passion.[8] In each case, the poet's self — first the self as artist in a putatively deficient medium (since rhyme, like music, is addressed to the sensual ear), and second the self as embittered lover — rises to pit itself in some "philosophic" way against its own spontaneous, immediate, and "naive" response to the urn.

Undaunted, the speaker attempts a third time to "enter" the urn, and Keats proposes, in his fourth stanza, a new and more adequate hypothesis about the aesthetic experience offered by an artifact, and our aesthetic response. The urn, he suggests, is not just the illustration of a legend or tale about other people; nor is it just a representation, in archetypal and idealized form, of our human aspirations. Rather, it is most truly described as a self-contained anonymous world, complete in itself, which asks from us an empathic identification supremely free both of factual inquiry and of self-interest. Naive museum-goers demand either a known story, or the representation of a state visibly analogous to one of their own. It is easy to be merely narratively curious: "What men or gods are these?" It is even easier, by analogy with ourselves, to love a lover: "More happy love! more happy, happy love!" To the first of these naive responders, art is like a newspaper photograph, in need of an explanatory caption; to the second, art is like a mirror, in which he narcissistically luxuriates. But Keats, contemplating his third scene — a ritual sacrificial procession — foreign, ancient, remote from anything he has himself known — asks not about an antecedent legend but investigates instead the boundaries of representation:

What group has the artist now selected? To what altar is the heifer being led? From what town does the procession issue?[9]

Keats confronts in this way the necessary limits of representational art. All mimetic art represents some fragment of life, and implies a preceding dramatic disposition of its figures and a narrative chain of consequences for them, an antecedent and subsequent existence of these momentarily visible forms. The artist selects some element of life and focuses his attention on it, composing it so memorably that even if it is foreign to our life or experience—as a Greek ritual procession is not familiar in the way that the lust or love of the first two scenes might be—still we are so taken by this representation that we ask not the myth or history that will conveniently classify its characters and actions but rather the questions "Who?" "Whence?" and "Whither?"—not with detached anthropological or literary curiosity but with entire intimacy and yearning. If we could answer these last questions—and by hypothesis we cannot, since the urn is both visually limited and tacit—we would know origins and ends. Who are we; whither are we led by that mysterious priest; whence have we come to this place where we stand? The self-complete world of the work of art exerts a force drawing us to a pathos not our own, not visibly reflecting our own immediate experience. In imagining the little town where the procession began and the green altar where it will end, Keats allows for the continuing naiveté of belief never entirely lost even in the most self-forgetful aesthetic response. In this last hypothesis, the sense of solid reality created by the urn draws us into a cooperative venture in which, by extrapolating outward to altar and town, we "see" (as in certain optical illusions) much more information than is actually provided. Given a created procession, we ourselves cooperatively create its destination and its origin—its religious whither and whence.

While this third hypothesis—in which the audience, prompted by the visible artifact, engages by its interrogation in an act of cooperative mutual creation with the artist—is more satisfying than the purely mimetic, historical hypothesis of the artifact-as-illustration given in the first stanza, or the purely expressive and allegorical one of the artifact-as-mirror proposed in the second and third stanzas, it is also, because the most sophisticated hypothesis, the most alienating. We might be grateful to the urn while it was instructing us in historical or legendary truths about divine or human action; we might warm to it while it represented, through a universal archetype, truths of emotion at once eternal and personal. But once we recognize that it is primarily neither culturally instructional (a "sylvan historian") nor flatteringly truthful to our narcissistic wishes—that it is neither about someone else nor about us, but rather about its own inventions into which we are enticed and on which we exercise our own pathos in return—we see it as necessarily artificial, a work in a given medium by a given hand. The return out of trance into consciousness, exhibited once in *Nightingale*, is here deliberately made to occur three times, with each exit from a scene into which one has entered. While we are "within" the urn, we are not outside it; while we are outside reflecting on it, we are not "within" it. Like the figures on the urn, we cannot at once be in the town where we live and on the urn.

I have been speaking, on the whole, as though Keats, looking at an urn, were pressed, by the intensity of his feelings, to three successively more complex and intelligent responses. In point of fact, of course, Keats invents his three urn-scenes—of orgiastic pursuit to music, of courtship to music, and of religious observance—to which his three hypotheses of response will be attached. The first turbulent scene is invented as one likely to stimulate archaeological questions which could be satisfied by the "truths" of a museum notice: "This scene represents a ceremonial orgy in honor of the god such-and-such; participants attempted ecstatic sexual experience by the use of intoxicants, and ritual music was played on the kind of pipe represented here," and so on. The second idyllic scene is invented as one which has the tendency to evoke psychological "truth" of an easy reductiveness: "In every civilization we find the eternal pair, youth and maiden; we recognize here the idealized posture of youthful first love and pastoral song." But the third religious scene is invented as one presenting the real test of aesthetic response. Once we pass (as museum visitors) beyond a wish for the explanatory factual truths of historical or cultural captions, and beyond the narcissistic stage of being interested only in "lyric" art which we can see as a reflection of something in ourselves, we can confront art as it is in itself, in its ultimate formal anonymity and otherness. It is not "they"—men or gods. It is not "I" or "we." Or it is not primarily these. It is itself. And, by its nature, it draws us to itself; we do not impose our concerns upon it.

Keats's triple hypothesis engenders the compositional rhythm of the poem, its large structural form. Whereas *Nightingale* traces first a withdrawal from the world, then an engagement with the music of the bird, and later an involuntary disengagement at the admission of thought (a single parabolic trajectory), the *Urn*, as I have said, repeats a comparable form three times, once for each scene. I recapitulate here in formal terms what I have already described thematically. The opening address to the urn—grateful, but equilibrated and archaeological—gives way to a mounting voyeuristic excitement, as the beholder surrenders to the orgiastic scene. This excitement is not allowed a gradual subsidence. Instead, at the very moment of its interrogatory climax, it is admonished by a reproof of the sensual, as the wild ecstasy is replaced, in a striking whitening of voice, by soft pipes which play "not to the sensual ear" but rather "to the spirit ditties of no tone." Yet a second time, while seeing the young lovers on the urn, the speaker's excitement is heightened; he feels, this time, not the excitement of a voyeur, but that of a passionate sympathizer. This fever of identification, defensively over-prolonged through an extra stanza, is suddenly cooled, in the midst of its exclamatory *accelerando* (just as the earlier factual questions had been broken into in mid-career), by the memory of human passion, with its paradoxical simultaneous cloying and persisting thirst. In both of these cases, the irruption of the reflective mind is sudden, unforeseen, and apparently unpreventable: mind bursts in—whether in questions or in reflection—on receptive sensation as a force no longer able to be repressed. Keats's easy sense of being able to outwit the "dull brain"—with its perplexing questions[10] and its retarding of trance—has vanished forever. The brain breaks in; and what is more, Keats welcomes it, and entertains it; he is genuinely interested in meditating on the relation between heard and unheard melodies, on art addressed to the ear vis-à-vis art addressed to the spirit. And in fact the brain is never really banished; even to the orgiastic figures it had addressed its intellectual questions; even in describing the lovers it incorporates its knowledge of earthly change in the elegiac and contrastive language through which the sympathy for them is addressed.

When, the third time, the speaker bends to the urn, he has lost his voyeuristic and narcissistic motives. The speaker is—really for the first time—the truly aesthetic spectator, viewing the scene with a speculative curiosity which is no longer idle nor hectic. He no longer makes a self-absorbed, contrastive referral to his own human case, but rather extends himself in a generous loss of self in the other. He enters into the life of the religious scene, prolonging it forward and backward with tenderness and feeling, investing the procession with the weight of life's mysteries of whence and whither without altering its otherness, both cultural and historic. The priest remains mysterious, a figure for Fate leading life on (derived as he is from the priest in *Psyche*, he is yet the devotee of no one deity); the little town remains unknowable, a figure for the invisibility of origins; the green altar remains unseen, and undescribed (unlike Psyche's fane), a figure for a veiled end.

When this last intensity of engagement with the urn fails (as, like the preceding ones, it must), it fails because Keats has seen too far into the core of an eternal destruction. This destruction is not melodramatic and fierce, like the mutual ravening of all created beings which Keats had flinched at in his epistle to Reynolds. That earlier destruction was something outside aesthetic experience, which nonetheless blighted that experience—"It forces us in summer skies to mourn: / It spoils the singing of the nightingale" (*Dear Reynolds*, 84–85). Here, in the *Urn*, no such sensational interference from the outside is envisaged: the destruction of aesthetic reverie arises rather from the necessary obliteration inherent in process itself. All processions, by the very fact of their existence as processions, leave their origins behind; all travel is sacrificial of its origins. There is no agent for this destruction: the townsfolk are not banished by an enemy; if their little town has a citadel, Keats tells us deliberately that it is a peaceful one. The mysterious priest has something of the folk-tale force of a pied piper: we are all led willingly on, by many pieties, into life and then out of it. Life's sadness does not lie in the bitterness of sexual rhythms with their ultimate exhaustion, those rhythms underlying the Nightingale ode; it does not even lie, as Keats had thought, in the perplexing intellect which interrupts or retards sensual reverie; rather, it lies in the very existence of origins, processions, and ends, in the fact of process.

These precocious insights left Keats with a poem four-fifths complete, with its great fourth stanza—expressing his furthest reach—already written. The poem had begun, we recall, with a comparison of the urn with rhyme—to the disadvantage of rhyme. The urn's whole and simultaneous visual art, where everything can be present (and presented) at once, seemed to Keats, fresh from his disillusion with the nightingale, sweeter than a temporally experienced art like music or poetry. The reason for this preference is exposed in the second and third stanzas: what is seen whole and simultaneously need never come to an end, whereas the defect of a temporal art, like the song of the nightingale or the rhyme of the poet, is that it bids adieu, and fades. Visual art is not fugitive—or so it would at first appear.

But as Keats explores his successive responses to visual art through his invented scenes on the urn, he discovers that there is a rhythm of engagement and disengagement by which the mind imposes its own temporality on the stasis of visual art. To the first scene, the beholder attributes a rhythm of pursuit and escape, a more excited version of the rhythm of the later procession. The inflamed men or gods come from somewhere; the maidens loth are struggling to escape to some haven. This invention of origins (Tempe? Arcady?) and ends (escape) accounts in part for the rhythms of engagement and disengagement. But a far more powerful force toward disengagement resides in every spectator's intermittent awareness, in contemplating any work of art, that the scene before his eyes is not a real but a represented one. Keats's first involuntary disengagement is caused by this knowledge; having seen the pipes and timbrels represented, he knows that they are *not* real, that they pipe unheard except to the spirit. This art is a dumbshow, and the pipes are in fact silent; but Keats, in an effort to mitigate the strict knowledge of disengagement, avoids the uncompromising word "silent" and calls the pipes, instead, "soft." We of course know that they are so soft as to be "unheard"; they play ditties "of no tone." The word "silent," though here repressed, waits in the wings and appears, insistently, in the last two stanzas.

Keats's response to the urn therefore becomes a classic case of the dilemma which the psychologists of perception (using the classic figure of the duck-rabbit) call the dilemma of figure and ground. If the spectator focuses on one aspect, the other recedes into the background, and vice versa. In this case, the dilemma is that of subject matter and medium, of "men" and "marble." While Keats pressingly interrogates the urn's figures, he cannot think of them as other than real: "What men or gods are these? . . . For ever wilt thou love . . . O mysterious priest . . ." On the other hand, as soon as he allows his consciousness of the marble medium to arise, he loses his sense of the figural representations as "real," and a disjunction in tone marks the breaking of the spell.[11] There are, as I have said, three such disjunctions in the poem (I italicize the moment of the tonal reversal):

> What pipes and timbrels? What wild ecstasy?
> *Heard melodies are sweet . . .*

> For ever panting and for ever young; '
> *All breathing human passion far above . . .*

> What little town . . .
> Is emptied of this folk, this pious morn?
> *And, little town, thy streets for evermore*
> *Will silent be.*

In concluding his poem Keats wished, it seems to me, to give equal credence to each side of these junctures, to recognize fully both his participation in the represented "reality" and his awareness of the constituting medium removing those representations from actual life. Since, in Keats's view, one cannot experience sensory participation in the represented scene and intellectual awareness of the medium at one and the same time,[12] and since attention can change focus so rapidly from what is being represented to the medium of representation and back again, Keats has to affirm two wholly incompatible responses, never simultaneous, one always canceling the other, but both of them authentic, both of them provided by the artifact, both of them "aesthetic."

It was in his second stanza that Keats had most wonderfully allowed the two responses, to matter and to medium, free play. He permits there a rapidly alternating perception first of one and then of the other, and he uses identical language for the two experiences in order to show that they compete on identical terrain. Commentary often refers to the impossibility of deciding which are "bad" and which "good" of the many "can's" and "cannot's" in this stanza. To the piper and the youth, Keats says in turn, "Thou canst not leave thy song," which is meant to be good but has overtones of coercion; "Never, never canst thou kiss," which is surely bad; and "She cannot fade,"[13] which is surely good. In this stanza, the poet still sees medium and subject matter in (to quote Wordsworth) "a constant interchange of growth and blight." The marble medium confers certain benefits ("She cannot fade") and certain limitations ("Thou hast not thy bliss"). The lines focus alternately on life matter — the beauty of the maiden, the ardor of the lover — and on the coercions of the marble medium — "Never, never canst thou kiss." The quick shuttling back and forth in the speaker's mind between immersion in the fervent matter and recognition of the immobile medium represents a tension as yet unconceptualized in the poem (that is, one not yet "philosophically" or "reflectively" analyzed).

In the following stanza, the third, Keats defensively attempts to suppress interrogation by suppressing one half of his response, his awareness of the limits of the medium. Thus he hopes to enter wholly into the static happiness of the represented matter, which attempts a return to Psyche's timeless bower: "Ah, happy, happy boughs! . . . And happy melodist . . . More happy love! More happy, happy love! / For ever warm . . . " The difference between this bower and that of Psyche is that into this bower has intruded the vocabulary of time, in the thoughts of shed leaves and springs that have been bidden adieu. And the undistinguished nature of the language of this stanza demonstrates the necessary failure of invention when the momentum of the poem is deliberately halted, stalled in its most recent perception. The needle of receptive sensation sticks, we might say, in its last phrase. The strain of maintaining timelessness in the vocabulary of time climaxes in the return of the repressed, as the sexual consummation prohibited by the atemporal visual medium of the urn takes place violently in Keats's recollection, leaving "a burning forehead, and a parching tongue."

Keats returns to the problem of subject matter and medium at the end of his poem. Shocked by the "deceiving" ability of representational art to persuade his belief not only in the represented procession but equally in the green altar and the fantasized town, he recoils intellectually from participation in subject matter into pure awareness of medium, becoming the apparently detached, but in reality the cheated, spectator. He no longer anthropomorphizes the urn into bride, child, or historian—all names which had been prompted by a wish to assimilate the artifact itself to its representational function—but rather addresses it as pure medium, as an Attic shape, a fair attitude, embroidered by the chisel of its carver with marble men and maidens.[14] But, as in the earlier attempt to suppress the intellect in the third stanza, one half of the response-field cannot be maintained alone. Marble men and maidens suddenly "swell into reality"[15] and walk on real earth "with forest branches and the trodden weed." It is hopeless to try to maintain a detached attitude: the scene *is* cold marble and it *is* trodden weeds, both and each, one moment the carved, the next the real.

The dilemma the urn presents is one insoluble to description. We can, if we like, see the whole ode as Keats's extreme test of his negative capability, in a moment when "Things cannot to the will / Be settled, but they tease us out of thought." He had written those words to Reynolds after composing his first sketch for the fourth stanza of the *Urn*, a sketch in which an easy "pictorial" simultaneity is preserved by a refusal to inquire into the expressive limits of painting, or into origins and ends. There, Keats had invented a present-tense "natural" scene which looks neither before nor after:

> The sacrifice goes on; the pontif knife
> Gleams in the sun, the milk-white heifer lows,
> The pipes go shrilly, the libation flows:

A white sail shews above the green-head cliff,
Moves round the point, and throws her anchor stiff.
The mariners join hymn with those on land.
                                    (*Dear Reynolds*, 20–25)

The ode will not permit itself such easy solutions as this eternally present one.

Aesthetic experiences, as well as intellectual ones, ask us to exist in "uncertainties, Mysteries, doubts, without any irritable reaching after fact & reason" (*Letters*, I, 193). Certain concepts, too, provoke this uncertainty; one of these, in Keats's view, is the concept of eternity. Is eternity an infinite sequence of temporal successions or rather an unchanged permanency? Keats has fluctuated between the two senses of "eternity" earlier in the ode, in his repeated use of "ever," "never," "for ever," and "for evermore." The first notion of eternity—as an infinite sequence of active, continuing, successive motions—is expressed in phrases like "For ever wilt thou love" and "For ever piping songs for ever new" (phrases that remind us of the gardener Fancy, who breeding flowers will ever breed new ones); while the second notion of eternity—as unmoving, fixed, and deathlike—arises in the lines about boughs that cannot shed their leaves and streets that "for evermore / Will silent be." One sort of "forever" (the *Psyche* "forever") belongs, as I have said, to the "swelling reality" represented by the subject matter, love "for ever panting"; the other sort of "forever" belongs to the static limitations of the nontemporal medium. One sort of "forever" is expressive and warm—"for ever piping" and "for ever warm"; the other sort of "forever" is silent and cold, like the streets forevermore silent and the cold Pastoral. As "artificial" artifact rises into the ascendant over "natural" action in the mind of the perceiver, the "silent" streets give birth to the generalizing phrase "silent form," and the "marble" men give birth to the phrase "Cold Pastoral!" (When we last saw the word "pastoral" it was natural and vegetative in the "pastoral eglantine" of *Nightingale*; now it is no longer associated with nature, but with art, and with genre.)

Perhaps there is no formulation adequate to the alternating awareness of subject matter and medium, of "nature" and "artifact" in aesthetic response. But it seems to me that the ending of the *Urn* has been unfairly criticized because neither Keats's intention nor his accomplishment has been entirely understood. (Though Keats's leaving his intent obscure may represent a flaw in execution, it does not excuse us from attempting to penetrate that intent.) The fiction of the ode is that of a poet coming, in woe, to a work of art, interrogating it, and being solaced by it. We know that Keats had himself remarked on how differently we contemplate things when we see them not equally but in distress of mind. "Difficulties," he said, "make our Prime Objects a Refuge as well as a Passion" (*Letters*, I, 141). He was speaking here of our aims rather than of our objects of contemplation, but we may say that in the ode he sees the urn as a refuge as well as a passion, as a friend to man in woe. Instead of repudiating, as he had done in the Nightingale ode, the tranced Fancy which makes illusion swell into reality, he now thinks of conscious representational artifice as a refuge, enabling man to "enter into the existence" of other modes of being, as he entered into the existence of the sparrow picking about the gravel (*Letters*, I, 186). (It is significant that the word "Fancy" is not used here, nor in subsequent odes; that word does not denote the truth-value that Keats is now attributing to art.)

There are lesser and better ways of entering into the existence of other beings. Keats had already explored one mode, which precluded all memory of the world left behind, in his meditation in *Nightingale* on lyric as pure, spontaneous, nonrepresentational melodiousness evocative of rich sensations. Now, by adding the truth of representation, and the truth of "unnatural" artifice consciously shaping a form, to the beauty of sensation, Keats can explore more complicated modes of aesthetic response — those which I have here named, too crudely, as voyeuristic, narcissistic, and disinterestedly aesthetic. All of them, however, cause that journey outward from habitual self into some other thing which seems, such is the force of creation, to swell into reality. On the other hand, the philosophic mind knows that in truth — at least in the truth of "consequitive reasoning" as Keats called it — the art object (here the urn) exists in a given medium (here the carved marble). "A complex mind," says Keats, is "one that is imaginative and at

the same time careful of its fruits—who would exist partly on sensation partly on thought—to whom it is necessary that years should
bring the philosophic Mind" (Letters, I, 186). Sensation and
Thought are respectively aligned, in this famous letter to Bailey, to
Beauty and Truth. Truth is, for Keats, the property of the conscious or waking mind, that mind which both sees aspects of life
and meditates on them conceptually, Adam's mind which woke to
the truth of Eve. (I use Keats's own vocabulary, however imprecise,
as the one least falsifying to his thought: "The Imagination may be
compared to Adam's dream—he woke and found it truth," as he
explained to Bailey.)[16] Keats had decided to omit the question of
truth from his poem of sensation, Nightingale, but he found he
could not continue to write without admitting to the precincts of
verse the perplexities of the brain as well as the delights of sensation. The urn's original charming names of bride, child, and sylvan
historian, fictively naturalizing metaphors, are all projects of sensation rather than of thought; thought must treat the urn as artifact.
When Keats allows philosophical thought to accompany his sensations of visual response, that thought sees the emotions and acts of
the beautiful represented forms, but also recognizes the gap in
psychological continuity between perception of matter and perception of medium. Allowing thought as well as sensation full play,
Keats recognizes that his own voluntary submission to the art object entails not only empathy but also the detached recognition of
its specific medium—causing that successive rhythm of entrance and
exit which he had found so painful when he believed it to be caused
exclusively by the deceptive cheating of a temporally dissolving
Fancy. Now, seeing the dialectic between empathy and reflection as
an ineluctable process of consciousness, he can regain an equilibrium
of feeling before the urn, and give it a self-elucidating speech which
will be true to its paradoxical union of stimuli to sensation and
thought alike.

The urn, as we last see it, is not a historian but rather an
epigrammatist. It is, astonishingly, no longer silent, as it had been
during Keats's prolonged interrogation. It finally speaks because the
speaker has ceased to ask it those historical and extrapolatory questions which it is not equipped to answer. The urn is only a "silent

form" when the wrong kinds of truth are asked of it. As soon as Keats sees it as a friend of man (rather than as a historian or an archaeologist) it speaks, and becomes an oracular form, saying (as oracles often do) two things equally true. It says "Beauty is Truth" when we are looking at it with the eyes of sensation, seeing its beautiful forms as actual people, alive and active. It says "Truth is Beauty" when we are looking at it with the eyes of thought, seeing it, as the mind must see it, as a marble inscribed by intentionality, the true made beautiful by form. The two messages do not coincide; they alternate. Like a lighthouse, the urn beams one message, then the other, as we respond alternately to its human verisimilitude (which solicits our empathy) or to its triumphant use of its resistant medium (which solicits our admiration). The urn can speak of nothing but itself, and its self-referentiality is nowhere clearer than in the interior completeness of its circular epigram, which encounters our ironic sense of its limitation. When the urn says, commenting on its own motto, that that is all men know on earth and all they need to know, we realize that it makes that announcement from the special perspective of its own being, the timeless being of the artwork in the Platonic realm where Truth and Beauty are indistinguishable. It speaks to us from its own eternity, at once so liberating and so limited. Keats's choice of a circular frieze, rather than a linear one, confirms the urn's self-enclosing and self-completing form.

Nonetheless, the urn, unlike the uncaring, "natural" Nightingale, speaks to man.[17] It is, in the phrase Keats used as well for Milton, "a friend to man," and it exemplifies the "great end" attributed, in *Sleep and Poetry*, to poetry, "that it should be a friend / To sooth the cares, and lift the thoughts of man" (246–247). The art of the urn-sculptor is, like the art of the poet in *Psyche*, mimetic, but it is mimetic in a philosophical way, not a photographic one; it does not copy some lost historical model, but rather it chooses evocative human postures. It is beautiful, like the song of the nightingale, but it is, in a way the bird's song cannot be, representationally true. Although it is expressive, it is not solely self-expressive, like the bird's song; although it has been made by an artist, it does not exhibit his motives (as Keats's earlier urn, in *In-*

dolence, had borne his motives Love, Ambition, and Poesy). Rather, it expresses a variety of cultural motives, not a homogeneous or personal set, and is therefore a broadly socially expressive form. And it is deliberate, a reworking of nature with tools, even a violation (by its chiseling) of nature, not a spontaneous ecstatic outpouring or budding.

The poet himself utters the closing words in which the urn's motto and commentary are encapsulated as a quotation:

> When old age shall this generation waste,
> Thou shalt remain, in midst of other woe
> Than ours, a friend to man, to whom thou say'st,
> "Beauty is truth, truth beauty,"—that is all
> Ye know on earth, and all ye need to know.

The last two lines are spoken by the urn,[18] which places special emphasis on the mottolike epigram before going on to comment on its unique worth. But the whole last sentence of the poem is the sentence of the speaker who, in his prophecy, recounts what the urn will say to succeeding generations. The speaker has reached, by the end of the poem, a prophetic amplitude of statement, looking before and after. With his philosophic mind, he foresees the time when his own generation will be wasted by old age, as previous generations have been in their turn; in that time to come, another young generation will be feeling woe as he has felt it, and will come to the urn, as he has come, for refuge and solace. In its generosity this picture of parallel relations between generations represents an advance over the cruel representation, in *Nightingale*, of hungry filial generations each treading the past parental generation down. In his closing stanza, Keats is now above and beyond his own past immediate encounters with the urn-scenes; his detachment is now comparable to the detachment of the urn itself. But his mind is more capacious, in this last stanza, than the being of the urn is. Keats's mind here encompasses past, present, and future; youth, woe, age, the wasting of time, and the coming of another generation—all those horrors from which he had so strenuously averted his gaze in *Nightingale*. Keats's mind judges and places the single experience of seeing the urn in the total human experience of the life and death of generations. The sublimity—and ecstasy—of art is therefore granted as one moment along the span of life, a moment in which, by the intensity of art, all disagreeables are made to evaporate "from their being in close relationship with Beauty & Truth" (*Letters*, I, 192). The disagreeables—age, death, woe—have reasserted themselves in the mind of the speaker both during the poem (in his reflective moments) and at the end of the poem. But he gives the last, solacing word to the urn, because it utters that word afresh to each new generation—yet he encapsulates that last word in his own last overarching sentence of praise for art.

The divinity physically worshiped in this ode is the art object, the urn. The divinities conceptually celebrated are the twin divinities of Beauty *and* Truth, Sensation *and* Thought. The divinity imaginatively celebrated is that greeting of the spirit that takes place between the audience and the art object. The object provides the beautiful carved forms of the three scenes; the spirit moves to enter into and share the life of each scene, and even, in the third instance, helps to extend that life into imagined new creation. Together the object and the spirit create the aesthetic reverie, real and unreal at once. If it is true that, as we read Keats's fourth stanza, our sense of a beautiful train of anonymous figures led by a mysterious priest from obscure origins to an ultimate sacrificial rite in an unknown place is all we know of beauty and truth on earth and all we need to know, then Keats's urn has kept its promise to our generation as to his.

IF WE NOW turn to a more exact inquiry into the language of the *Urn*, we must raise, first of all, the central question it provokes. The ode has become notorious for one of its stratagems of language—the resort to the Platonic absolutes, Beauty and Truth. It omits only Goodness, sometimes (as in Spenser's *Hymns*) called Love. Keats's resort to the Platonic dyad governs the whole poem: it means that he had set his mind resolutely on an assault on philosophical language, as he then conceived it. His earlier approach in *Nightingale* to the philosophical problem of the relation of "life" to "art" tried to treat the problem metaphorically, opposing day to night, waking to dreaming, silence to song, suffering to ecstasy, and so on. In the *Urn*, Keats determines not to resort to descriptive metaphor alone, but also to confront intellectually; not only to find images, but to enunciate propositions; not "to console," but "plainly to propound" (Stevens). The pictorial and descriptive language which had governed *Nightingale* had, even there, been adequate only to the central rapt trance; the "real" world of "life" had called up in Keats his antiquated personifications of spectre-thin Youth, palsied Age, lustrous-eyed Beauty, and pining Love; while the pain of his own mortal lot, once he readmitted the perplexing mind, had called up a propositional utterance of a defensive explicitness, "Thou wast not born for death, immortal Bird!" These elements in *Nightingale* give birth to several elements of the diction of the *Urn*. The *Urn*'s implicitly contrastive judgments (boughs that, unlike real boughs, cannot shed their leaves; love, unlike human love, forever panting; and so on) spring directly from *Nightingale*'s contrastive emphasis on the immortality of the bird; and the urn's constant Lover and unfading Maiden are clearly, as I have said above, derivations-by-contrast from the prospectively fading Beauty and faithless Lover of *Nightingale*. But the *Urn*-language ("She cannot fade, though thou hast not thy bliss, / For ever wilt thou love, and she be fair!") is deliberately stripped of *visibilia*. Beauty is robbed of her lustrous eyes and the Lover has not even so expressive a verb as "pine"; he simply "loves," she is simply "fair." Evidently the reader who comes to the *Urn* expecting throughout the ode the rich intensification of language that he found in *Nightingale* will be disappointed: where are his Keatsian luxuries? Of course they are not entirely absent; but Keats is placing stern and deliberate shackles on himself in the central part of his poem, deciding to mistrust his proliferating adjectival fancy and to write instead in the plainest outline. By "the plainest outline" I mean first of all his choosing the simplest possible emblems of desire (a lover loving, a maiden being fair, a piper piping, trees in leaf), and second his choosing the plain language of pure, unqualified proposition (rhyme's tales are sweet, but sculpture's tales are sweeter; heard melodies are sweet, but unheard ones are sweeter;

songs to the sensual ear are dear, but those to the spirit are more endeared; human love saddens, cloys, and parches, but that on the urn is far superior).[19] Thus, for the first three stanzas (with some exceptions which I will mention later), the wish to write with a sober and unmistakable truth both of figural presentation and of intellectual assertion led Keats to a certain baldness of unequivocal judgment ("more sweetly," "sweeter," "more endear'd," "far above"), wholly unlike the native tentativeness which sprang, in him, from his exploratory and negatively capable sensibility. The wish to be truthful and to speak in propositions rather than in descriptions also led him to state the obvious in the barest of skeletal statements, aligning a series of blunt verbs:

thou	canst not leave thy song
nor ever	can those trees be bare
never	canst thou kiss
she	cannot fade
thou	hast not thy bliss
for ever	wilt thou love, and she be fair
ye	cannot shed your leaves
nor ever	bid the spring adieu

These sentences employ forms of extreme propositional simplicity; they are verbal "yes" and "no" markers:

leave song?	No
be bare?	No
kiss?	No
fade?	No
have bliss?	No
love for ever?	Yes
be fair?	Yes
shed leaves?	No
bid spring adieu?	No

In being addressed to figures (the melodist, the lover, and the boughs) who presumably would know whatever the poet is telling them about their state, the sentences might also seem to display a false ingenuousness or whimsicality. And yet we know the power of these stanzas; and we all agree that the fiction they adopt, as the speaker describes to the urn-figures the mixed blessing of their state, is a way for Keats to displace first-person utterance. (He does not, incidentally, address the maiden as he does the male lover and the male piper; the two males are fantasy-figures for himself as bold lover and unwearied melodist, and his empathy joins them, not her.)

In the absence of adjectival sensuality, Keats attempts by two means to give his "propositional" language some richness. He repeats central words (as in "ye soft *pipes* play on, / Not to the sensual *ear*, but more end*ear*'d, / *Pipe* to the spirit . . . / *For ever piping* songs *for ever* new"). But even more than to the repetition of words, Keats resorts to the repetition of syntactic patterns, to a rigid, hypnotic pattern of apostrophe followed by either assertion or negation in a chain of "ever" and "never," "not" or "no." The pattern is just varied enough so as not to be absolutely predictable: a "canst not" is followed by a "can" and by a "never canst" and "cannot"; in the midst of the declarative "can's" and "cannot's" comes the sudden, touching "Yet, do not grieve" — the first sketch for the poet's later consolation of Autumn, "Think not of them." The semantic and syntactic repetitiveness rises in the third stanza of the ode to a form of babble, in which what is being said is palpably subordinated to the effect of incoherent envy — "Ah happy, happy boughs! . . . and happy melodist . . . more happy love! more happy, happy love! For ever warm . . . for ever panting." It has usually been assumed that Keats lost control of his poem in this stanza; Bate (p. 513) speaks of the "strain" here comparable to that felt in "Already with thee!" in *Nightingale*. It is perhaps misguided, though, to think of Keats as a helpless spirit to whom poems happened; it is more probable that instinctive aesthetic aims led him compositionally down certain paths — in this case, the path of propositions — which exacted a certain price. The trouble with propositions, for someone of Keats's earlier aesthetic inclinations, was that they seemed not to embody feeling. A statement of what is or is not true is, of itself, emotionally neutral; and Keats's first set of propositions about the figures on the urn, following his initial questions, attempt the form of that declarative neutrality: "Thou canst not leave / Thy song"; "[Never] can those trees be bare"; "She cannot fade"; "For ever wilt thou love." Dissatisfied with blank propositional statement, Keats suppresses questions and rewrites the propositions, turning the original declarative mode to an exclamatory form: "Ah happy, happy boughs! *that cannot shed your leaves*; and happy melodist *for ever piping*; more happy love! *for ever panting*." Keats's revolt against the propositional form is already evident in his interpolations of feeling in the apostrophes "*fair* youth" and "*bold* lover" as well as in his pained "do not grieve" and his sympathetic "though thou hast not thy bliss." He is even false to the strictly propositional form (itself expressively appropriate to the eternal present tense of the atemporal urn) when he moves into the future tense of prophecy: instead of the more proper "Forever dost thou love; she is forever fair," he offers what he regards as a consolatory vista of future years to his bold but unsatisfied lover: "For ever wilt thou love, and she be fair!"

One cannot, however, write every passage twice, first saying what is or is not, and then rephrasing it with an "applied" emotional coloring by affixing to every declarative statement an exclamatory addendum. These two stanzas, then—stanzas two and three—urge us, by their very inefficiency as stratagem, backward to the language of the beginning of the ode and forward to the language of the last two stanzas.

I have already spoken of Keats's wish to incorporate representational "truth" in this ode. This thematic wish necessarily provoked a second—a desire to incorporate propositional "truth" in the language of the poem. Keats's resolve to incorporate "truth" in this ode led him to the poem's first naive view of truth as a set of simple answers to simple questions, names and stories to answer who and why. Keats then passed on to a second hypothesis: if truth is not identificatory names and stories (the truth of fact or of history), perhaps it is true declarative propositions (the truth of philosophy)—but to be true to emotion as well as to fact, the "philosophical" propositions must be invested with rhetorical coloration, and therefore he is led to attach his exclamation (the truth of feeling). Finally, some of his propositions must state not only what is, but in what order relative things are to be placed, in what way some are better than others (the truth of value); consequently, we see Keats resorting to judgmental or hierarchical propositions of the sort "X is sweeter than (or more endeared than, or far above) Y."

But Keats cannot all command the strings, and his language wishes to escape his new puritanical effort to say what is true—factually, philosophically, emotionally, and judgmentally—rather than to narrate or complain or describe or wish, as he had chiefly done in the earlier odes. The language escapes its propositional aridity in the opening five lines of the ode, and it also escapes in the fourth stanza—those two passages where the poem becomes most beautiful, and most itself. The first stanza of the *Urn* offers us a far more complex mind, holding far more intellectual possibilities in view, than any single stanza of the earlier odes. It contains some reminiscence of earlier work, including the sense of past mythology borrowed from *Psyche* (as "What men or gods are these?" recalls "Who wast thou?"), and Keats's self-presentation as poet present in all previous odes. But the urn's initial appellations, in their intellectual complexity, are unlike any epithets in *Indolence* or *Psyche* or *Nightingale*. "Thou still unravish'd bride of quietness" and "Thou foster-child of silence and slow time" offer us a different depth from the descriptive "Thou light-winged Dryad of the trees," though they are cut to the same syntactic pattern. A Dryad has fairy wings and belongs in trees; but a bride and unravishment and quietness are not necessarily related to an urn, nor is a foster child necessarily linked to silence or time. The epithets in *Indolence* ("a fair maid, and Love her name"; "Ambition, pale of cheek"; "my demon Poesy") and in *Psyche* ("O latest born and loveliest vision"; "O brightest"; "the gardener Fancy"; "the warm Love") are like the epithets in *Nightingale* ("immortal Bird"; "warm South"; "deceiving elf") in being simple and conventional in their expression and in their categories of reference. But the complex mind writing the *Urn* connects stillness and quietness to ravishment and a bride (as John Jones says, p. 220, surely the bridal Urn is Eve, Adam's dream as he awoke and found it Truth); this complex mind also interrelates silence, the lapsing of ages, death, and fosterage; it connects history to the woods, and stories to flowers, and it judges sculpture against poetry; it puts legends with leaves, interweaving both with the haunting presence of the invisible in culture—all in relation to a carved form and its auxiliary ornament; it alternates men with gods, the natural with the pastoral, Tempe with Arcady; it joins music to activity, and ecstasy to struggle. The mind generating this first stanza is surely a more interesting and fruitfully confused mind than the one which generated the opening of *Indolence* or *Psyche* or *Nightingale*. It is a mind striving against its tendency to exclude. (In *Indolence* the mind had wished to exclude its own compulsion toward action, temporality, and form; in *Psyche* it had wished to exclude both time and the embodiment of reverie in a physical medium; in *Nightingale* it had wished to exclude its consciousness of suffering.) Now nothing is to be excluded—neither the past nor the present, neither the peaceful nor the ecstatic nor the violent, neither men nor gods, neither truth nor legend, neither sexuality nor chastity, neither figuration nor location, neither origins nor ends, neither activity nor stillness, neither life nor art, neither music nor silence.

We find our satisfactions variously in art; but one of the greatest satisfactions is our sense that the artist is being faithful to all he knows of experience, and is determined, within the limits of his medium, to exclude nothing. The *Urn* (unlike *Indolence, Psyche*, and *Nightingale*) originates in a decision to embrace representationally all that is; and to tell, in some way, the truth about it. But after the inexpressibly fruitful first stanza, for two stanzas Keats writes a more lax verse, first condemning himself, in the service of philosophical truth, to the enunciating of propositions, and then, in the service of the truth of feeling, turning the same propositions into exclamations. Finally he utters the proposition which I believe voices the generating motive of the poem—the necessary self-exhaustion and self-perpetuation of sexual appetite.

It may be true that one needs only that paradoxical human sense of cloying and thirsting to engender, by contrast, the unfading love and beauty of the couple on the urn. But we must recall here the two forms of sexuality on the urn—the mad pursuit of the maidens loth and their consequent struggle to escape, and the contrasting entirely idyllic portrait of the loving lover and the fair beloved (each scene accompanied by its appropriate music). It seems to me that the somewhat theatrical evoking of cloying and parching reflects a Byronic sexuality of pursuit and struggle rather than Keats's new, scarcely as yet believed in, hope for a permanent tie to Fanny Brawne. In his words of July, just after writing the odes, "For myself I know not how to express my devotion to so fair a form: I want a brighter word than bright, a fairer word than fair . . . In case of the worst that can happen, I shall still love you" (*Letters,* II, 123). The second-scene figures on the urn, then, represent in themselves not only things unattainable (eternity, immobility) but also things Keats believed in—love, constancy, fidelity, beauty, and truth. To these constants, the cloying and parching did not apply; the only power which can touch the verities, Keats believed, was death. The true opponent to the urn-experience of love is not satiation but extinction. It is not the transience of erotic feeling but the transience of life itself which is the obstacle the ode must confront; and it does so in its greatest invention, its fourth stanza.

The great imaginative discoveries of this stanza—its invisible altar-goal and its invisible town-origin—are not inventions of sensation but of thought. The green altar and the little town correspond, in being "what-is-not-on-the-urn," to the fading youth and palsied age and groaning men of *Nightingale*—those things not present in the Nightingale's world. It is evident now how completely Keats has abandoned his *Nightingale* idea of a suffering world and a pain-free art. Art, on the urn—by including struggle, resistance, and sacrificial procession as well as love and youth—has begun its effort to be all-inclusive, to let in "the disagreeables." What is excluded on the urn, then, is only what we cannot ever know— whence we came, whither we are going, those mysteries of eternity. Keats reverses the coloration we might expect for the point of origin and the point of sacrificial conclusion; while we might have expected the sacrificial to be the empty and the desolate, and the point of origin to be leafy, populated, and pristine, Keats displaces his fear of death onto the abandoned town, which itself takes on the qualities of the life we shall have vacated when we die. In exhibiting, in this third scene, our social role rather than our private role—in placing us all as members of a linked cultural procession of pious folk—Keats sacrifices the pride of solitary position that had made him, in *Indolence*, the self-sufficient dreamer refusing the social solicitations of Love or Ambition or Poesy. A similar solitariness had led him to cast himself in a starring (if "tuneless") role as Psyche's priest-poet (and, displaced as Cupid, as Psyche's lover). The social sympathy stirring in *Nightingale* (for the condemned youth and the palsied old) led Keats only to an anguished flight away from such sympathies. In the *Urn*, social sympathy leads Keats to a self-abnegating place in the anonymous (almost, we wish to say, choral) procession. In refusing human music to the sacrifice, Keats takes an even more ascetic position. The orgy had its pipes and timbrels; the calmer tableau of love had its happy melodist; but the only sound in the scene of sacrifice is the premonitory lowing of the heifer (a transmutation, of course, of the ecstatic song of the nightingale). Both pipes and hymns had been included in Keats's first imagining of the sacrificial scene in the epistle to Reynolds ("The pipes go shrilly, the libation flows: . . . / The mariners join hymn with those on land"). The new absence of art-music at the close of the ode is a striking omission, given Keats's insistence in the *Urn* on melodies heard and unheard, and given the careful insertion of art-melody into the first two scenes of lust and love. The effect produced is of a falling-silent of accompaniment, and of the incapacity of music to express either the final animal utterance of the victim or the final silence of the little town. Even unheard melodies do not encompass that pathos. The easy, natural music of *Indolence* ("the throstle's lay"), the internal music of *Psyche* ("tuneless numbers," a "delicious moan / Upon the midnight hours") and the full-throated spontaneous music ("full-throated ease," "such an ecstasy!") of *Nightingale* will never again rise spontaneously in Keats. Lamia's delusive music vanishes with the palace it supports; and there is no music in *The Fall of Hyperion*. The great recovery of music in *To Autumn* comes in the final acoustic "noise" of bleats, whistles, and twitters.

As I have said, these felicities of the fourth stanza of the *Urn*—the invoked but invisible origin and end, the absence of art-music—are inventions of thought, not of sensation. And yet the language of this greatest stanza of the ode (especially in light of its contrast with the other stanzas and other odes) demands comment. The stanza returns, as we recall, to the third-person questioning of the first stanza, in asking (though with a different, nonfactual, tonality), "Who are these coming to the sacrifice?" It then begins to recapitulate the second stanza by replicating its second-person addresses ("Ye soft pipes . . . Fair youth . . . Bold lover") in its second-person address to the priest ("O mysterious priest"). The heifer with its "drest" garlanded flanks has replaced *Psyche*'s rosy sanctuary "dress[ed]" with the wreathed garlands on the trellis, as adornment for the sacrificial morn replaces adornment for the lovenight. The *Ode to a Nightingale* is, like *Psyche* (and, in its prolongation of drowsiness into the morning, *Indolence*), a night-poem; the *Urn*, by coming into the light of day and rousing itself on "this pious morn" to sacrificial activity, exhibits a stoic bravery, to be continued in the later odes. After the one-line overture "Who are these coming to the sacrifice?" the three equal movements of three lines each give the fourth stanza an equanimity and spaciousness not found in the other stanzas of the ode. The last question of the poem, though it follows the direct question to the priest, returns to the third-person formulation of the opening questions ("What men or gods?")—"What little town . . . is emptied" today? The town's three competing imagined locations (by river, or by sea shore, or mountain-built) make the town literally unknowable. The greater becomes our surprise, then, when the tender second-person address, hitherto reserved to things or persons visible on the urn (pipes, boughs, lover, melodist, priest), is extended, with an effect of indescribable pathos, to the invisible and unknowable little town:

> And, little town, thy streets for evermore
> Will silent be; and not a soul to tell
> Why thou art desolate, can e'er return.

The *Urn*'s earlier "can's" and "cannot's" are echoed in the line "not a soul . . . can e'er return," just as the future tense of the bold prophecy "For ever wilt thou love" is echoed in "Thy streets for evermore / Will silent be." The "for evermore" and "e'er" echo their happier counterparts earlier as well.

When an urn is shifted round, *Indolence* had told us, "the first seen shades *return*"; and Keats had imagined that he could command the *Indolence* phantoms to fade, and "be once more / In masque-like figures on the dreamy urn." But now, refusing the cyclical recurrence of his first view of the urn-figures, and his illusion that they can leave and return to their places on the urn at will, Keats puts a final interdict on all his shades: not a soul "can e'er *return*." It is the frequent internal echoes from ode to ode such as this one (of which we cannot suppose Keats to have been unconscious) which create much of the depth of the odes when they are read together.

In admitting the perpetual silence of the streets of his little town, Keats ceased to struggle, with volleys of questions, against the foster-child of silence. Not a soul will come back from that undiscovered country. In resolving to remain in the presence of the urn without any further questions, Keats exemplifies his own Negative Capability; "not a soul to tell why" is a complete capitulation to mystery, comparable to the acquiescence in ignorance voiced in the epithet "mysterious" applied to the priest. The absence of music in the fourth stanza stands for speechlessness, and for inexpressibility.

After the tranquil and sovereign language of the scenes, visible and invisible, of the fourth stanza, we are shocked—all readers are shocked, to a different degree and in different ways—by the language of the close of the ode. In defending Keats's intent and decisions here, I mean only to defend the necessity of this stage in his noble exploratory progress toward "philosophizing" and toward a language suitable for "philosophizing" in. If, at this point, Keats decided that the language for thinking, even in poetry, must be the abstract and propositional language of philosophy (as he knew it), that was a mistake he was encouraged in by the example of Wordsworth and Coleridge. The language of the close of *Urn* cannot be entirely assimilated to the language used earlier in the ode, and this is a flaw; but we can begin to consider Keats's aims in closing his poem by looking at the epithets by which he characterizes the urn. They are different from his epithets-from-a-devotee in earlier odes, and even from the epithets in earlier lines of this ode. In other odes, and at the beginning of this ode, Keats is often a passive subject, content to be worked upon by his imaginings, ineffectually refusing their solicitations (*Indolence*) or aspiring to participation in a better realm (*Nightingale*) or, at most, proposing to copy a past devotion (*Psyche*). His function as dreamer (*Indolence*), liturgist-priest-lover (*Psyche*), or audience of sensation (*Nightingale*) precludes a critical intellectuality. But the interrogatory mode of *Urn*, which permits the brain full activity, interrupting sensory trance to make judgments and extended reflections, allows as well for consciously intellectual epithets, which attempt a mastery over the object to which they are attached. As I said earlier, "bride of quietness" is a far more complex formulation than "Dryad of the trees" or "amorous glow-worm of the sky"; and yet "bride of quietness," "foster-child of silence," and "sylvan historian" are still epithets of wonder and empathy and pathos, rather than epithets engendered by a critical mind. Attempting to allow the perplexed brain full freedom in his ode, Keats becomes in his last stanza the nineteenth-century intellectual man who is acquainted with archaeological terms and literary genres. "Attic shape" and "Pastoral" are epithets not of rapt subjection but of active intellectual mastery. "I will name you," says Keats, "not in terms you engender upon me ('bride,' 'child') but in terms by which I classify you according to scholarly, intellectual, or critical convention. I have called your youth 'fair' and your maiden 'fair'; those were the words of one entering into your pastoral fiction; now I will call you, yourself, by the standards of aesthetic judgment, a 'fair *attitude*.' I have called you, in awe, the 'foster-child of silence'; now I will call you, in sober truth, a 'silent *form*.' I have called you, imaginatively, a bride and a child, which you in fact are not; but now I will give you a relational name to which you can, in waking certainty, lay functional claim; you are 'a *friend* to man.' "

There are of course fluctuations in feeling, from frigidity to affection, in these epithets of mastery, as commentators have pointed out. I wish simply to make clear that they are all epithets by which Keats attempts to assert his own intellectual rights over the urn, saying that his mind must judge and interpret, as well as respond to, the urn's offering of itself. A flowery tale may be expressed by the urn more "sweetly," perhaps, than it could be by rhyme; but

Keats's rhyme wishes to be philosophical, as the urn, being non-discursive, seemingly cannot be. And yet he will make the urn philosophical. In his final act of intellectual mastery (and generosity), he will give the urn language. He will give it words, ascribe to it a philosophical utterance—his supreme gift to the urn which, until now, could speak only by its pictures.

In writing words for the urn to say, Keats has disturbed his readers. The urn's delphic utterance has the granite solidity possessed only by the most immovable propositions, those which approach tautology: "I am who am," or (another Keatsian one from the *Letters*, I, 279, also cited by Sperry, p. 279), "Sorrow is Wisdom." The attribution of truth to representational art, and the coupling, common in aesthetics, of the terms Truth and Beauty, as the desiderata of art, did not, for Keats, render the terms unproblematic. On the contrary, his own repeated raising of the terms in the *Letters* points to his worrying the problem. His exclusion of "the disagreeables" from previous odes, and their partial inclusion in *Urn*, points up the direction of his concern. He still excludes human death from the urn (except insofar as it is represented by the emptied and invisible town); but by addressing the town in the second person Keats has rendered the deserted town not absent and invisible, but present and engaged with, thereby allowing the pathos of the disagreeable to coexist with truth.

The wish to include the "disagreeable" thought that all art is fictive, medium-bound, and artificial rather than warm, human, and alive accounts for the chilly tone of some parts of the closing stanza. In using the words "shape," "form," "attitude," "marble," "brede," and "Pastoral," Keats is declaring that he will speak in aesthetic, worldly, factual, and critical terms about the urn as an artifact, as an object situated in medium and genre. But the urn has another existence—its virtual existence inside our experience of it. In that existence it exerts its immediate force, scene by scene. Keats must find a concluding language for that warm empathetic experience as well as for the cooler experience of evaluation and taxonomy. He says, thinking once again of the epistle to Reynolds (where he had declared "to philosophize / I dare not yet!"), that the urn "tease[s] us out of thought / As doth eternity." In the epistle, he says that this state—in which one is led beyond the capacities of thought—is one of purgatorial blindness (Keats's purgatory is a realm occupying the vertical space between earth and heaven):

> Things cannot to the will
> Be settled, but they tease us out of thought.
> Or is it that imagination brought
> Beyond its proper bound, yet still confined, —
> Lost in a sort of purgatory blind,
> Cannot refer to any standard law
> Of either earth or heaven? — It is a flaw
> In happiness to see beyond our bourn —
> It forces us in summer skies to mourn:
> It spoils the singing of the nightingale.

This great passage (*Dear Reynolds*, 76–85), written a year before the odes, wishes to place happiness above insight; and it gives rise directly to *Nightingale*'s attempt to keep the bird's singing unspoiled by human mourning. However, this passage already foreshadows the purgatorial emphasis of the letter, a year later, on soul-making. In the *Urn* Keats has (temporarily) left purgatory behind (he will return to it in *The Fall of Hyperion*); he also has decided to change his emphasis, when he talks of art, from the "immortal" (a word implying a being which cannot die, though like the nightingale it may have been born, and can live in time) to the "eternal" (a word which removes all considerations of birth, death, and existence in time). The urn exists (as we enter its "reality") in eternity, and from its vantage point there, where Truth and Beauty are one and the same, it befriends man in woe by making him free of its realm. Its utterance ("That is all / Ye know") is to be linked to other consolatory utterances in Keats, notably the two I have mentioned earlier, "Yet, do not grieve," and "Think not of them." These reassurances are almost maternal: we must think of the urn as saying what it can to us in our perplexity. The urn speaks of knowledge itself; of the sum of our knowledge; and of what we need to know. Since "knowledge" is for Keats a word of "philosophical" weight, the urn's double use of "know" ("all / Ye know . . . and all ye need to know") in its address to him (and us) is intended to allay his doubts about the propriety and relevance of a philosophical ambition to his work as man and poet. What word but "know" could end this ode where Keats's project was to admit Thought and Truth to art? What but a propositional sentence, and a repetition by a pun on the two meanings, partitive and summary, of "all," could end this ode which chooses statement over description, and inclusiveness over exclusion? The "mysterious doors / Leading to universal knowledge" (*Endymion*, 1, 288–289) could not remain forever shut. The eternal Urn must speak differently from the immortal Bird.

In inventing a language for eternity, Keats resorted to two distinct forms. One is eternally or Platonically true; one is accommodated to human ears. Since we fear that our knowledge is incomplete and insufficient for our state, the urn inclines to us to tell us that what we know (however limited) is sufficient for us, thereby releasing us from the torment of insufficiency. To that degree, the urn speaks our language. But in its oracular condensation of our knowledge into a riddling motto, the urn speaks the only language that Keats can invent which he believes adequate to an eternal being—a language in which he represents in an accommodated propositional form and its converse (X is Y — Y is X) a reality which can only be conceived of as the simultaneous and identical existence (in another realm) of X and Y.

The urn's creed exemplifies, in its bare propositional form and in its use of the diction of Platonic abstraction, Keats's pledge to make truth his best music (*Endymion*, IV, 773). In speaking to men of the extent and sufficiency of their *knowledge* (rather than of their dreams or visions), the urn ratifies the participation of the perplexing brain in aesthetic experience. We recognize in the intellectuality of this last stanza the complex mind (under a different aspect) which we came to know in the opening stanza of the ode. It still perceives finely and concretely (the forest branches, the trodden weed); it still wishes to see the whole (as it saw the totalizing anthropomorphic "shape" of the sylvan historian, it now sees the art-historical Attic "shape" of the vase) as well as the parts; it still aims to incorporate the philosophical diction which speaks of time and eternity, truth and legend, pastoral and thought, with the diction of sensation, which gives visual impressions of men, maidens, and even a heifer (the latter a presence quite unthinkable in *Indolence, Psyche,* or *Nightingale*). But in removing itself from the rapt visual and emotional awe of the first stanza, in recalling its own state of sexual woe, in foreseeing its own end in the wasting of its generation, in deciding on its final austere, intellectual epithets for the urn and in putting words into the urn's mouth, the mind of the last stanza represents itself as finally the master of its aesthetic experience, which it can recall at will, speculate on, and find a language (however imperfect) for. Sensation, this mind declares, must coexist with Thought, Beauty with Truth; and the language of Beauty must find a coexistence with the language of Truth.

For the rest of his life Keats was engaged in an investigation of what the language of Truth might be, and whether or not it differed from the language of Sensation, and, if so, how it differed. It is clear from the *Urn* that he believed, at the time he wrote this ode, that the language of Thought was one which expressed itself in propositions purporting to encode truths, of which the perfect form was "X is Y" (the "fallen" form of the Platonic "X is identical to Y"); that it used the abstractions proper to philosophical discourse (of which the chief specimens were words like "Beauty" and "Truth"); that it made intellectual judgments, often expressing a hierarchy of value; and that it was a language of perplexity which interrogated sensation before arriving at propositional formulation. By contrast, the language of Sensation, or of Beauty, seemed to be descriptive and exclamatory, to follow serially upon the registerings of the senses, to be concrete and intense, and to render the synaesthetic convergences, as well as the discreteness, of sensual experience. It was a language not of eternity but of time and space; of things past and passing; of luxuries and of visions. It wished to set aside the "dull brain" which, by thoughts of mortality, perplexed the self's relish in sensation and retarded its flight into trance. The concept of such a language of Sensation represents, I need not say, my abstraction into pure form of Keats's early tendency to luxury. In fact, Keats's perplexing brain is never entirely absent, even in the earliest verse; and "curious conscience . . . burrowing like the mole," was, from the beginning, seeking in Keats's poetry a language of its own.[20]

The language of Sensation did not seem adequate to Keats as a vehicle either for tragedy or for heroism. His powerful association of the language of Sensation with the language of lyric led him to think that maturity of mind would have to entail a forsaking of lyric for the epic or dramatic (following the ardors rather than the pleasures of verse, after the manner of Milton); the language of Thought (or even the language of Deed) might then supersede the language of Sensation. We now see *The Fall of Hyperion* as Keats's chief self-conscious effort to write the poetry of Thought, and *Otho the Great* as his attempt to write the poetry of Action. In neither did he succeed as he had hoped. The poetry of Action and the poetry of Thought were both, as we now see, better realized in the ode *To Autumn*.

But before arriving at the conflation of sensation, action, and thought, Keats had to absorb into his ode-world yet another realm, the realm of the "lower" senses. In *Psyche*, as we recall, he had puritanically suppressed all the senses in favor of a dialogue with his own soul, full of historical reminiscence and interior Fancy, defining art as an imitative imaginative activity which preexists (and does not perhaps need) any embodiment in a sense-medium. In *Nightingale*, by focusing on the activity of a single sense (that of hearing) he had been able to include artist, audience, and artifact in his trio of bird, self, and song, but at the price of exalting Beauty and Sensation alone and eliminating representational Truth (including Greek myth) and its poetry of Thought. In the *Urn* the artist is long dead, and only the artifact and its audience remain, but in this art corresponding to the sense of sight, Truth as well as Beauty has become constitutive of creative expression, and the mind is permitted its allegorizing, interrogatory, and propositional functions. Keats's successive scrutinies of natural, creative, but resultless reverie (*Indolence*), of tuneless, imitative numbers (*Psyche*), of wordless, spontaneous, beautiful *melos* (*Nightingale*), and of silent, truthful, objectified representation in a resistant visual medium (*Urn*) are all experiments exhibiting a certain defensiveness in one whose medium, after all, was words, whose art was conscious poetry, whose talent was deeply mythological, and who knew of other senses besides those two "high" ones, sense and hearing. Haunting these odes, up to this point, is the absence of any real exploration of the "lower" senses of taste and touch; and each of these odes is itself incomplete as a metaphor for Keats's total experience of art as he knew it in poetry—its dependence on the senses, its inception in reverie, its fertile, constructive activity in the mind, its powerful embodiment within a resistant medium, its reception by the greeting spirit, its representational validity, its allegorizing tendency, its luxurious beauty, its philosophical truth, its momentary glimpse of divinity, its sense of active intellectual and critical power and mastery. The simple movement of entrance and exit, even in its triple repetition in the *Urn*, is simply not structurally complex enough to be adequate, as a representational form, to what we know of aesthetic experience—or indeed to human experience generally. In the *Ode on Melancholy* Keats will at last admit the "lower" senses to his world of eternal forms, will take on the heroic mastery of action instead of passive subjection or conceptual mastery alone, and will argue the proper relation between psychological experience and aesthetic form. He will also attempt in *Melancholy* to use all his "languages" at once—the language of Greek mythology, the language of allegorical frieze, the language of descriptive sensation, the language of heroic quest, the language of gothic medievalizing, the language of the courtly-love (or "Provençal") tradition, the temporal language of fugitive experience, and the propositional language of eternal verities. If this rich amalgam is, as it proves to be, aesthetically grotesque, it exhibits nonetheless a mind unwilling to abandon any of the linguistic or symbolic resources it has so far discovered.

V

The Strenuous Tongue:
The *Ode on Melancholy*

Infant playing with a skull;
Morning fair and storm-wreck'd hull;
Night-shade with the woodbine kissing . . .
Muses bright and Muses pale
Bare your faces of the veil.

> *Welcome joy, and welcome sorrow*, 12–14, 24–25

A mimic temple, so complete and true
In sacred custom, that he well nigh fear'd
To search it inwards; whence far off appear'd
Through a long pillar'd vista, a fair shrine.

> *Endymion*, II, 257–260

Even bees, the little almsmen of spring-bowers
Know there is richest juice in poison-flowers.

> *Isabella*, 103–104

To raise a trophy to the drama's muses.

> *To George Felton Mathew*, 7

          Mistress fair,
Thou shalt have that tressed hair
Adonis tangled all for spite; . . .
And the hand he would not press . . .
                      Who
Has a mistress so divine?
Be the palate ne'er so fine
She cannot sicken.

> *Fancy* [draft], 89–91, 94, 100–102

She dwells with Beauty—Beauty that must die;
  And Joy, whose hand is ever at his lips
Bidding adieu.
            —*Ode on Melancholy*, 21-23

Ode on Melancholy

No, no, go not to Lethe, neither twist
   Wolf's-bane, tight-rooted, for its poisonous wine;
Nor suffer thy pale forehead to be kiss'd
   By nightshade, ruby grape of Proserpine;
Make not your rosary of yew-berries,
    Nor let the beetle, nor the death-moth be
      Your mournful Psyche, nor the downy owl
A partner in your sorrow's mysteries;
    For shade to shade will come too drowsily,
      And drown the wakeful anguish of the soul.

But when the melancholy fit shall fall
   Sudden from heaven like a weeping cloud,
That fosters the droop-headed flowers all,
   And hides the green hill in an April shroud;
Then glut thy sorrow on a morning rose,
    Or on the rainbow of the salt sand-wave,
      Or on the wealth of globed peonies;
Or if thy mistress some rich anger shows,
    Emprison her soft hand, and let her rave,
      And feed deep, deep upon her peerless eyes.

She dwells with Beauty—Beauty that must die;
   And Joy, whose hand is ever at his lips
Bidding adieu; and aching Pleasure nigh,
   Turning to poison while the bee-mouth sips:
Ay, in the very temple of Delight
    Veil'd Melancholy has her sovran shrine,
      Though seen of none save him whose strenuous tongue
   Can burst Joy's grape against his palate fine;
His soul shall taste the sadness of her might,
    And be among her cloudy trophies hung.[1]

*T*HE CANCELED first stanza of the *Ode on Melancholy* describes a heroic romance quest, a voyage to the ends of the earth to seek out the fabulous Melancholy, a female goddess. The stanza asserts that the hero must be willing to go even to Hades in his quest, and that he will in the event fail to find the goddess archetypal to his state; the voyage will end in frustration. The hero's equipment comes from Petrarch and Burton: the references to the courtly-love conventions of the unhappy lover in his storm-swept bark, blown by sighs and dashed with tears, suggest that the origins of the poem lie in Love-Melancholy; and the sections on Love-Melancholy in the second volume still remaining of the *Anatomy* that Keats possessed[2] are more heavily underlined and marked than are any other portions.

In the ode, the hero's ghastly bark is built of human bones, his mast is an empty "phantom" gibbet[3] (we do not know for whom it is destined), his sail an eclectic patchwork of creeds ("My Creed is Love, and you are its only tenet," Keats wrote to Fanny Brawne in October 1819—*Letters*, II, 224), his wind a groan, his rudder a severed dragon-tail (attesting to his past heroism), his ropes the slain Medusa's snake-hairs (he has confronted her and killed her). Though Keats rejected this stanza, he kept in his ode the notion of the questing activity of a newly strenuous hero, who refuses the opiates of drowsiness and indolence in favor of transcendent Platonic search. The protagonist in the earlier odes had been placed in a position of inactivity in the world, and had always been defined as a poet: for the first time, in *Melancholy*, the hero fares abroad, and traverses the known and unknown perilous seas, and is defined as ambitious lover and hero rather than as poet. The wakefulness rejected in *Indolence* and bitterly experienced at the end of *Nightingale* is here pursued as a positive good—pursued at first, however, too defensively and too far.

The formal pattern of the *Ode on Melancholy* in its three-stanza published form is one of desperate action and equally desperate reaction, of thesis and antithesis, followed by a third stanza which finds a synthesis both unexpected and satisfying. The first stanza rehearses (by countercommand) the temptation to suicide ("Go not to Lethe"), while the second stanza flees just as far away from shade and nightshade as the first, by implication, had approached them. If a peaceable and healthy spirit was, as Keats said in April (*Letters*, II, 106), his new ideal, then both the excess of suicidal longing and its converse, the excess of forcing and vexing the powers of life, were equally repellent to him: "It is as if the rose should pluck herself, / Or the ripe plum finger its misty bloom." In a proper spirit,

> the rose leaves herself upon the briar,
> For winds to kiss and grateful bees to feed,
> And the ripe plum still wears its dim attire,
> The undisturbed lake has crystal space.
> (*On Fame*, 9–12)

The opposite of the peaceable and healthy man is the "fevered man" who "cannot look / Upon his mortal days with temperate blood." Keats's hero in *Melancholy*, in flushed reaction against his earlier despairing temptation to distill poison, becomes the fevered man and goes out to pillage nature, glutting his sorrow on flowers and rainbows, imprisoning his mistress's hand, and feeding deep on her eyes in lieu of drinking wolf's-bane.

I have been speaking as though the ode were descriptive of its speaker, like the other odes, where the speaker refers to himself as "I" or "we" and reserves second-person address for various immortal spirits, from the *Indolence* shadows to the *Urn* figures. *Melancholy* alone among the odes uses, as its constitutive trope, admonition or exhortation; the poet addresses admonitions to himself, borrowing the mode of Hamlet's self-lacerating soliloquies, crossed with the mode of advice-to-the-perplexed that Keats found in Burton ("I may say to most melancholy men, as the Fox said to the Weasel that could not get out of the garner, When you are lank again, seek the narrow chink where, when lank, you entered; the six non-natural things caused it, and they must cure it").[4] But the self-admonition of the ode lasts formally only through the two stanzas of extremes—the stanza of suicide and the stanza of glutting. In its search for the temperate mean, the poem appears to leave admonition behind, coming to rest (in its final stanza) in the more neutral territory of third-person description. I will return to Keats's motive for the use in this ode of the second and third person, rather than the first, but here I need only remark that by its very nature self-admonition in stress cannot use a temperate rhetoric. It requires the rhetoric of the goad: "No, no, go not there, let not this be; but rather glut, imprison, feed."

This forcible self-propulsion on the part of the poet out of the world of opiates into the world of violently taken pleasure puts the diction of the two worlds into an apparent contrast of high relief; but in reality the seamless continuity of the admonitory form ("Do not do this; rather, do that") shows the negative and positive commandments to be more alike (in being equally in the rhetorical mode of self-goading) than they are different. The components of both sets of commands even resemble each other. The obliterating waters of Lethe are not unlike the weeping cloud which obliterates the green hills in a shroud; the lethal nourishment offered by wolf's-bane and the ruby grape of Proserpine is paralleled by the glut offered by the rose and the peonies; the mournful Psyche finds a counterpart in the raving mistress; the down of the owl is matched by the soft hand of the mistress, and so on. The vocabulary, though superficially mythological in the first stanza, is there more truly a vocabulary of the natural mythologized; and the natural substrata—the tight-rooted wolf's-bane, the deadly night-shade's ruby grape, the yew-berries, the beetle, the death-moth, and the downy owl—are actually near-cousins to the droop-headed flowers, the morning rose, the salt sand-wave and the globèd peonies—all the items of nature in the second, nonmythological stanza.

Of course, we must ask why, in Keats's compositional choices, the first stanza indeed contains mythology, and the second none, and the third neither mythology nor nature but allegory; and that question, together with the question of the employment of the second and third persons instead of the first, will take us far into the design of the poem. We might begin by saying that the presence of mythology in the first stanza reflects the central problem of the poem—the search for a mythological figure in the underworld, whether Proserpine or Psyche, who will replace, when the speaker commits suicide, the natural mistress he will leave behind. Proserpine, the goddess of the Underworld, can by joined only by the hero's committing suicide; but the second goddess mentioned, the *Psyche* death-moth, is a figure for an internalized death-wish, making it the entire spiritual principle of the speaker. The search for the goddess-partner, or death-mistress, is resolved in two ways at the end of the poem, after the speaker has resisted the temptation to commit suicide. In the closing stanza we are first given a flurry of allegorical figures with whom the earthly mistress is said to dwell—mortal Beauty, fleeting Joy, and aching Pleasure—all immortal figures with whom the poet may dwell while remaining with his earthly mistress. But in the second, subsequent resolution of the poem, the focus changes from the company surrounding the mistress to the company surrounding the hero, who bursts Joy's grape and can therefore enter, in the temple of Delight, the *penetralia*, or inmost shrine, that of the goddess Melancholy, where his soul will become one of the goddess's eternally suspended trophies, in the company of other phantom-souls so distinguished.

The language of these two resolutions is of a piece; it is the allegorical frieze-language earlier used to describe the urn-presences in *Indolence*, the personages of the world of sorrow in *Nightingale*, the figures on the urn.[5] Keats's allegorizing here attempts to come nearer to his ideal of Truth (to which, as we recall, he had made his vows in the *Urn*) than it had been able to do in *Nightingale*, where he had only barely escaped the ridiculous (in thinking of making allegorical Youth grow old) and had settled for having the Platonic absolutes undone by time, as Youth grows pale and thin and dies, Beauty cannot keep her lustrous eyes, and Love fails in constancy after only a single day of pining. In *Indolence*, the absolutes had not even been allowed an honorable ideal status, but were demoted to the status of vain imaginings:

> O folly! What is Love? and where is it?
> And for that poor Ambition—it springs

From a man's little heart's short fever-fit;
For Poesy! — no, — she has not a joy.

By contrast, in the *Urn* the absolutes are preserved from either satire or decline. On the urn (if only there) Love is always love, Beauty is always fair. I believe that the advance in conceptualization of the absolutes which *Melancholy* reveals (which I will now take up) suggests that *Melancholy* was written after the other great odes but before *To Autumn*.

I call this new form of conceptualization an advance because in *Melancholy* each of the mistress's companions is defined by a post-positioned clause which has a restrictive intent. There is no undying Beauty; rather, mortality is shown to be inherent in Beauty — there is only Beauty-that-must-die. (This is different from a Beauty that cannot keep her lustrous eyes; prophecy is one rhetorical mode, the restrictive predication of intrinsic necessity is another.) There is no lasting Joy; the very gesture iconographically identifying Joy is his hand ever at his lips bidding adieu. And there is no distillable sweet tincture of pure Pleasure; all pleasure is metabolized to poison not after, but during, the moment of the ingestion of that pleasure. Keats's *Melancholy* frieze is less perfect than some of his previous friezes because he does not yet know entirely how to create it. The frieze in *Nightingale* is, so to speak, a cinematic one of time-lapse photography, as we see Youth grow pale, and Beauty unable to keep her lustrous eyes, and Love decline from today to tomorrow. The circular and self-joining frieze on the urn is of course perfect, but it can be so because its figures, halted in an eternal present, incorporate in themselves no possible change. (The iconic *Indolence* figures, though carved on an urn, seem to be able to move off their urn at will and to change their iconic posture from profile to full-face, a conception so intellectually incoherent that Keats never reverts to it.) In *Melancholy*, Keats wishes to create a frieze in which change is not represented as temporally caused but intrinsic. He succeeds brilliantly with one clearly visual figure, that of "Joy, whose hand is ever at his lips / Bidding adieu," a figure which recalls with some self-irony on Keats's part the early dream of the impossibility of lips bidding adieu between Cupid and Psyche, the incident of disillusioning adieu in *Nightingale*, and the hostile adieu of *Indolence*.

The figure of Joy, a figure suitable for placement in a temple, incorporates all these adieux (the word is used in all the odes except *To Autumn*) into one gesture, iconographically succinct, painful and equable at once. But the other *Melancholy* figures are not visually well realized. "Beauty that must die" asserts but does not visualize the mortality of Beauty, and the extraordinary notion of the metabolizing of nectar to venom remains an internal and unvisualizable conceit of Pleasure, intensely suitable to the poem's intellectual progress toward truth and its inclusion of the "lower sense" of taste, but not appropriate for a visible frieze of companions in a sanctuary.

The second resolution—that of the hero's own destiny and companions—adopts a spatial and visual metaphor of temple and inner sanctum, but neither Delight nor veiled Melancholy is conceived in any compelling visual way, and Joy's grape is not in any necessary way connected with the Joy whose hand is at his lips. In fact the only successfully visualized items in the temple are the cloudy trophies. And yet, by adopting the generic forms of the frieze and the temple Keats had led us to expect a visual equivalent to his conceptualization, a promise he could not entirely fulfill, but which led, I believe, to the majestic visual forms of *The Fall of Hyperion* and *To Autumn*.

We see, then, several organizing forms at work in this ode. The large structural form is that of a quest, and this form organizes the whole poem: "Go not to Lethe to find true Melancholy, but rather to nature, and Joy; burst Joy's grape with the strenuous tongue of a heroic seeker, and you will successfully find what others cannot, Melancholy's sovereign shrine and the veiled goddess herself." This quest-form, borrowed of course from *Endymion*, has not previously appeared in the odes (except negatively in *Indolence* where the speaker declines to act), and requires a departure, in its emphasis on action and power, from Keats's previous notions of what an ode-protagonist should be like. The active quest begun in *Melancholy* is further refined in *The Fall of Hyperion*, where it takes on epic grandeur, and where a supreme visualization of temple and goddess is invented to reward the protagonist's deathly struggle up the stairs. Like the initiate in *Melancholy*, the hero of *The Fall* reaches an inner sanctum. The quest-form will be put to better use in *Autumn*, where the quest is retained but the melodramatic accoutrements and self-goading seen in *Melancholy* are rejected in favor of a search more gently pursued and more generously rewarded: "Sometimes whoever seeks abroad may find / Thee." It is still necessary to go abroad and seek, but not to the ends of the earth—only so far, we are peacefully told, as to the neighboring fields. (The quest-theme of power and reward will also find a surprising extension in *Autumn*, but I postpone that subject to the final chapter.)

A second form, besides that of the quest, organizing the *Ode on Melancholy* is the opposition between the language of natural objects and the language of frieze, the one "realistic," the other "allegorical." These two languages live here in an uneasy coexistence. We feel that nightshade cannot grow in the temple, and aching Pleasure cannot stand in the salt sand-wave. And yet Keats's wish to make a rapprochement between the two languages is evident in the natural and realistic bee-conceit (significantly *not* the traditional allegorical image of honey-making) attached to the allegorical aching Pleasure. In *Nightingale*, as we recall, the allegorical frieze of human figures groaning and pining had to be abandoned in order that Keats might enter the "natural" realm of the bird; similarly, the allegorical figures on the urn stand "far above" all naturalistic breathing human passion. This earlier confrontation between sculptured figures and apparently natural objects is evident also in *Indolence*, the first ode where Keats makes explicit to himself the close relation between allegorical language and works of art. They belong together, he thinks; and both are opposed to nature.

What Keats chooses to allegorize is another topic. In *Nightingale*, he restricts the allegorical mode to the "real world" of groaning men and dying youths, opposing it to a "natural" world of the bird; in *Urn*, as in *Indolence*, it is rather the world of the unchanging ideal which attracts allegorical terms to itself (Youth, Melodist, Maiden) while human passion in the "real" world remains unallegorized. What this history reveals is that Keats wanted allegorical import in his poems but wanted natural description as well, and did not know how to combine them or which realms—human, subhuman, superhuman—to allegorize.

We learn from *Melancholy* that Keats has ceased to see himself reclining in passive "indolence," engaging in purely mental constructions of Fancy, or silent in rapt attendance upon some instance of musical or visual art. He is self-charged, now, to a quest as a seeker, as one who wishes to inhabit at once the world of globèd peonies and the world of Joy's grape, a world of the senses and a world of concepts. He has translated the allegorical world into a new relation with the sensual world: it is not intermittent, as in *Indolence*, not antithetical, as in *Nightingale* and *Urn*, not parallel, as in *Psyche* (where the interior world of mind contains a replica of the outer world of history and the senses), but rather a relation conceded as inextricable. However, the language of *Melancholy* is still stiffly dual. The sensual and the mental have not as yet found a common language faithful to both. The one speaks the language of particularity, the other of allegory.

The only figure participating in the mythological language of *Melancholy*'s first stanza, the naturally sensuous language of the second, and the allegorical language of the third is the figure of the female. She is the third organizing form of the poem (which I add to those of the quest and the polarity between the sensual and the conceptual). She is, in turn, the Melancholy of the allegorical canceled first stanza, the classical Psyche and Proserpine of the mythological actual first stanza, the angered human mistress of the naturalistic second stanza, and the veiled Melancholy of the allegorical close. In the canceled first stanza she represents an inaccessible goddess; in the actual first stanza she is desired as a domesticated mythological partner in sorrow; in the second stanza she appears as the principle of human erotic desire and love-melancholy; and in the third she is a conquering allegory. The recurrence of the female figure as the object of quest in Keats offers no surprise after *Endymion*,[6] but this penultimate ode suggests that his ideal solution to the problem of the embodiment of the female must embrace all her dimensions — religious, mythological, natural, domestic, and allegorical. The demon Poesy, Love, Psyche, the light-winged Dryad, the bride of quietness, the fair maiden, and the angered mistress — each of these embodies one or the other of these dimensions, but no one has as yet been human woman, Ceres, Proserpine, and Delight-Melancholy all in one.

Still, we see in this ode that Keats is moving toward a female figure who will be natural, mythological, and allegorical all at once, who will possess the knowledge of triple Hecate, the knowledge that Homer mastered and that Keats desires:

> Such seeing hadst thou, as it once befel
> To Dian, Queen of Earth, and Heaven, and Hell.
> (*To Homer*, 13–14)

And Keats is turning away from passivity, spectatorship, and visionariness of a dreamy sort in order to seek some self-image more strenuous and directed; here, he rejects both a deathly drowsiness and a frenzied intemperance in favor of large "peaceable" recognitions and an equipoise of joy and sorrow.

In *Melancholy*, the speaker does not appear as a poet, but rather as a man ravaged by love-melancholy; and the question of art, so explicit in the other odes, does not, strictly speaking, arise. It is of course implicit in the opposition of "mythology" to "nature" and the resolution of their quarrel in allegory. The ostensible subject of the ode is rather the inner breadth of emotional experience; its question, how to absorb willingly the plenum of melancholy as well as the fullness of delight. The aim of the ode is to know and explore, not to repress, the wakeful anguish of the soul, and to savor with a fine palate the grape of Joy burst by the strenuous tongue. In choosing wakefulness over sleep, in valuing anguish as one relishes a taste on a fine palate, in praising strenuousness over passivity, this ode marks Keats's taking a more confident appetitive stance toward all passions, no matter how contrary, painful, and conflicting. *Melancholy*'s advance over earlier odes in welcoming the whole breadth of emotion is as striking as the *Urn*'s advance over *Nightingale* in admitting representational and propositional Truth. However, *Melancholy*'s desire for emotional breadth has not yet found an adequate temperateness of expression, nor an adequate comprehensive symbol. Keats often knew what he intended before he found a language in which to say it properly. Just as the language of *Nightingale*, where Keats was on his familiar and perfected ground of sensuous description, is more immediately accomplished than the awkwardly-tried-out new propositional language of "Truth" in the intellectually more comprehensive *Urn*, just as the purely visionary or interiorized fane of *Psyche* is more consistent than the ambitious conflict-born shrine of *Melancholy*, so we must wait for Keats's painfully acquired faith in the value of wakeful anguish to find its proper language in *The Fall of Hyperion*, and for his dim apprehension of a better goddess than Psyche or Melancholy to find its proper language in his descriptions of Moneta and Autumn.

It must be remarked that Keats's appeal (in the second stanza of *Melancholy*) to an exacerbation of consciousness as a cure for melancholy goes directly counter to the temperateness he would have found recommended as a remedy in Burton (2.2.1.1). Glutting and feeding deep are, even when practiced on flowers and eyes, forms of intemperance. But, though from Burton we cannot derive glutting as a remedy, we can derive it as a symptom. Burton sees melancholy as a "fit" which comes and goes (1.1.3.4), and he connects melancholy not only with "misty fogs" in the brain "which dull our senses, and Soul clogs" ("The Argument of the Frontispiece," VIII–IX) but also with heat, "violent actions," and being "rash, raving mad, or inclining to it" (1.1.3.3). The sufferer in *Melancholy* is "had, having, and in quest to have, extreme" as befits someone in the throes of love-melancholy; his extremeness does not subside until the third stanza, and it is wrong to read the first two stanzas as pieces of sage advice. This is a personal poem in an impersonal guise, and retells the torments suffered in the relation with one's "mistress" (Burton's inevitable term for the beloved.) The disordered quest for roses and rainbows and peonies would be recognized by any psychologist as an attempt to replace a lost love-object with surrogate ones; and though there is no proof of such a conjecture, we may speculate that the angry mistress, though she does not appear for some time, was the cause (in terms of motivation) of the speaker's wish at the opening of the poem to find oblivion; he prefers oblivion to her wrath. I will return to the question of the angry mistress later, but I must first look again at Keats's conclusion.

Keats's conscious attempt to incorporate, in the close of the poem, the poisonous wine of wolf's-bane (transmuted to the bee-poison made of Pleasure), the ruby grape of Proserpine (transmuted to Joy's grape), the angry mistress (transmuted into the victorious trophy-taking goddess), and the weeping cloud (transmuted into the sacrificial cloudy trophies) marks a sedulous intent to finish out his completions. There are still unmistakable signs of strain (the fed-on eyes, for instance, resemble too much for comfort the tongue-burst grape). The eventual completion of the destiny of his hero presented certain difficulties to Keats: once the hero had abandoned a quest for Melancholy which would take him to death and Lethe, and had decided to live, the question of his status at the end of the poem had to be determined. In fact, the hero experiences something like a death; the grape that he bursts in joy, finding grief, echoes the bursting of Gloucester's heart, and leads us to think that the hero, too, dies spiritually a death like Gloucester's physical one:

> *His flaw'd heart*
> (Alacke too weake the conflict to support)
> *Twixt two extremes of passion, joy and greefe,*
> *Burst smilingly.*
> (italics indicate Keats's underlining)

As the hero's heart seems to burst with the mingled sadness and joy of the grape that is burst and destroyed in the savoring, his soul becomes fixed as one of Melancholy's cloudy trophies, in her temple, his tomb. Keats marked the passage in Shakespeare's sonnets which may have occasioned, in this ode on love-melancholy, the tomblike close:

> Thou art the grave where buried love doth live,
> Hung with the trophies of my lovers gone.
> (Sonnet 31)

(On the other hand, we may also recall the gibbet of the canceled beginning of the ode: what is hung on this gibbet, at the end, is the soul of the Petrarchan lover dead for love.) The cloudy soul-trophy has joined the huge cloudy symbols of a high romance, and the quest-hero has in fact participated in the apotheosis removing him from the world of tragic circumstance, an ending not wholly appropriate to the attempt of this ode to give full credence to experience in this world.

Where we find the speaker of each ode at the end of the poem is significant. In *Indolence*, he is still embedded in the flowery grass, in nature, in a drowse; in *Psyche* he is vicariously awaited for a love tryst within the casements of the fantasy-fane; in *Nightingale* he has awakened from sense-fantasy into anguish, and from solitude in art into the suffering social world; in *Urn*, he is the intellectual contemplative spirit, aware of truth, consciously shaped art, and society; in *Melancholy* he is transubstantiated, allegorized through emotion, into a spiritual trophy. This latter disembodiment-into-art, as the man becomes the trophy of the Muse, represents a dangerous victory for the Belle Dame, though it also represents Keats's first full incorporation of his own certain death into the odes.

The company whom Keats chooses in each ode is also significant. In *Indolence*, preferring solitude in unformed visions and dreams, he rejects the company of Love, Ambition, and Poesy—those formed aspects of the self whom, the ode implies, he had previously accepted, and who now solicit his return to their fellowship. In *Psyche*, he rejects the Christian world which would banish (in the form of Psyche) classical myth; but he also rejects the objective and societal world in favor of a solitary ensconcing of himself with Psyche. In *Nightingale*, Keats also initially rejects the social world, but he does so in favor of a solitary vertical communion with an abstract artifact purged of human reference (except insofar as that reference is projected by the reverie of a listener); in *Urn* he at last admits social human life, both when it is arrested for scrutiny outside the corruption of time, and in the temporal shared experience of generations. *Melancholy* reverts to a conflation of *Psyche* and *Indolence*: in the company, a goddess is present, but so are Beauty, Joy, Pleasure, and Delight, hypostasized human aspects like *Indolence*'s Love and Ambition. A Psyche-priest no longer, the votary is now himself the sacrifice. This is a development we might have anticipated from the conjunction of priest and sacrificial victim in the *Urn*, but the price of the hero's becoming a victim, in this later version of Keats's tale, is that in his last appearance he is deprived of all society, as he becomes a lifeless trophy hung in the goddess's shrine, himself a voiceless cloud, an ex-voto as art object. As Keats considers, through these mutations, the problem of the solitude of the poet, and what he should choose, or hope for, or receive, or give, in the way of society, he still sees no obvious or secure way to establish a relation with a living group. To this problem, as to all the others raised in the odes, both *The Fall of Hyperion* and *To Autumn* will address themselves.

In respect to its language, the *Ode on Melancholy* exhibits more confusion than any other of the odes. It began, in the canceled first stanza, with language drawn from at least six sources—the homiletic-prophetic ("Though you should do X, you would fail to achieve Y"), the religious ("creeds"), the Petrarchan (a bark, a mast, a sail, groans to fill out the sail, a rudder, cordage), the heroic (the effort of the underworld quest to find "the Melancholy"), the gothic ("dead men's bones," a "phantom gibbet," a sail "blood-stained and aghast"), and the mythological (a dragon, Medusa, Lethe). These disparate registers of language sit ill together, and they suggest various dispersed aims for the poem without defining one aim as central. We gather that the object is either an Orphic journey to the underworld in search of a Muse, or a futile quest like Childe Roland's, in which the hero will follow in the footsteps of his doomed predecessors, all those dead men who have come to a bad end on the phantom gibbet. Or it may be that the hero is going to slay "the Melancholy," as he has slain Medusa and the dragon. Or he is a lover, in the classic Petrarchan bark, and the groans and blood are his own, the marks of cruelties inflicted on him by his richly angry mistress. The prophetic speaker remains shadowy; he speaks from a depth of experience, as yet unknown to the hero whom he addresses, about the probable results of such voyages. The speaker's sympathy seems to lie at least partly with Medusa (so reduced to a bald skull, having suffered her large uprootings) and with the dragon, its tail still "hard with agony" though severed long ago. Even in such a brief sketch rationalizing the elements of the canceled first stanza, we see incoherent elements; we have not found a place for the creeds which, stitched together, are to make up the sail; and it would seem that the phantom gibbet is reared only after the dead men (whose bones make the bark) have died, and so may be destined only for the hero himself. Woodhouse, per-plexed by the creeds, suggested the substitution of "shrouds," presumably as more consistent with the dead men and the idea of sails. But the religious motive generating "creeds" claims greater emphasis in the unfolding of the poem. The ode is evidently, in this first canceled stanza, aiming for a Renaissance syntax of melodramatic suspense, with its multiple concessives: "Although you should do A, and B, and C, and D, and E, you would fail." The tone is not one of meditation (as in the odes immediately preceding) but of action contemplated by the hero, and doomed to failure, dramatically, by the Burton-like speaker.

In canceling this stanza,[7] Keats abandoned the Petrarchan melodrama of the ship and the dead predecessors, but very little else — surprisingly little, thematically speaking, in view of the entire dissimilarity between the canceled first stanza and the actual one. The homiletic-prophetic is still the putative language of the speaker, but its rhetoric is no longer directed to outward narration of quest-failure; in turning inward, it is no longer the speech of an initiate to an ephebe, but has become rather the dialogue of the mind with itself, losing its former character of hectoring in proud bad verse. Now the speaker yearns, almost to capitulation, toward his own double absorbed in his rituals of sorrow. Religion remains, translated from the doctrinal (creeds being always repellent to Keats) to the liturgical, linked by the phrase "sorrow's mysteries" to the ritual of sacrifice performed by the urn's "mysterious" priest. The heroic quest is touched very lightly ("Go not to Lethe") and its fuller expansion is reserved for the ending of the poem, where Keats will praise the "strenuous" tongue. The mythological dimension of the canceled stanza is preserved in the mention of Lethe, Proserpine, and Psyche; and even the canceled gothic leaves its traces in poisonous wine, wolf's-bane, nightshade, rosary, yew, and death-moth. Keats's initial leaden and programmatic use of the Petrarchan vocabulary perhaps ensured its disappearance when he began to revise; and yet, since he was capable of making almost any anterior literary style bear his own stamp, we may deduce, from his refusal to set the whole tenor of his piece to the Petrarchan tune, his own sense that he was writing about a topic larger than the melancholy of love. If, as I believe, the poem originated in love-melancholy, Keats's decision to drop the Petrarchan frame is all the more striking. (In demoting the mistress, in his second stanza, to a subordinate though climactic position, he takes the same road toward reducing the emphasis on love.)

If we look to see what the melancholy soul who is being admonished in the actual first stanza wants to have, we see that his desires are several. He wants to drink something (either the waters of Lethe or the wine of wolf's-bane); he also wants his "pale forehead" to be flushed by the ruby claret of Proserpine; but since that contact is represented as a kiss, we may say he wants erotic experience as well as a draught of vintage. He wants as well a garland—in this case a rosary of yew-berries—which we may perhaps ally to that of the sacrificial heifer; he wants an emanation from himself (whether beetle or death-moth) to symbolize his mournful soul; and he wants company in his sorrow's mysteries, preferably the bird of dark wisdom, the downy owl.[8] These desires are not, by the other, admonitory half of his mind, condemned *as desires*; they are condemned only insofar as the *objects* chosen to satisfy those desires are not ones of which the speaker can approve. The speaker, in effect, promises to offer a better vintage, a better eroticism, a better garland, a better soul-emanation, a better company, by which the wakeful anguish of the soul may be preserved alive, not drowned in Lethe. To take poison, whether nightshade or wolf's-bane, is to become that "sod" feared in *Nightingale*; as Keats wrote later from the ship taking him to Italy, "I wish for death every day and night to deliver me from these pains, and then I wish death away, for death would destroy even those pains which are better than nothing" (*Letters*, II, 345). If Keats is not to "drown his sorrows" (and his use of the verb "drown" may have been occasioned by just this cliché) in poisonous drink, he must await the next advice of his inner daemon, to be offered in the second stanza. It should be noticed that the actual first stanza retains the melodramatic syntax of the canceled first stanza, replacing concessives (Although you do X) with negative exhortations (go not, make not, let not), continued until, after six injunctions, the suspended consequent is permitted to appear in the closing lines,

> For shade to shade will come too drowsily,
> And drown the wakeful anguish of the soul.

The negative injunctions are in fact more subtle, in their undertow of attraction, than the canceled prophetic gothic concessives. It is because of the undertow of attraction, as I have said, that I am led to call this a poem of self-advice, a personal poem impersonally phrased. And the self-advice in the second stanza, then, may be seen to be as suspect as that in the first: the first shows the homilist subversively attracted by what he reproves; the second shows the homilist covertly repelled by what he advises.

In the narrative frame of the poem, the second stanza represents a flashback, presenting two occasions which might lead to the suicidal expedients conjured up in the first stanza. The first occasion is a causeless melancholy (what Burton calls melancholy interrupt, "which comes and goes by fits," 1.1.3.4), falling, according to Keats, "sudden from heaven like a weeping cloud"; the second is love-melancholy, caused by a tirade of anger from one's mistress. In short, the structure of the second stanza is that of two parallel if unequal blocks, the first of seven lines, the second of three, joined by "or":

$$
7 \begin{cases} \text{When fit falls} \\ \\ \text{Then glut sorrow on} \end{cases} \begin{matrix} \\ X \\ Y \\ Z \end{matrix} \quad or \quad 3 \begin{cases} \text{If mistress shows anger} \\ \\ \text{[Then] emprison hand} \\ \text{let her rave} \\ \text{feed on eyes} \end{cases}
$$

But there exists in the stanza a competing structure, because the "or" which joins blocks I and II exists in a "false" parallelism, emphasized by anaphora, with the "or" of possible objects of gluttony:

$$
\text{Then glut thy sorrow} \begin{cases} \text{on a morning rose,} \\ or \text{ on the rainbow of the salt sand-wave,} \\ or \text{ on the wealth of globed peonies,} \\ or \text{ if thy mistress, etc.} \end{cases}
$$

This structural overlapping has the effect of making the whole clause about the mistress seem yet another object of the verb "glut," and therefore places it less as another occasion for a melancholy fit than as another object for satiety: this parallelism reduces, as I have said, the status of love-melancholy (actually, the only explicit melancholy instanced in the poem) to one experience among many. The false symmetry of the three "or's" enables the syntax of the second stanza to resemble that of the first, with a long postponement of the climax to the end. Each of the stanzas of *Melancholy* (including the canceled one) is composed of a single sentence; in each, the syntax conducts a sustained quest of its own for resolution, as increment by increment it amasses itself to a conclusion. In this, *Melancholy* is unlike the other odes, which interrupt, with exclamations or questions, the syntactic momentum.

If it is generally felt, as I believe it is, that the middle stanza of *Melancholy* suffers by comparison to the two flanking it, it must suffer on account of its thought and language, since it is not noticeably different from its companions in syntax or speaker. Thought and language, in this stanza, seem both enfeebled. The first stanza's religious, erotic, companioned world of drowsy temptation is in every way — with its wine, and kiss, and ruby grape and rosary and partner and mysteries — more interesting than its opposite, which offers to the senses a more commonplace set of satisfactions — the rose (for sight and perhaps smell), the rainbow of the salt sand-wave (for sight and taste),[9] the wealth of globèd peonies (for touch), and peerless eyes (for sight, and for taste, since one is to feed upon them). In the second stanza the mistress is antagonistic, unlike sorrow's congenial conspirators Psyche and Proserpine; the religious appetite for mystery is not satisfied; and, most of all, the hero seems aimless in the order of his glutting: the list (a rose, a rainbow, the wealth of peonies, eyes) seems composed without much care for variety or perspective, though the appropriateness of rose and peonies as erotic female surrogates is clear. Keats has taken some care to distribute his glutting among the senses, but even here we remain relatively undirected, and the noble earlier phrase "sorrow's mysteries" does not suggest a sorrow that can be dealt with by gazing at a rose. The flowers are the more there to be savored, we are to suppose, because "fostered" from their drooping by the showers of the melancholy fit (rather as slow time, generally thought of as destructive, had "fostered" the urn).

But the green hill, not a partner to anything in the first stanza, makes an unexpected and arbitrary entrance, and departs never to be seen again. As for the mistress, everyone has felt the literary impropriety of the language used in the passage concerning her. The injunction to "feed deep, deep upon her peerless eyes" brings the Spenserian and Petrarchan language of peerlessness into uneasy conjunction with the predatory. The lover is transformed into something ravening his lady while she raves (Keats, with his talent for puns, could not help thinking of words like "ravish" and "ravening" as he wrote "feed" and "rave"). The echoes of *Venus and Adonis* and *Troilus and Cressida* in the imprisoning of the hand are evident;[10] but I think that Keats also, in this ode as in others, has *Hamlet* in mind.[11]

The second stanza of the *Ode on Melancholy* has made, we notice, a notable turn into "realism," sacrificing at once the underworld voyage, Greek mythology, emblematic insects and birds, liturgical acts and appurtenances, and in fact the soul itself. This clean sweep perhaps makes the language of the second stanza seem impoverished after the riches of the first. But we cannot doubt that Keats intended this purgation of the mythological and liturgical, just as he intended the purgation of the Petrarchan apparatus. One intent of the stanza is to come violently into the light of day, to wake up, to banish all bowers and "shades." Consequently, the hero could not glut his sorrow on "the night's starred face" or on fast-fading violets. When Keats reflected, in the last letter he wrote, on "all that information (primitive sense) necessary for a poem," the two instances he gave of that information were "the knowledge of contrast" and "feeling for light and shade" (*Letters*, II, 360). The *Ode on Melancholy*, in its first two stanzas, sacrifices the latter—a chiaroscuro—in favor of contrast, of an attitude of yes against no, this against that. Wordsworth's "Come forth into the light of things, / Let nature be your teacher," is the purport of Keats's second stanza; but for Keats that aesthetic of plain sight meant the sacrifice of everything symbolized by wine, kisses, mythology, religious veneration, and mystery—or so the second stanza, by its repression of all these things, implies. It is a poverty, the light of day; and therefore a glut is, for Keats, impossible within it. It is for that reason that we feel the strain of the declared glut, and that we find the intensity of "feed deep, deep," an empty one. The added assonantal and empty "peerless" offers no satiety.

If we say that Keats's duty at this point was to find for his deprived hero some diet more imaginatively rich than the clichés of morning rose and peerless eyes could offer, and that the diet must include surrogates for the fatal pleasures — erotic, religious, palatal, and societal — denied him after he is told to forswear them in the first stanza, then we see to what ends Keats was pressed in concluding his poem. His first stratagem was to find a middle ground between the rich mythology of the beginning and the starved (if glutted) naturalism of the middle, by reintroducing those allegorical figures that had haunted him, though variously named, through the other odes. Love, Poesy, and Ambition he had called them in *Indolence*; Youth, Beauty, and Love were their names in *Nightingale*; in the *Urn* they were the Melodist, the Lover, and the Maiden. They are his allegorical frieze-figures, as I have said, and they appear here again, this time named Beauty, Joy, and Pleasure. They are the company the hero will find, and they live in the shrine of Melancholy, found within the temple of Delight. These two additional figures are invoked in the round, as sculpture, while the others are seen in relief (like Joy) or only conceptually.

This stratagem replaces the Psyche of the first stanza with Delight, and Proserpine with Melancholy, so the hero, at the end, does not lack goddesses, as he had in the second stanza. The third stanza replaces the beetle, the death-moth, and the owl — companions from the literature of emblems — with companions from the literature of allegory, Beauty, Joy, and Pleasure. It replaces the religion of sorrow's mysteries and rosaries of yew-berries with worship at a "sovran shrine" within a "temple" — reinstating religious allusions and architectural constructions missing in the "natural" second stanza. It replaces the ruby grape and poisonous wine with Joy's grape and nectar. It replaces the kiss of nightshade with the sipping mouth of the bee and the lips of Joy; and it replaces the mistress's hand of the second stanza with the hand of Joy. It replaces the poisonous wine by that poison into which Pleasure is transmuted. The purely sensational delights of the second stanza have been replaced by emotional experiences of a deeper sort, the dangerously protean Joy and Pleasure of the close.

We encounter intellectual difficulties with the conceptualizations of the last stanza. We have seen Keats's allegorical figures in their simplest form in *Indolence*: Love, Poesy, and Ambition are unchanged and unchangeable, Idea translated into figure, figure given name—"a fair maid, and Love her name" or "Ambition, pale of cheek." We recognize these as Spenserian masque-figures. We next meet, in the sequence of the odes, an allegorical couple, Cupid (also called "the warm Love") and Psyche; they represent allegory interchangeable with myth; they too are Spenserian. *Nightingale* is, as I have said, the first of the odes to make allegorical figures change before our eyes, as we see Youth grow pale and spectre-thin and die. The allegory-in-motion is clearly in Keats's mind in *Nightingale*, and he attempts the motion in another way, by negating stability. In allegory Beauty always keeps her lustrous eyes, and in allegory Love forever pines. By saying "Beauty cannot keep her lustrous eyes," Keats denies permanence without, however, showing us change.

In the *Urn*, Keats might seem to be returning to his static practice in *Indolence*, but I think there is a difference between the two usages. The personages on the urn are pictured in motion but are frozen at an active instant of that motion. There is by contrast no motion associated with the fair maid named Love; even pale Ambition, though "ever watchful" adjectivally, is not actively "watching," in a tensed verb. But the melodist on the urn is "forever piping," and the lover is "winning" near the goal. Insofar as allegorical figures represent Ideas, or Platonic absolutes, they are not allowed to be in motion. The solution of the *Urn*—of freezing an Idea in motion (Love in act) so that it remains an absolute Idea—is not allowed by Keats, in later odes, to stand. He finds it, evidently, an evasion of change; hence we find the interesting figures in the temple of Delight, which incarnate the idea of the inextricable simultaneity of opposites (rather than change over time), which forms the intellectual basis of the *Ode on Melancholy*. The "weeping cloud" of *Melancholy* is the same cloud that appears in the journal-letter to the George Keatses (*Letters*, II, 79) and its "bursting" is the bursting of Joy's grape:

> Circumstances are like Clouds continually gathering and bursting—while we are laughing the seed of some trouble is put into the wide arable land of events—while we are laughing it sprouts it grows and suddenly bears a poison fruit which we must pluck.

Between the writing of this passage (with its bitterness about the poison fruit which we must pluck) and the ode's bursting of Joy's grape lies an evolution in Keats's view of his metaphor. The poison fruit survives in the nectar-turned-poison of Pleasure; but the final palatal claim is given not to grief but to Joy. The Idea of simultaneity—"while we are laughing it sprouts it grows"—is the one which, much developed, and in a more benign aspect, will generate the *Autumn* ode: "While barred clouds bloom the soft-dying day, . . . / Then in a wailful choir the small gnats mourn." Blooming and mourning coincide.

As Keats tries to make his Platonic Ideas incorporate change and process, he moves away from simple temporal prophecy ("Beauty cannot keep her lustrous eyes") and into necessitarian prediction ("Beauty that must die"). This latter is an intellectual formulation with no conceivable visual equivalent; so Keats tries once more, with "Joy, whose hand is ever at his lips / Bidding adieu," producing a figure like Ambition ever watchful; but this time the emblematic attribute is a gesture of motion (and in that sense comparable to the "forever piping" of the melodist on the urn), but it is an entropic motion, unlike that of the lover on the urn, whose motion (winning near a goal) is anti-entropic. The gesture of Joy is admirably suited to Keats's purpose: it is visual, it has instant iconographic significance (Keats may have seen funeral steles with the comparable farewell gesture of the hand on the shoulder), and it is symbolic of a process of closure. But it is a static pose: Joy is "ever" posed thus. Keats tries once again, and achieves, at the expense this time of visual coherence, an intellectual figure coming closest to what he has in mind, a Platonic Idea absolutely incorporating entropy—a change for the worse—into itself. The image in Keats's letter of the seed sprouting into a fruit passes over the intermediate stage of the flower; here he arrests the process at the stage of the flower (the stage at which the second stanza of the ode, with its focus on flowers droop-headed or otherwise, is also arrested). The flower, with its nectar of Pleasure, is here still innocent: it is some power in the bee that can change nectar into venom. And yet the metamorphosis is not attributed to the bee, but helplessly to Pleasure itself: "aching Pleasure nigh, / Turning to poison." This passage in the ode may be compared to Keats's outburst on lust written on the margins of his Burton: insofar as women are flowers, and Keats the bee, he confusedly blames himself for distilling a venom from their sweetness, and yet at the same time blames the nectar itself for its instability and its lack of resistance to metamorphosis.

The beautiful verbal situation of Pleasure between "aching" and "turning," and the wholly satisfying rhyme of "lips" and "sips," mark Keats's hitting his stride in this ode, so that we are ready to expatiate with him in his "Ay"—that word he will turn to again, and for the same purpose, a sigh, in *Autumn*: "Ay, where are they?" Deprived of his solitary Lethean bower, he turns to its social parallel, a shrine, this time not a mythological one, as in *Psyche* or *Urn*, but an allegorical one: an outer temple of Delight enclosing an inner shrine of Melancholy. Here, space—the distance from temple door to inner sanctum—substitutes for time (the time it takes the initiate to pass from simple Delight to the more complex intertwined Delight-and-Melancholy). Though visual, the image of temple and shrine is related neither to the frieze-figures nor to the emblematic and naturalistic bee (himself a poetic descendant of the moth and beetle of the first stanza), but rather to the initial bower. In one final effort, Keats invents a heroic figure—significantly unnamed, but human, not allegorical—to represent the idea he has been pursuing. We recall that in order to end the poem he needed (given its beginnings) a heroic quest, religious feeling, sensuality, soul-emanation, a governing metaphor of taste, a mythological richness, and a tone of prophecy not hectoring but meditative. And yet, if he is not to break the poem in two, he needs also to preserve some link with the naturalism of the second stanza, with its elements of a weeping cloud, growing things, a feast for the eyes, and a peerless mistress. In his redefinition of the hero as one who has found the power to taste Joy to the full, Keats redefines heroic strength; in making the hero the initiate who can enter the Holy of Holies, he recalls his secular religion of soul-making. In making the fruit to be tasted not a poison fruit but Joy's fruit, Keats absolves circumstance and finds a figure—in the inextricability of tasting and bursting—which is neither entropic nor anti-entropic alone, but both at once, a bidding-adieu and a winning of the goal in one act.

The minatory "Though seen of none" distinguishes the solitary hero in an accolade which dismisses the lingering morbidity of the first stanza as well as the combined sentimentality and predatoriness of the second. The language of the last six lines of the ode shows Keats's complex imagination working at its most rapid pace. Each word carries weight and aura at once. Authority is borne by the asseverative "Ay," the intensive "very," the distinguishing "sovran," and the stern "seen of none save him," as well as by the concluding prophetic revelation of the destiny of the hero as cloudy trophy. The naturalism of the weeping cloud returns in Melancholy's veil and in her cloudy trophies: tears are the veil, as silent tears are the substance of the trophies.[12] The hero tastes sadness as one tastes tears; even as one might taste the salt sand-wave. The growing flowers of the second stanza have become (for the first time in the odes) fruit—not the ruby grape of Proserpine, that poison fruit, but the grape of Joy. The triumph of the stanza comes in its last line, another of Keats's "false" syntactic parallels. We expect that some enlightenment will follow "His soul shall taste the sadness of her might, / And—" If I were to invent an epistemological ending, it might read, for instance,

> His soul shall taste the sadness of her might,
> And know the melodies her choir had sung.

We expect, after the "And," a verb parallel to "shall taste"—an active verb, prolonging the experience of the hero. Instead, the hero silently dies upon the bursting of the grape—and we realize that it is his heart that has broken in the tasting. A later version in the *Letters* (II, 352) reads: "Oh, Brown, I have coals of fire in my breast. It surprised me that the human heart is capable of containing and bear-

ing so much misery." So we are unsettled by the lack of parallel syntax; when we find a passive verb form rather than an active one, and
feel the full force of the passive phrase—"be hung"—we realize we
are hearing the posthumous fate of the hero. Hung as an ex-voto of
tears on the walls of the sovereign shrine, his soul finds its companions among the other trophies—those other souls whose heart has
broken with joy and misery. Keats was perhaps remembering, in
the hung trophies, that phantom gibbet on which the hero was to
find himself hung at last, just as, in the surrounding trophies, he
was recalling the dead men, his predecessors in the quest. The
strenuous tongue is a direct (and less phallic) descendant of the
dragon's tail still hard with agony, just as the mistress's dwelling
with Beauty is a descendant, figuratively speaking, of Melancholy
,dwelling in a Lethean isle.

In making the *Ode on Melancholy* his ode on the sense of taste,
Keats had to depart entirely from his original first stanza, which
had included no imagery of taste at all. I assume he was governed in
this departure by his realization that he had already written odes on
hearing and on seeing; in choosing to dwell on taste he made the
crucial passage, for him, to the "lower" senses. The earlier odes,
hymns to the higher senses, subordinated smell and touch. *Melancholy* has the daring to be a hymn to the "strenuous tongue" (and its
energy) and the "palate fine" (and its spiritual discrimination among
joys). The brave predication "His soul shall taste" has of course
properly religious antecedents ("O taste and see," for example) as
does the ecstatic juice of the grape. It should be noticed that the
grape here yields only its own juice, not wine; Keats's intoxication
will never again, after the repudiation of wine in *Nightingale*, be
that of any earthly drink. (He makes a point of his sobriety not only
here, but also in *What can I do to drive away*, in *The Fall of Hyperion*,
and in *To Autumn*.)

In carrying through his small drama of the hero who, passing
through the temple of Delight, dares to enter the sovereign inner
shrine and find within veiled Melancholy, the hero who tastes Joy
to the full through his own savoring and fine-judging palate,
thereby breaking his heart and becoming a trophy of tears within
the shrine, Keats allowed his fears to extend into death and beyond

—beyond the death of Beauty, or the adieu of Joy, beyond even the metamorphosis of Pleasure into lethal poison: he passed into that region he had visited before in *Endymion*, the Cave of Quietude. The cave is the only place outside of *Melancholy* where the cloudy trophies would not be out of place: this den of remotest glooms is surrounded by dark regions where the spirit sees "the tombs of buried griefs." In this deepest den, one can sleep "calm and well":

> There anguish does not sting; nor pleasure pall:
> Woe-hurricanes beat ever at the gate,
> Yet all is still within and desolate.
> Beset with plainful gusts, within ye hear
> No sound so loud as when on curtain'd bier
> The death-watch tick is stifled. Enter none
> Who strive therefore: on the sudden it is won.
> Just when the sufferer begins to burn,
> Then it is free to him; and from an urn,
> Still fed by melting ice, he takes a draught.
>   (*Endymion*, IV, 526–535)

The parallels with the end of *Melancholy* are evident, as are those with the journey homeward to habitual self, linked by Keats to a parching tongue:

> A homeward fever parches up my tongue—
> O let me slake it . . . !
>   (*Endymion*, II, 319–320)

This parched tongue and the "parching tongue" of the *Urn* are relieved at last by the bursting of Joy's grape, itself also envisaged in *Endymion*:

> Dost thou now please thy thirst with berry-juice?
> O think how this dry palate would rejoice!
>   (II, 327–328)

We are justified in seeing Keats as willing to end *Melancholy* in the desolate region envisioned in the Cave of Quietude. But by including the rejoicing of the palate, he can enter the Cave of Quietude (its shape reproduced in the temple of Delight, as, later, in the skull of Moneta) without the repining expressed in "Forlorn" or "Cold Pastoral." Desolateness is no longer blamed on deceitful fancy or deceitful art or deceitful perception; it is seen not simply as a consequence of joy, not even as inextricably balanced against joy, but actually as a component within joy itself and indistinguishable from it, just as savoring is indistinguishable, experientially, from bursting. (Of course, savoring can be distinguished *conceptually* from bursting; and Keats will attempt a conceptual sequestering of tragedy in the theater of Moneta's brain.) In conceding the inextricability of joy and death, Keats finds himself able to think through and beyond death into his posthumous fate; and he can conceive of death as something to be nobly envisaged rather than ignobly suffered.

It is not to denigrate the *Ode on Melancholy* that I have represented it as a poem engaged in a continual and provisional hunt for its adequate means. In spite of its rather formulaic clarity of structure—"Not this; but that"—and its explanatory coda, it has no clarity of means. Uncertain at first whether it wants to be Petrarchan or mythological or religious or Homeric, uncertain later whether it wishes what it counsels against (drowsiness) or whether it likes what it recommends (glutting sorrow in flowers), it recovers itself brilliantly at the end, gathering together as many as it can of its desires—desires for death, for wakeful anguish, for joy, for intensity, for erotic response, for a sovereign mistress, for a society of those sorrowing, for a heroic quest, for mythological resonance, for natural experience, for the "lower" senses. It finds the end of its quest for intensity in the drama of self-transmutation by heartbreak into a cloudy trophy, an immortality of tears.

The importance of *Melancholy* to the sequence of the odes lies chiefly in its admission of the "lower" senses to the realm of highest experience. The price it pays for that admission is a great uncertainty of language; by comparison with this ode its predecessors are marvels of consistency. But there was a disembodied nonphysical quality in the shades of *Indolence*, the shrine of *Psyche*, the singing of the nightingale, and the "experience" postulated of the figures on the urn—and that disembodied ideality has emphatically disappeared in the physical conjunction of strenuous tongue and burst grape. Without the *Ode on Melancholy*, Keats would not have found his way to the rich embodiments of the autumn ode. Without *Melancholy*'s experiments in allegorical figuration, he might not have invented Autumn amid her store. But the *Ode on Melancholy* is silent. It has not found any place for music; its speaker and hero are not poets, they exist distinct from the speaker-poet of all the preceding odes.[13] A further attempt must have seemed to Keats a necessary effort; the degree of the seeming effortlessness of the last ode (by contrast to the unwieldy movement of *Melancholy*) is a measure of the intellectual and spiritual work that preceded its composition.

If *Nightingale* presses toward the realm of Sensation and Beauty, and the *Urn* presses toward the realm of Thought and Truth, *Melancholy* represents the new notion, of incalculable significance for Keats, that a poem could press toward Sensation and Truth. We find here the link between Sensation and Truth which visual beauty (as in the *Urn*) could offer only in alternating emphases; and which "senseless, tranced" sensation in *Nightingale* could not offer at all. *Melancholy* is clearly a "Truth" poem in its myth of quest: since perception and sensation are immediate, not remote, the quest for "the Melancholy" must mean, in the canceled first stanza, a quest for the true essence of the experience, the allegorical form that will reveal its Platonic nature—a quest rewarded in the arrival at the veiled figure within the temple of Delight. It is also a Truth poem in its (canceled) successful confrontations of the dragon and Medusa: by looking the most threatening male and female forms in the face, by seeing the truth of what they are, one overcomes and slays them. It is also a Truth poem in its refusal of drugs, in its adherence to "wakefulness" even in anguish, and in its final penetration beyond the portals of the temple of Delight into its inmost shrine. If *Melancholy* does not remove the last veil from the mysterious face of Truth—an act which Keats will be able to accomplish only in *The Fall of Hyperion*—it nonetheless pursues Truth, Vision, Wakefulness, and Quest almost to their last sanctuary, and certainly further than they have been pursued in earlier odes. The surprising, striking, and almost miraculous discovery of *Melancholy* is that Truth can be pursued in Sensation rather than in

Thought alone. The rather random "realistic" sense-feedings on a rose here, a wave-rainbow there, the riches of peonies elsewhere[14] provide a quick enlivening of the temperature of sense-response (away from the drowsy sense-lulling of the opening) in order that the aching pleasure of the emblematic bee-mouth can raise the temperature still higher; this ensures the tension which will give the allegorical burst grape and the tasting of sadness their most acute form.

Of course there are intellectual difficulties with the proposition "Sensation is a path to Truth"; these are brought into visible and paradoxical form by Keats's use of emblematic and allegorical Sensation (rather than sensual sensation) in the last stanza. What is the tongue that bursts Joy, as one would burst a grape? And what is the palate that savors that Joy? It is the "palate of the mind," as Keats later called it in *I cry your mercy*; if it should lose "its gust," he says, he would forget life's purposes. The recognition that his own mind worked in ways which were best described by the vocabulary of Sensation, rather than by the vocabulary of Thought (logic, propositions, "consequitive reasoning"), meant, for Keats, that *thoughts* could be symbolically represented by a train of described *sensations*. If the reader can recognize those sensations as ones experienced by the palate of the mind, he will take them in as what Eliot was to call an objective correlative; but where Eliot considered that the objective correlative was the correlative to *feeling*, Keats considers it the correlative to *thought* (and therefore his own version of Truth, with its concomitants Vision, Wakefulness, Dark Passages, and Quest).

It follows that the last stanza of *Melancholy* must employ the vocabulary of Thought (those abstractions which for Keats represent Ideas—Beauty, Joy, Pleasure, Delight, and Melancholy) as well as the vocabulary of Sensation (aching, poison, sipping, a bursting grape, palate, and taste). The propositional language of Truth ("Beauty . . . must die") yields to a language of iconic situation ("hand . . . ever at lips") and of sensation ("burst Joy's grape"). The last two lines, phrased in a proposition prophetic in its tense, ring the changes of the ode's language. In bald description of linguistic registers, we might read:

His soul [Truth] shall taste [Sensation] the sadness [Emotion]
of her might [Erotic Veneration],
And be among her cloudy [Naturalistic] trophies [Heroic]
hung [Sacrifice].

I have said least about the language of Emotion, which rather
evades the Keatsian categories of Beauty and Truth. In deciding to
make the subject (and the allegorical divinity) of this ode an intense
emotion, rather than a passive state (Indolence), a mythological
goddess (Psyche), a natural entity (a nightingale), or an artwork (an
urn), Keats here begins to worship a complex emotional state, the
acute nexus of pleasure and pain, from which, he realizes (remembering the thoughts grown from pleasant pain in *Psyche*), his
creativity has always sprung. The melancholy fit fosters the droop-
headed flowers; what else, then, should he worship but this?

In embodying into divinity his own inner melancholy state, Keats
moves away from the avoidance of introspection which, in *Indolence*,
ensured the irreality (as ghosts and phantoms) of parts of himself
(Love, Ambition, Poesy) he wished not to acknowledge. He recalls
in part his wish in *Psyche* to build a proper sanctuary for his love-
goddess, but Psyche is not, I think, an externalized part of his own
self so much as an object for himself as priest and Cupid. In *Melancholy*, he has built a double sanctuary and peopled it and installed his
goddess within it — an exteriorizing of inner states of delight and
melancholy of which he was incapable in *Psyche* in any explicit or
self-reflective way. He has, in short, passed to conscious self-representation in writing. No longer the audience listening to, or looking
at, an object (bird or urn) he cannot become, he becomes the object
of his own self-scrutiny. The achievement of deliberate self-ob-
jectification in part accounts for this ode's being an address to the
self, making the self the object of attention. The "new" wakeful
self, split off, can address the "old" self addicted to indolence,
drowsiness, dreams, and death; and can equally address, implicitly,
by the range of its closing language, another "old" self which had
been wont to separate Sensation and Thought, Beauty and Truth,
description and "philosophizing." Yet this explicit self-representation is still expressed in the vocabulary of the soul's own emotions—

sorrow, anguish, mournful melancholy, joy, pleasure, delight, sadness. The one named allegorical figure who is objective, not a sensation in the soul, is Beauty, derived from the mistress, herself a "naturalistic" objective reality among the roses and rainbows and peonies (themselves masquerading as naturalistic and objective, though with clear symbolic function). The mistress is that "material sublime" that Keats knows must constitute his aesthetic medium:

> O that our dreamings all of sleep or wake
> Would all their colours from the sunset take:
> From something of material sublime,
> Rather than shadow our own soul's daytime
> In the dark void of night.
>   (*Dear Reynolds*, 67–71)

I take this to mean that Keats found it petty that our daydreams and night dreams on the whole repeat—and not in a finer tone—our spiritual concerns during the waking hours. He would prefer that daydreams and night dreams represent sublime sunsets or exhibit "Titian colours touch'd into real life" (*Dear Reynolds*, 19). Certainly the *Ode on Melancholy* shadows the soul's daytime anguish, though the second stanza may be attempting some frantic grasp of the material sublime. Keats's instinctive knowledge that the material sublime was his true path had to wait upon his recognition that sensation in him was, *when aesthetically ordered*, a way of thinking and a presentation of Truth.

The difference between the rather randomly strung sensations of much of *Endymion* and the far more moving sensations of the ode *To Autumn* is not a difference of material—intellectual or emotional or imagistic—so much as it is a mastery of arrangement, or "stationing." The stationing of sensations was Keats's most original way of thinking and truth-telling. It saved him from a weak "philosophical" language of propositions and an equally weak "sensational" language of emotions (like that at the end of *Melancholy*). The theory that Truth can be attained by experiencing sensation to the full (including both physical and emotional sensation) is presented and worked out in *Melancholy*, but not yet successfully exemplified. Once Keats realized that it was in the *ordering* of sensation that Truth and emotion both could be expressed, and that the whole world of phenomena could be taken as his palette, he was ready for his magisterial exemplification of the theory in *To Autumn*. It takes all its colors from the sunset.

The *Ode on Melancholy* offers a therapeutic theory of aesthetic experience. In *Nightingale*, aesthetic response is finally judged useless, a cheat. *Melancholy* sees it as a recourse against depression, an alternate to opiates. When the melancholy fit falls, causelessly (or so Keats first sees it), Keats is tempted by a set of natural winged creatures (owl, beetle, death-moth), opiates (Lethe), and poisons which can perform the same functions as the nightingale and its song—like that winged creature and its enrapturing song, they offer an escape from consciousness. Rejecting that temptation, Keats flees to the visually beautiful—to a rose, a wave-rainbow (the rainbow he will use again in *Lamia*), peonies, his mistress's eyes. The visually beautiful, without ideational or moral import, parallels the tonally beautiful in *Nightingale*; Keats here feasts on pure color and shape as he had there feasted on pure sound. But whereas his response in *Nightingale* had been passive as he received the song-as-opiate, his new view of aesthetic response treats it (tentatively) as an active, even predatory undertaking; he gluts his sorrow on flowers, and feeds deep, deep, on his mistress's eyes. The mania of this response corresponds to the preceding depression which sought opiates; the exacerbated Delight is here pursued just as, in the canceled first stanza, the Lethean Melancholy had been suicidally sought. The disjunction of human experience in this ode resembles that in *Nightingale*; though the poet has advanced to an active aggression against his melancholy in lieu of a passive distraction from it, the violent mood-swing from suicidal longing to forced aesthetic pleasure does not provide a comprehensive theory of art, as we can infer from some remarks on glutting one's eyes or throat which Keats made elsewhere. He wrote in July 1819 that "the parties about here who come hunting after the picturesque like beagles . . . raven down scenery like children do sweetmeats" (*Letters*, II, 130), and on 5 September of the same year he included a later-canceled passage of *Lamia* in his letter to Taylor:

A Glutton drains a cup of Helicon,
Too fast down, down his throat the brief delight is gone.

(*Letters*, II, 159)

The shape of the first two-thirds of *Melancholy* may be compared to the erratic swings of a needle—ninety degrees to the left of the equilibrium, then ninety degrees to the right. The needle comes to rest in the third stanza, at its central balance, free of the pressures to left and right. In its longing after erotic partnership the first stanza harks back to *Psyche*—Keats's "mournful Psyche" is to be the death-moth—while in its appetitiveness the second stanza foreshadows the active seeking abroad of *To Autumn*. The problem posed by the ode is to find a description of aesthetic experience which will include an opiate, though not a fatal one; a female, though not an erotic partner (by its nature, the erotic cannot achieve the aesthetic stance); and an active search, though not a randomly predatory one, for Delight. Keats's solution is to turn, as he has also done in the *Urn*, to the realm of essence, the Platonic one of the eternal Good, True, and Beautiful. The Beautiful in Keats's realm incorporates a necessary death as Joy bids a perpetual adieu, and as aching Pleasure is metabolized to poison as the bee-mouth sips. These essences are not referred to a stable base; they are presented in a partly statuesque, partly conceptual way. Dissatisfied with this manner of formulation, though not with its import, Keats rewrites his union of the permanent and the transient, melancholy and joy, but this time refers the experience to a single figure, an ephebe being initiated into the *penetralia* of life. Veiled Melancholy, in her sovereign shrine within the temple of Delight, is seen of none save him. Keats's fine solution alters the deep feeding on the mistress's eyes to the bursting of Joy's grape by a strenuous tongue; the sexual force of the tongue retains the aggression of the earlier search for beauty, but, by aiming the experience at a fine palate, makes the experience a discriminating rather than a random one. The taste becomes a spiritual one, experienced by the soul, rather than the sensual taste of the ruby grape of Proserpine or the visual glutting of the eyes; active pursuit is followed by a form of victimage as the ephebe's soul is suspended among the trophies of the goddess. The attitude of the artist to the natural and human world is here Keats's aesthetic question: so long as aesthetic relish is violently disconnected from human feeling it is predatory and unreal, as Keats implies by his appending to the excesses of the second stanza the equilibrium of the third. In the predatory mode, one lets one's mistress rave in anger; one neither listens to her words nor experiences one's own wrath or shame at her anger—instead one feeds irrationally on her peerless eyes. This deflection of emotion into visual relish is, in Keats's eyes, a form of perversion. The poem is concerned with the ways of responding to melancholia rather than with aesthetic questions as such; yet in its final recognition of the mixed nature of all joy, pleasure, and delight, of the inevitability of death in human experience, and of the presence of the metaphysical in the existential, it prepares the way for *Autumn*. In rising above the disillusion of immediate emotional experience to a generalized view of existence, it avoids the bitterness of *Nightingale* and enables a larger view comparable to that aimed for at the end of the *Urn*. Finally, in its emphasis on which responses are worthy and which unworthy, it allows into the poem questions of moral import which were largely excluded by the purely mental focus of *Psyche* and by the trance of *Nightingale*. Beauty, in this poem, can no longer exist separated from Truth: Beauty (to speak truthfully) is a Beauty-that-must-die. No Divinity, Keats here proposes, can live except in the shadow of its opposite; it is in the temple of Delight that Melancholy has her sovereign shrine (just as in *Autumn* fruition and death are seen to be inseparable). The locus of the beautiful and the pleasurable is the normal and equilibrated, if strenuous, experience of the fine palate bursting a fruit into savor, of a bee-mouth sipping nectar, not the first depressed realm of poison-eating nor the second manic realm of glutting on flowers and feeding deep on human eyes. Keats will, in the last ode, emphasize these perceptions of the centrality and normalcy of aesthetic response, will recall the inextricability (within *ordered* sensation) of Beauty and Truth, and will move into a position of primary importance the sacrificial tenor of existence. The simple tripartite structure of *Melancholy* resembles superficially that of the ode *To Autumn*, but the difference in order and density between the successive enumeration of opiates and visual delights in

Melancholy and those of the fruits of the earth in *Autumn* will be evi-dent when we reach the last of the great odes. The pattern of *Melan-choly* is one of moral injunction, both direct ("Do not do this, do that") and indirect ("Seen of none save him"). This pattern becomes a dead end for Keats; he will not adopt it again. But he will invent moral exhortation coming from a source outside himself in the per-son of Moneta; as he passes, with the bursting of the grape, from reverie and spectatorship into the realm of action, he feels the need of a rule of conduct. It is not until *To Autumn* that he succeeds in embodying, in a presentational and sensuous mode, not only the in-tellectual insights evident in its meticulous ordering of detail, but also the ethical imperatives that *Melancholy* (and, as we shall see, *The Fall of Hyperion*) voice in a homiletic rhetoric.

VI

The Dark Secret Chambers:
The Fall of Hyperion

There lies a den,
Beyond the seeming confines of the space
Made for the soul to wander in and trace
Its own existence, of remotest glooms . . .
Dark paradise! where pale becomes the bloom
Of health by due; where silence dreariest
Is most articulate; where hopes infest;
Where those eyes are the brightest far that keep
Their lids shut longest in a dreamless sleep.
O happy spirit-home! O wondrous soul!
Pregnant with such a den to save the whole
In thine own depth.

 Endymion, IV, 512–515, 538–545

The sacrifice is done.

 The Fall of Hyperion, 241

In the dusk below
Came mother Cybele! alone — alone —
In sombre chariot; dark foldings thrown
About her majesty, and front death-pale.

 Endymion, II, 639–642

Though an immortal, she felt cruel pain.

 Hyperion, I, 44

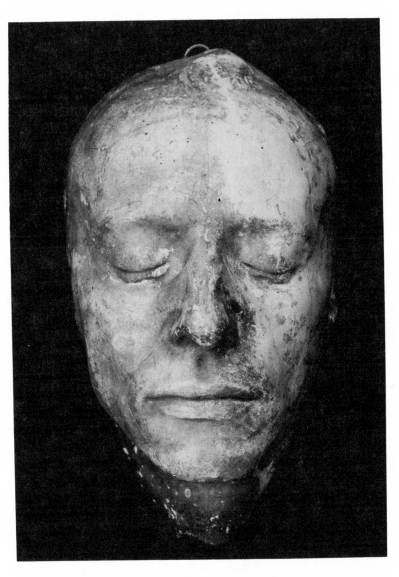

Then saw I a wan face,
Not pin'd by human sorrows, but bright blanch'd
By an immortal sickness which kills not;
It works a constant change, which happy death
Can put no end to; deathwards progressing
To no death was that visage.
    — *The Fall of Hyperion*, I, 256–261

From *The Fall of Hyperion*, I

"Majestic shadow, tell me where I am:
Whose altar this; for whom this incense curls:
What image this, whose face I cannot see,
For the broad marble knees; and who thou art,
Of accent feminine, so courteous."
Then the tall shade in drooping linens veil'd
Spake out, so much more earnest, that her breath
Stirr'd the thin folds of gauze that drooping hung
About a golden censer from her hand
Pendent; and by her voice I knew she shed
Long treasured tears. "This temple sad and lone
Is all spar'd from the thunder of a war
Foughten long since by giant hierarchy
Against rebellion: this old image here,
Whose carved features wrinkled as he fell,
Is Saturn's; I, Moneta, left supreme
Sole priestess of his desolation." —
I had no words to answer; for my tongue,
Useless, could find about its roofed home
No syllable of a fit majesty
To make rejoinder to Moneta's mourn.
There was a silence while the altar's blaze
Was fainting for sweet food: I look'd thereon
And on the paved floor, where nigh were pil'd
Faggots of cinnamon, and many heaps
Of other crisped spice-wood — then again
I look'd upon the altar and its horns
Whiten'd with ashes, and its lang'rous flame,
And then upon the offerings again;
And so by turns — till sad Moneta cried,
"The sacrifice is done, but not the less
Will I be kind to thee for thy good will.

My power, which to me is still a curse,
Shall be to thee a wonder; for the scenes
Still swooning vivid through my globed brain
With an electral changing misery
Thou shalt with those dull mortal eyes behold,
Free from all pain, if wonder pain thee not."
As near as an immortal's sphered words
Could to a mother's soften, were these last:
But yet I had a terror of her robes,
And chiefly of the veils, that from her brow
Hung pale, and curtain'd her in mysteries
That made my heart too small to hold its blood.
This saw that Goddess, and with sacred hand
Parted the veils. Then saw I a wan face,
Not pin'd by human sorrows, but bright blanch'd
By an immortal sickness which kills not;
It works a constant change, which happy death
Can put no end to; deathwards progressing
To no death was that visage; it had pass'd
The lily and the snow; and beyond these
I must not think now, though I saw that face—
But for her eyes I should have fled away.
They held me back, with a benignant light,
Soft mitigated by divinest lids
Half closed, and visionless entire they seem'd
Of all external things—they saw me not,
But in blank splendor beam'd like the mild moon,
Who comforts those she sees not, who knows not
What eyes are upward cast. As I had found
A grain of gold upon a mountain's side,
And twing'd with avarice strain'd out my eyes
To search its sullen entrails rich with ore,
So at the view of sad Moneta's brow,
I ached to see what things the hollow brain
Behind enwombed: what high tragedy
In the dark secret chambers of her skull
Was acting, that could give so dread a stress
To her cold lips, and fill with such a light
Her planetary eyes; and touch her voice
With such a sorrow. "Shade of Memory!"

Cried I, with act adorant at her feet,
"By all the gloom hung round thy fallen house,
By this last temple, by the golden age,
By great Apollo, thy dear foster child,
And by thy self, forlorn divinity,
The pale Omega of a wither'd race,
Let me behold, according as thou said'st,
What in thy brain so ferments to and fro." —
No sooner had this conjuration pass'd
My devout lips, than side by side we stood,
(Like a stunt bramble by a solemn pine)
Deep in the shady sadness of a vale,
Far sunken from the healthy breath of morn,
Far from the fiery noon, and eve's one star.
Onward I look'd beneath the gloomy boughs,
And saw, what first I thought an image huge,
Like to the image pedestal'd so high
In Saturn's temple. Then Moneta's voice
Came brief upon mine ear, — "So Saturn sat
When he had lost his realms." — Whereon there grew
A power within me of enormous ken,
To see as a God sees, and take the depth
Of things as nimbly as the outward eye
Can size and shape pervade.[1]

I N *Hyperion* (which was composed before the odes) and *The Fall of Hyperion* (composed chiefly after the first five odes, but before the ode *To Autumn*), Keats brings up for examination, as in *Psyche*, the inner operations of the working brain. The wide hollows of Apollo's brain in *Hyperion* and the dark secret chambers of Moneta's skull in *The Fall* become urns of knowledge and of art, art as yet, like that of *Psyche*, disembodied. But the decorative fancifulness of *Psyche*'s garden is the comedy of which the *Hyperions* are a tragic version. In the *Hyperions*, in a great widening of vision, the content of art is affirmed to be not merely the anonymous erotic and religious scenes on the urn but also all political and spiritual history:

> Knowledge enormous makes a God of me.
> Names, deeds, gray legends, dire events, rebellions,
> Majesties, sovran voices, agonies,
> Creations and destroyings, all at once
> Pour into the wide hollows of my brain,
> And deify me, as if some blithe wine
> Or bright elixir peerless I had drunk,
> And so become immortal.   (*Hyperion*, III, 113–120)

In this speech of Apollo, Keats seeks a solution to the temporal evanescence of art. The art of space will prove, in the *Urn*, as fugitive as the art of time in *Nightingale*; in the bold leap of the two *Hyperions*, Keats has chosen to turn from art as medium (Apollo's music) to art as mentality, and to the notion of mentality not as a realm exempt from history, as in *Psyche*, but as a realm which, by incorporating history, becomes therefore superior to mental categories of time and space. The mind is imagined as a container: Keats emphasizes its hollowness. The urn is not conceived of as a container (and therefore interpretations dwelling on its possible function as a resting-place for ashes are wide of Keats's mark); the urn is represented as a self-bounding frieze (its practical function, whatever it might be, slighted in favor of its representational surface and its harmonious total outline). In *Psyche*, though the fane and garden are placed within the brain (which is consequently in some sense a container), Keats treats the brain as a constructive agent, as a working force and a breeding gardener, rather than as a container. Here, however, in *Hyperion*, the brain is preeminently the storehouse of memory, where life, history, and process exist in synchronic and not diachronic form.

This notion of a nonlinear shape of history-in-the-mind struck Keats late in the composition of *Hyperion* (probably, as Stillinger conjectures, p. 638, in the spring of 1819) and threw into relief his preceding labored epic debate in the poem on time, history, and change. Familiar as that debate is, I must recapitulate it briefly here, because in its painstaking articulation of positions we find the Keatsian basis both for Moneta's face in *The Fall* and for the ode *To Autumn*.

In bursting *Melancholy*'s grape, Keats allowed, as I have said, irreversible change and death into the odes (the little town, though desolate, is in its "identity" unchanged, since it can be imagined and addressed; the grape's "identity" is sacrificed in being burst). The attitude or attitudes one can adopt in thinking of death preoccupy Keats in the first *Hyperion*, too; and its solutions influence those of the odes. Some of these attitudes are rather woodenly acted out by the dethroned Titans; others are suggested by Keats himself in his role as the impersonal narrator of *Hyperion*. We must examine them to understand the meaning of Moneta's face and its metamorphosis into the figure of Autumn.

The first attitude explored in *Hyperion* is that of conscious acceptance of a "posthumous" existence. We see the Titans as cloudy trophies, so to speak, of their previous sovereign state: "Forest on forest hung above his head / Like cloud on cloud," says Keats of the fallen Saturn. This "posthumous" existence — one which has internalized the knowledge of mutability — is felt as a contrastive one. That is, the nostalgic memory of the former existence or identity serves as the point of view from which the current existence is described — the new existence is realm*less*, *un*sceptered, voice*less*, nerve*less*, list*less*, deadened, still, silent fallen, sunken, shaded, sodden, old, and time*less*. The life that has been lost was one possessing change (morn, fiery noon, and evening star), health, light, joy, eminence, air, seeds, motion, heat, utterance, and youth. So much can be gathered from the Keatsian contrastives of the opening of *Hyperion*, but the poetry, in addition to being nostalgic and embittered in some lines, embodies elsewhere, notably in the steady nobility of the tragic opening of the poem, a tonality that we associate with Keats's North Star vision, an open-lidded, solitary steadfastness. The pathos that later invades the descriptions ("His old right hand lay nerveless, listless, dead") can be thought either to strengthen or to weaken the poem, depending on one's preferred Keats. But the opening, in spite of its open use of words like "sad" and "sunken" and its contrastive language ("voiceless," "deadened"), is not nostalgic. It is conclusive. It redescribes the pastoral *locus amoenus* in a shocking but beautiful way, turning it from nature to art by setting as its centerpiece an aged marble god instead of a panting, lovesick youth:[2]

> Deep in the shady sadness of a vale
> Far sunken from the healthy breath of morn,
> Far from the fiery noon, and eve's one star,
> Sat gray-hair'd Saturn, quiet as a stone,
> Still as the silence round about his lair;
> Forest on forest hung above his head
> Like cloud on cloud. No stir of air was there,
> Not so much life as on a summer's day
> Robs not one light seed from the feather'd grass,
> But where the dead leaf fell, there did it rest.
> A stream went voiceless by, still deadened more
> By reason of his fallen divinity
> Spreading a shade: the Naiad 'mid her reeds
> Press'd her cold finger closer to her lips.

The grateful shade of the pastoral covert is here, but transmuted; this bower provides not protection from too hot a sun or too harsh a wind but rather imprisonment from sun and air alike; the pastoral "vale" (the word on which Keats had raptly dilated in his notes on *Paradise Lost*) is here, but as the lair of a proud eminence now sunken;

the necessary stream is here, but robbed of its music; the mythological *genius loci* is here in the presence of the Naiad, but she is a cold and silent and asexual presence;³ the forest of sylvan pastoral surrounds Saturn, and (as we later learn) the moon herself is not absent — she sheds "her silver seasons four upon the night." But the whole bower is transformed by the immobile central presence of the sculptural Saturn, still as a stone and bearing his gray hair; his iconographical vegetative counterpart is the Shakespearean and Miltonic fallen dead leaf. Opportunities for nostalgia abound, but the light seed and the feathered grass are untouched by it. The voice that speaks this opening has perfect command of stationing and phrasing alike; Keats's wonderful command of order in *To Autumn* begins here. Time (morn, noon, and eve), space (forest on forest), and relative positions (Saturn deep in a vale far sunken from light and air, the Naiad amid her reeds) are all magisterially "placed." The first sentence descends to the central Saturn and rises from him again; the second, after its negations ("no," "not," "not"), subsides into an absolute and balanced placing: "Where the dead leaf fell, there did it rest." And the third sentence brings into beautiful parallel the voiceless stream, the fallen divinity, and the gesturing Naiad. She, of course, is related by close cousinship to *Melancholy*'s "Joy, whose hand is ever at his lips / Bidding adieu," but her gesture, though progressive or intensified, admits no change of direction, no reversal from silence toward utterance. She is silence and chill, a Muse as voiceless herself as her medium or matrix, the stream. It is true that the dead leaf has fallen, the stream goes by, the Naiad presses her finger closer — that is, time exists in this vale — but the leaf rests where it falls, the stream cannot resume its voice, the Nymph's finger-pressure cannot be reversed nor her cold finger warmed; matters are settled, here in Saturn's lair, for silence, death, and a chill that can only increase, as the finger is closer pressed. This is Keats's first sketch for what will become Moneta's progressive and self-intensifying sickness.

The pathetic fallacy — that the rest of nature suffers with Saturn — is in this passage lightly refused. Saturn's reign has stopped, but time has not stopped. In the later *Fall of Hyperion*, the pathetic fallacy is explicitly rejected, as Saturn is made to groan in outrage,

"Still buds the tree, and still the sea-shores murmur. / There is no death in all the universe, / No smell of death" (422–424) — musings addressed to "solitary Pan," who continues to make nature fruitful and musical in spite of the vicissitudes of individual or even dynastic tragedy. (Keats here registers this perception of untroubled natural persistence for safekeeping, so to speak, and returns to it in *Autumn*.) The *Urn* refuses to let the boughs shed their leaves; when the dead leaf falls at the beginning of *Hyperion* we see a severer and more tragic form of the burst grape.

This pastoral, with a gray-haired, palsied *senex* as its "human" actor (when Saturn speaks it is "as with a palsied tongue," 93), is fruitlessly defended against in the subsequent *Nightingale*, which vows to flee the sight of palsy shaking a few sad last gray hairs. But Keats found he could not forget this sorrow, and the odes may indeed be thought of as the lyric choruses to the Titans' tragic drama.

As I have said, Keats's first and deepest attitude toward decline and change, in *Hyperion*, is to see them as irreversible — to see that the dead leaf rests where it fell — and to place them squarely within the *locus amoenus*. But the poem had to be continued; and to continue it, more superficial attitudes are explored in turn. Thea, for instance, suspects some worse calamities to come; but this perception cannot alter, though it can deepen, the first sense of disaster. Saturn hopes (like Milton's Satan) for the reversibility of change, anticipating a final victory over the rebel Olympians by the one Titan still throned, Hyperion. Hyperion will come, Saturn hopes (123–127),

> to repossess
> A heaven he lost erewhile: it must — it must
> Be of ripe progress — Saturn must be King.
> Yes, there must be a golden victory;
> There must be Gods thrown down.

Saturn's second optimistic hypothesis hopes, if not for reversibility, at least for the repeatability of origins (141–145):

> Cannot I create?
> Cannot I form? Cannot I fashion forth
> Another world, another universe,

> To overbear and crumble this to nought?
> Where is another Chaos? Where?

To the acceptance of posthumous existence, to the hope of reversibility, to the hypothesis of another chaos to be formed, Keats adds yet one more attitude to decline. Hyperion's response in his not yet dethroned state is, as Sperry has pointed out (p. 188),[4] to exhibit nervous torment — to ache, to pace, to become "distraught" in his eternal essence by seeing new horrors, so much so that he cannot see, for pain, the beauty of his surroundings (241–244):

> The blaze, the splendor, and the symmetry,
> I cannot see — but darkness, death and darkness.
> Even here, into my centre of repose,
> The shady visions come to domineer.

Hyperion's rebellion against circumstance takes the form of wishing to disturb necessity — "if but for change" to accelerate the dawn. His impiety is rebuked by the narrator (292–293):

> He might not: — No, though a primeval God:
> The sacred seasons might not be disturb'd.

Keats's own future impiety in the *Urn* is precisely to disturb the sacred seasons and forbid the leaf to fall. He repents in *To Autumn*, and like Hyperion learns how to bend his spirit to the sorrow of the time.

Coelus, Hyperion's father, suggests that, allegorically interpreted, the fall of the Titans is the discovery of the passions; through consciousness and feeling, man falls irreversibly into mortality. The Titans, says Coelus, used to live "in sad demeanour, solemn, undisturb'd," like the sacred seasons. Now they are ignobly worked on by "fear, hope, and wrath; / Actions of rage and passion," visible in them as in "men who die" on the "mortal world beneath." Coelus, who is the first incarnation of the powerless voice later to become that of the gnats adrift on the wind, explains the impotence of utterance in the face of change:

> I am but a voice;
> My life is but the life of winds and tides,
> No more than winds and tides can I avail.

The most that Coelus can do is the most that the narrator of *To Autumn* can do: "Keep watch on [the] bright sun, / And of [the] seasons be a careful nurse." The guarantors of the procession of the seasons are the stars: "And still they were the same bright, patient stars." The gaze of these patient eremites is the forerunner of the patient look of Autumn over the last oozings.

In the Miltonic parley of Titans in *Hyperion*, Asia, like Saturn, hopes for future glory through historical change, Enceladus speaks for reversibility through revenge, and Oceanus announces that the Titans have fallen by reason of progressive evolutionary necessity, being replaced by a fairer race, while Clymene reinforces Oceanus' optimistic interpretation by describing the irresistible music of the young Apollo. It is impossible not to feel that in spite of his tragic and resigned "posthumous" beginning, Keats wishes to share Oceanus' hopes in "the grand march of intellect" (*Letters*, 1, 282) which here produces the deified Apollo. Like Hyperion, Apollo is to be a sun-god, but unlike the nature-god Hyperion he is also the god of art. He represents the power of art to incorporate and replace nature, as composition on the "artificial" lyre replaces poor Clymene's "natural music" from a seashell. He also represents knowledge and forethought triumphing over circumstance, and Keats therefore considers him a more suitable hero than Endymion:

> One great contrast between them will be—that the Hero of the written tale [i.e., *Endymion*] being mortal is led on, like Buonaparte, by circumstance; whereas the Apollo in Hyperion being a foreseeing God will shape his actions like one.
> (*Letters*, 1, 207: 23 January 1818)

In taking the progressive view, Keats has rather forgotten the old Titans with whom he began, and their experience is put aside in favor of the creation of Apollo: "Apollo is once more the golden theme!" The "Father of all verse" addresses Mnemosyne, who tells

him, in an odd reshaping of the Adamic dream, that he had dreamed
of her, and, waking, had found not Eve but a lyre at his side:

> "Yes," said the supreme shape,
> "Thou hast dreamed of me; and awaking up
> Didst find a lyre all golden by thy side,
> Whose strings touch'd by thy fingers, all the vast
> Unwearied ear of the whole universe
> Listen'd in pain and pleasure." (*Hyperion*, III, 61–66)

This unhappy melodist, the not-yet-deified Apollo, plays music of
pain and pleasure to the vast, unwearied ear of the whole universe;
it is easy to see that he is transmuted, on the urn, into the happy
melodist unwearied, who pipes songs of pleasure alone. Like the
Titans, Apollo is unhappy, but his unhappiness comes from stasis,
and his appetite is for change; his unhappiness comes from ignorance, and his appetite is for knowledge; his unhappiness takes
place on the green ground of vegetative nature, and his appetite is
for the celestial (III, 96–100):

> Are there not other regions than this isle?
> What are the stars? There is the sun, the sun!
> And the most patient brilliance of the moon!
> And the stars by thousands! Point me out the way
> To any one particular beauteous star.

Though Mnemosyne remains mute, Apollo is nonetheless transformed, reading a lesson in her silent face as Keats will read a lesson
in the silent form of the urn (III, 111–113):

> I can read
> A wondrous lesson in thy silent face:
> Knowledge enormous makes a God of me.

As Keats realizes that all the hypotheses of the Titans that he has
rehearsed sequentially (whether of progress or decline) and all
changes (whether welcomed or feared) are equally present in the hollows of the conceptualizing and recording brain, the previous labored

narrative toiling through sequential and conflicting attitudes toward mutability embodied in the speeches of different Titans seems slow and fruitless. Keats's lyric desire to ensconce all feeling into one suffering subject defeats his epic desire to tell a tale, and he decides to begin the massive recasting which he will entitle *The Fall of Hyperion*: both titles show his interest to lie more in the tragic decline and suffering witness of the Titans than in the hopeful unveiling of Apollo.

It has not been realized, I think, that Keats's source for the suffering witness and rebellious claims of the Titans (and especially of Moneta) is Spenser's Mutability Cantos, to which I suspect Keats returned before writing *The Fall of Hyperion* and *To Autumn*.[5] In these cantos (to recapitulate the matter relevant to Keats) a single remaining Titaness, Mutability, determines to assert her ancient right over that of the Olympians:

> She was, to weet, a daughter by descent[6]
> Of those old Titans that did whylome strive
> With Saturnes sonne for heavens regiment;
> Whom though high Jove of kingdom did deprive,
> Yet many of their stemme long after did survive.

The Titaness shows to men "proofe and sad examples" of her "great power" (relating her to Keats's Melancholy); she next embarks on her conquest of heaven, and her first act is to attempt to dethrone her Olympian counterpart Cynthia (both are moon-goddesses of mutability) — a struggle Keats would have read with special interest because of his having taken Cynthia as his goddess in *Endymion*. Mutability (in her allegorical genealogy, daughter of Earth and granddaughter of Chaos) confronts Jove and demands sovereignty. Jove

> marked well her grace,
> Being of stature tall as any there
> Of all the Gods, and beautifull of face
> As any of the Goddesses in place.

Jove shakes his lightning in wrath:

> But when he looked on her lovely face,
> In which faire beames of beauty did appeare
> That could the greatest wrath soone turne to grace,
> (Such sway doth beauty even in Heaven beare)
> He staid his hand.

Mutability appeals above Jove to the God of Nature—"the highest him, that is behight / Father of Gods and men by equall might." When the God of Nature appears, however, it is apparently a woman (though veiled) that we see, but Spenser quickly suggests that in reality the God of Nature is an androgynous form:

> Then forth issewed (great goddesse) great dame Nature
> With goodly port and gracious Majesty,
> Being far greater and more tall of stature
> Then any of the gods or Powers on hie;
> Yet certes by her face and physnomy,
> Whether she man or woman inly were,
> That could not any creature well descry;
> For with a veile, that wimpled every where,
> Her head and face was hid that mote to none appeare.

(Keats retains a hint of this same androgyny by never using a gender pronoun in reference to his figure of Autumn.) The veils of Dame Nature Keats will bestow on Moneta, together with the "terror" they evoke:

> And yet I had a *terror* of her robes
> And chiefly of the *veils*, that from her brow
> Hung pale, and curtain'd her in mysteries.
>   (*Fall*, I, 251–253, italics mine)

"Some do say," Spenser writes of Nature's ambiguous veil, that it was

>   so by skill devized,
> To hide the *terror* of her uncouth hew
> From mortall eyes that should be sore agrized;

> For that her face did like a Lion shew,
> That eye of wight could not indure to view:
> But others tell that it so beautious was,
> And round about such *beames* of *splendor* threw,
> That it the Sunne a thousand times did pass.
>
> (italics mine)

Keats borrows Spenser's splendor and beams (as well as terror and veils) for Moneta (but since she is a moon-goddess she cannot be linked, like Spenser's Nature, to the sun; that blessing is reserved to Keats's Autumn). Moneta's eyes, says Keats, "saw me not, / But in blank *splendour*, *beam'd* like the mild moon" (italics mine). I reserve, for my next chapter, the aspects of the Mutability Cantos that directly affect the ode *To Autumn*, and continue here with the last few passages relevant to Melancholy and Moneta.

Though Mutability successfully shows the seasons, months, and hours, as well as life and death, to be under her sway, Jove objects that he and his fellow Olympians are exempt from mutability. The Titaness retorts that even the Olympians are subject to her, and once again she turns first to her Olympian counterpart, Cynthia the moon:

> Her face and countenance every day
> We changed see and sundry formes partake,
> Now hornd, now round, now bright, now browne and gray;
> So that "as changefull as the Moone" men use to say.

The "hornd" moon may lend another detail to *The Fall*, where Saturn's temple is a "horned shrine" (I, 137): "I look'd upon the altar, and its horns / Whiten'd with ashes" (I, 237–238). Mutability's last triumphant claim makes the entire universe her trophy—a passage Keats must have recalled in the last line of *Melancholy*:

> "Then, since within this wide great Universe
> Nothing doth firme and permanent appeare,
> But all things tost and turned by transverse,
> What then should let, but I aloft should reare
> My Trophee, and from all the triumph beare?"

As we know, Nature finally pronounces against Mutability, offering two arguments, neither of which Keats found convincing. Nature first adduces the cyclicity of natural process (but Keats saw that individual men and dynasties know no such cyclical fate); second, she adduces the Last Day, when change will end (a religious dogma to which Keats could not subscribe). Rather, Keats allied himself with Spenser's own sublunary conviction that in everything but the Christian heaven, Mutability "beares the greatest sway." And though Spenser's chief emphasis in the Mutability Cantos has been on the classical view of the spontaneous decay of nature with the passage of gradual time, in his epilogue he invokes the much sharper biblical image of the sudden Grim Reaper; he rejects those "things so vaine / Whose flowring pride, so fading and so fickle, / Short Time shall soon cut down with his consuming sickle." As the "classical" entropic view of the two Mutability Cantos produces in Keats (in *The Fall of Hyperion*) another classical Titaness who is prey to an endless decline (unlike the Olympian Cynthia, who waxes as well as wanes), so the Epilogue to the Mutability Cantos produces in Keats a harvest reaper with a hook—but one deeply changed, as we shall see, from the usual iconographic form of the Grim Reaper.

The Fall of Hyperion, to which I can now turn, is cast in the form of a dialogue of the mind with itself. For all its pretensions to epic narrative, and for all its debt to Spenser, Milton, and Dante, its import is lyric. The two halves of the mind presented in the poem are symmetrical, as Keats sets bower against sanctuary, nature against art, Maiden-thought against dark passages, dreamer against poet, Paradise against mortality, our happy unfallen mother Eve against suffering Moneta, and so on. There are, in this poem, so many reminiscences of the odes that we can see the Induction to *The Fall* as a virtual recasting of ode material, and as a preparation for the writing of *To Autumn*, which will learn from both the *Hyperions*.

Once again, Keats attempts a new version of the *locus amoenus*. This one does not display Palsied Eld spreading a chill about the grove. Instead, in the center of the bower—where Cupid and Psyche had lain, where Keats himself had lain in *Indolence* and *Nightingale*, where in *Melancholy* the mistress had been placed in company with rainbows, waves, peonies, and roses—there is now an absence. The poet arrives as a latecomer; our first parents have preceded him at a feast ("a meal / By angel tasted or our Mother Eve"), leaving husks and shells (but also a continuing plenty) behind. Though this arrival has been read as an allegory of artistic belatedness, it can equally well be read as a testimony to Keats's consciousness of the mortality of generations (when he himself arrived at adulthood, he arrived alone, both his parents long since dead). We arrive, then, in a place where others have preceded us; we arrive provided for, but orphans. We then replace the bower of Maiden-thought with a sanctuary, leave nature for architecture; and we place in the sanctuary effigies of our vanished parents, as Keats places his brooding statue of Saturn[7] and his living but ghostly priestess Moneta—who assumes toward the poet a role combining both the sternness of male authority and the tenderness of maternal solicitude. The unemphasized and mute statue of Saturn is an ineffectual attempt at introducing a male presence to the shrine (in *Autumn*, the paternal presence will be transferred to the sun). Keats's invention of fallen parental Titan-presences represents an attempt to see himself as an adult, subject to the fate of previous generations, rather than as a privileged youth, an immortal Apollo who can never die. *The Fall of Hyperion* allows the sacrificial procession of the urn to proceed to its altar and go past it: "The sacrifice is done," Moneta tells the poet. It remains to be seen what postsacrificial vision, deprived of progressive or linear or exceptional movement, can be said to be. (*To Autumn* substitutes agricultural harvest for ritual sacrifice, and consequently treats harvest as retrospectively sacrificial, not as a prospective source of rich garners.)[8]

Keats's aim in *The Fall of Hyperion* is to transmit religious vision—the visions his soul perceives in its aspiring struggle. In still thinking of "the soul," he is still partially in the grip of his old vertical desire for wings: in fact, after the first step up the staircase, he starts up "as if with wings," and mounts up to the altar as angels "flew / From the green turf to Heaven." He has not yet entirely reconciled himself to a pair of patient sublunary legs (as he will somewhat when he "seeks abroad" in horizontal motion in *To Autumn*). The soul had been for Keats an important leading-idea in the previous odes: in *Indolence* it was his soul that was a lawn; it was Psyche the soul whose priest he would be in his *Ode to Psyche*; it was its own "soul" that he said the nightingale poured forth in music; it was "the spirit" that he preferred to the sensual ear in *Urn*; and it was the soul of the hero that would taste the sadness of Melancholy's might, becoming her cloudy trophy. Against this persistence in a dualism of spirit and body, Keats will set, in his autumn ode, the sensual eye and ear as the prerequisite and sole channels to religious intuition, and all talk of "the soul" or "the spirit" will disappear.[9]

My concern here cannot be with the whole of *The Fall*,[10] but only with those parts intersecting with and reflecting the five earlier odes and anticipating *To Autumn*. It must be said, first of all, that the intent of *The Fall of Hyperion* is to *tell* (not to experience) a dream. This open-eyed and conscious relating of a past dream is for Keats very unlike a lapsing into a dream state; it suggests his new deliberateness of composition. The sober certainty of waking truth here preserves a memory of the dream, and saves Imagination from that "dumb enchantment" — a phrase harking back to *Nightingale* — of the senseless trancèd thing. The bower of *The Fall* contains no stream (unlike *Psyche*'s bower or the bower of the old Saturn; the nightingale's bower needs no noise of waters because music is being provided by the bird, while the other, refreshing, function of water in the *locus amoenus* is not needed in *Nightingale* since no bodily life flourishes in the death-trance of suspended consciousness caused by the bird's song). Instead of a "natural" stream or a fountain, we find in *The Fall* a transparent liquid distilled by civilized art from some unknown source and placed by some agency in a cool drinking vessel. This juice, because transparent, is to be distinguished from the purple vintage desired in *Nightingale*; it is domineering but not intoxicating; the fact that wandering bees sip it suggests that it is the nectar of the gods (which Keats had seen in Neptune's Palace, *Endymion*, III, 925). In any case, it does not numb the brain like Keatsian intoxicants, but instead confers visionary powers. The old conflict between intoxication (wine) and sobriety (Joy's grape) is here mediated by this "bright elixir"; but the potion does not deify the drinker (as Apollo in *Hyperion* is deified); it only empowers him to a new knowledge of reality. Keats's emphasis on his own mortality and that of all men is explicit: in drinking, he pledges not the "humans" or "living" of the world (as he might have done), but rather "all the mortals of the world," as well as "all the dead whose names are in our lips." Though the drink is said to have properties like those of opiates (the Asian poppy) and poison, and though to an observer its effects simulate those of intoxication (Keats sinks down "like a Silenus on an antique vase"), its inner effects, as I have said, are illuminating rather than obscuring. By this means too, then, Keats insists on coldness and clarity, as he does in "telling" his dream. (He will relent in *Autumn* and allow the intoxicating poppy to return; in every way *Autumn* is more humane than *The Fall*, allowing for lulling charities forgone in the strict former examination of conscience.)

The arbor-roof of trellis vines and the floral censers of *The Fall*'s garden recall, as I have said earlier, *Psyche*; the white heifers in Proserpine's field and the antique Silenus on a vase recall the *Urn*; the poison and potion recall *Melancholy*; and the winged upstarting recalls the aching for wings in *Indolence* and *Nightingale*. The old sanctuary spacious enough to include clouds under its roof resembles the shrine of *Melancholy*, and the liturgical paraphernalia (robes, golden tongs, censer) seem relics of *Psyche*. Keats is attempting, then, at the beginning of *The Fall*, to bring the whole force-field of his imaginative phantasmagoria—the realms of Flora, Pan, and Ceres, the realm of Proserpine and the realm of *Psyche*, the shrine of *Melancholy* and the figures on the urn—into focus. We have seen before, in *Psyche*, the transmutation from natural bower to architectural fane (one of Keats's most necessary imaginative movements); and here the feast of summer fruits (itself remembered from Porphyro's laden dishes and baskets of gold and silver) is halfway, with its empty shells and grape stalks half-bare, to the stubble-plains of Autumn. Keats's slumber and his waking represent a motif repeated from *Indolence, Psyche, Nightingale,* and *Melancholy*; but here there is no disappointment at the difference between sleep and waking. Keats notes as fact simply that the bower has gone, and that he finds himself in an old sanctuary, an eternal domed monument, where the moth cannot corrupt (the biblical moth seems to have crept in by way of *Melancholy*). The resemblance of the shrine of Saturn within the temple to the shrine of *Melancholy* is evident. We meet, instead of *Psyche*'s priest, Saturn's priestess. Moneta stands, veiled, at the altar beneath the (apparently) seated image of Saturn. Keats, standing before her at the altar, cannot see the face of the seated image, because the face is blocked by the bulk of its marble knees above his head; he therefore is forced to ask whose temple this is. Moneta answers:

> "This old image here,
> Whose carved features wrinkled as he fell,
> Is Saturn's; I, Moneta, left supreme
> Sole priestess of his desolation."

The word "desolation" tells us that we have reached another version of the little town; but here the sacrifice is done, and the sacrificial fire is burning low, and will not be offered more fuel, though fuel abounds. It is Moneta who has performed the symbolic sacrifice (a sacrifice, as in the *Hymn to Pan*, of spice-wood, not of a living being like the heifer; this substitution of symbol for reality is now a sign of Keats's conscious acceptance of the synecdoches of art); it is finally Moneta herself, as one of the Titans, who is the real sacrificial victim. Her face bears the signs of her continuing affliction: as Sperry points out, she shares a "sickness" with Keats himself, who, suffering from "a sickness not ignoble," that of dreaming, finds himself before her as before a mirror.

Keats has needed to decide, here as in *To Autumn*, what shall be sacrificed (here, sweet spice-woods) as the symbol of human tragic destiny; and what animate being (here, Moneta) will represent tragic emotion. It is easy to see why Keats, once he had resolved to carry the sacrifice through to its symbolic end (an end he had foreseen in *Sleep and Poetry* when he said his spirit would be "a fresh sacrifice" to Apollo), had to forgo the heifer of *Dear Reynolds* and the *Urn*. In *Melancholy* the grape is the sacrificial object, and its double—the human being embodying tragic fate—is the soul of the poet transformed into a cloudy trophy. In *The Fall*, because the sacrifice is the uninteresting spice-wood (less interesting than Joy's grape), all narrative interest is displaced onto Moneta's face, the repository of tragic emotion. As Moneta reveals her mysteries by parting her veils, Keats sees the vision which becomes the Spenserian allegorical core of the poem:

Then saw I a wan face,
Not pin'd by human sorrows, but bright blanch'd
By an immortal sickness which kills not;
It works a constant change, which happy death
Can put no end to; deathwards progressing
To no death was that visage; it had pass'd
The lily and the snow; and beyond these
I must not think now, though I saw that face.

This first segment of the Keatsian description of Moneta's face recalls many of the narrative arguments of the first *Hyperion*—those which pondered the fact of change, asking whether it was irreversible or reversible; whether it had beneficent purpose; and whether, if painful and irreversible, it was at least a subject for revengeful action. Since the subject of the inquiry was the fate of the gods, the fate of the imagination itself was in question, as Hartman makes us see.[11] Keats was not quite sure how he should represent the dynastic doom of his Titans, but decided (at least in the case of Saturn) to represent the change as the coming of old age. He had, in the past, represented the doom of the gods as an alienation resulting from simple neglect on the part of men: Psyche remained forever young, forever entwined with Cupid, keeping her ancient place so much that one could enter a forest and start a wing. It was our estrangèd faces, Keats implies, that had caused her to be forgotten. This pleasing fiction (as it later seemed to Keats) about the immortality of human myths could not persist in the face of the obliteration by time of successive historical cultures: the relief that the urn has been preserved, almost miraculously, by being fostered by silence and time, hides the apprehension that most works of imagination have in fact perished. In making his Saturn, unlike his Psyche, grow old, and in showing that his seated marble image felt the stroke (its immortally smooth features wrinkling as the Titans fell from power), Keats implied, but did not progress to, the scene where Saturn would die. "The gods are old; the gods are mortal" is (for all Oceanus' optimism, or Enceladus' cry of revenge) the central theme of the first *Hyperion*. But the portrait of Moneta's face conjures up a new view of the fate of the gods. Moneta is not old; her face shows none of Saturn's wrinkles. Instead, she is ill. (There had been some tangential mentions of illness in the first *Hyperion*—Saturn is palsied, Thea feels "cruel pain" about her heart, and the grouped Titans feel their hearts "heaving in pain, and horribly convuls'd / With sanguine feverous boiling gurge of pulse"—but the emphasis was on age.) Keats's new invention—that tragic destiny is a continuous process, not a mortality but an immortal progressive illness—has more relevance to his own sense of life, we feel, than to his concern about the vanishing of successive cultures. It is consciousness itself, as Keats had suspected in *Nightingale*, that is the irreversible sickness. Moneta's countenance is appropriately bloodless in its blanched pallor; the active fever of the suffering blood has abated here in memorial recollection. There is no prospect of cure, but neither is there any prospect of death.

Keats, we may speculate, drew for the details of Moneta's face not only upon the deaths he had witnessed in his own family but also upon the corpses he would have seen in his surgical training. The tone of the medical diagnostician is present in the description of Moneta's sickness: an unschooled observer would have been able to say only that her face was wan and pale, but Keats, seeing her pallor, immediately offers both a diagnosis ("blanched by an immortal sickness which kills not") and a prognosis ("deathwards progressing / To no death") based on known stages of the disease ("It had pass'd / The lily and the snow"). There are various distinctly corpselike aspects to Moneta; her veils, like Glaucus' cloak, are shroudlike; "pale," they "curtain'd her in mysteries." Her eyes are half open, but they are "visionless entire" like those of the dead; her lips are cold; and she is constantly addressed as a shade. The narrator possesses anatomical knowledge; behind Moneta's brow he imagines "the hollow brain" (as though the marks of bone fusion on the skull denoted chambers, sheltering the divided lobes of the brain).

The original narrative predicament of the Titans has been internalized into a spiritual predicament, as if historical event in itself were nothing (as Stevens says) "until in a single man contained." In having passed the (spring) lily and the (winter) snow, Moneta's face has passed beyond the circle of the seasons, including the "seasons

four" of the waxing and waning moon. There is no seasonal cyclicity to Moneta's face; it is the face of a blanching to blankness (Keats
uses the Miltonic "blank" and also transforms it to its French verb-
doublet). The description of Moneta's face has affinities with
Wordsworth's passage on the Simplon Pass, where the poet sees
that the "woods decaying, never to be decayed, / The stationary
blasts of waterfalls . . . / Were all like workings of one mind, the
features / Of the same face . . . / Characters of the great Apocalypse." The encompassing power of memory is itself immune to
change; immersed in change, it rehearses change on its tablets. All
the white light of Moneta's face is a moon-light, reflected light —
not the sunlight of primary experience, but the light of experience
reflected on in conscious apprehension.

The next segment of Keats's description focuses on Moneta's
"planetary" eyes, which "in blank splendor beam'd like the mild
moon." Moneta's name is derived from the moon as well as from
the admonitory Juno Moneta, and if Apollo is the Sun and Inspiration and Music, she is the Moon and Memory and Thought. In emphasizing her cold lips, Keats links her to the Naiad of the opening
scene with the cold finger; in venerating her eyes filled with light,
Keats makes her an icon of intellectual knowledge, far removed
from sensuous perception. Her womb has been displaced upward,
so to speak, to her creating brain:

> I ached to see what things the hollow brain
> Behind enwombed: what high tragedy
> In the dark secret chambers of her skull
> Was acting, that could give so dread a stress
> To her cold lips, and fill with such a light
> Her planetary eyes.

This "forlorn divinity, / The pale Omega of a wither'd race," is
beyond, in experience and suffering, any pregnancy except that of
thought. Her eyes take no interest in the external world:

> But for her eyes I should have fled away.
> They held me back, with a benignant light
> Soft mitigated by divinest lids

Half closed, and visionless entire they seem'd
Of all external things—they saw me not,
But in blank splendor beam'd like the mild moon,
Who comforts those she sees not, who knows not
What eyes are upward cast.[12]

Like the nightingale, Moneta comforts those she sees not, and knows not whether anyone beholds her. This remoteness of Moneta's is however not preserved; in point of fact she does (like the urn) speak to Keats, listen to him, and guide him. But the blank appearance of the visionless eyes tells us that Keats is still concerned with art's indifference to its audience, as he was in *Nightingale* and to a lesser extent in the *Urn*.

Keats's portraits of the Titans are drawn, on the whole, from *Paradise Lost*; but Moneta's face comes, as I have suggested above, only tangentially from Milton. It may owe something to the passage Sperry invokes from the tenth book, where Adam sees that death may be "not one stroak, as I suppos'd / Bereaving sense, but endless miserie" (809–810). On the other hand, Keats did not mark this passage in his copy of *Paradise Lost*. And Adam's vision scans the persistence of misery through generations, first in himself and then in his posterity ("Both in me, and without me, and so last / To perpetuity," 812–813). This notion of ill fortune repeated through history in different generations, in external ways, does not resemble very greatly Moneta's beautiful and ravaged face. Michael's revelations to Adam were probably one source of "the scenes / Still swooning vivid" through Moneta's brain; and it is true that the word "misery" links Adam's sorrow to Moneta's "electral changing misery." But if we are to understand Moneta through any source besides Spenser, it is not so much to Milton as to Keats's younger self in *Endymion* and *La Belle Dame sans Merci* that we must look, as well as to his reading in Burton and Shakespeare; I begin with the latter, reserving *Endymion* for the last.

In the *Anatomy of Melancholy*, Keats marked the end of the passage in which Burton sought to establish the limits of representation:

What therefore Timanthes did, in his picture of Iphegenia, now ready to be sacrificed, when he had painted Chalcas mourning, Ulysses sad, but most sorrowful Menelaus, and shewed all his art in expressing variety of affections, he covered the maids father, Agamemnon's head with a vaile, and left it to every spectator to conceive what he would himselfe; for that true passion and sorrow in *summo gradu*, such as his was, could not by any art be deciphred.

(II, 3.4.2.4)

Keats takes up the challenge: to reveal "true passion and sorrow in *summo gradu*" is to disclose the face of the person who is to perform and to witness the sacrifice, to unveil passion and sorrow at their utmost pitch.

The observation, so un-Miltonic, that the pallor of Moneta "had passed the lily and the snow" comes from another source, one that Keats had emphatically marked with three lines. Moneta is linked through this source—Shakespeare's *Venus and Adonis*—to the *Ode on Melancholy*, through the passage where Venus imprisons the soft hand of her reluctant lover:

Full gently now she takes him by the hand
A lily prison'd in a gaol of snow.

Keats's absolute asceticism in *The Fall* takes this Shakespearean distinction between erotic whitenesses and presses it into service for a "medical" diagnosis of the degree of Moneta's pallor, as well as for an effect of progressive cold, as the face passes from the lily of chastity to the snow of physical chill. Keats may also be remembering, in inventing Moneta's face, another passage he had marked in Burton, quoting a speech from Drayton's *King John*. Matilda writes to King John:

I am not now as when thou saw'st me last.
That favour soon is vanished and past;
That rosie blush lapt in a lilly vale,
Now is with morphew overgrown and pale.

The passage (II, 3.2.6.3) is offered by Burton in his section on the cure of Love-Melancholy, by way of proof that even the fairest women soon decay in beauty. Moneta, by way of her pallor and the reference to the lily, is also related to the knight at arms with the lily on his brow, palely loitering, and to the "pale kings, and princes too, / Pale warriors, death pale were they all," of *La Belle Dame sans Merci*. But these male victims are not beautiful; "their starv'd lips in the gloam / With horrid warning gaped wide." Moneta is a compound creation made of both the pale victims and their fairy mistress with her wild eyes, but the compound image has suffered a desexualization in becoming a Spenserian Titaness and assuming parental authority.

Moneta also resembles the goddess Diana of *Two Noble Kinsmen*. In a passage Keats marked, Emilia prays to the moon-goddess Diana:

> O sacred, shadowy, cold and constant queen
> Abandoner of revels, mute contemplative,
> Sweet, solitary, white as chaste, and pure
> As wind-fann'd snow . . .
> And, sacred silver mistress, lend thine ear.
>
> (v, i, 137–140, 145)

The link with the moon establishes Moneta's descent from Diana, and therefore from Keats's own Cynthia to whom Spenser's Titaness is the moon-rival. But there are yet earlier foretastes of Moneta in *Endymion*, in its vignettes of maternal anxiety and suffering in the figures of Niobe ("very, very deadliness did nip / Her motherly cheeks," i, 342–343) and Cybele (with "front death-pale" and "dark foldings thrown / About her majesty," ii, 641–642). Both are solitary ("Poor, lonely Niobe!" and "Mother Cybele! alone—alone—") and act as foils to the paired erotic couples in the poem.

In *Endymion*, Cynthia herself has been "alone in chastity" before her glance lights on Endymion; the myth of the poem narrates her descent into erotic emotion and his ascent into the Olympian ethereal. But the face of Moneta shows that Keats was in the end compelled to return the moon-goddess to her original chastity and solitude, if he were to remain faithful to his original vow (in *Endymion*'s words): "I did wed / Myself to things of light from infancy." Light allows for no veiled faces, and no escape into the ethereal, but is finally a mandate to knowledge.

I turn now to the two figures in *Endymion* which chiefly prefigure Moneta. The first is the male figure of Glaucus, given (according to Lemprière) the gift of prophecy by Apollo, and linked by his prophetic gift to Moneta, who "fosters" Apollo. In the poem, Circe dooms Glaucus to an old age lasting a thousand years, an old age of love-melancholy, since he pines for his lost Scylla. He must evermore "wither, droop, and pine," be oppressed by "weary watching," by "long years of misery," by "long captivity and moanings." Circe has cursed him with bitter playfulness:

> Oh no—it shall not pine, and pine, and pine
> More than one pretty, trifling thousand years . . .
> . . . and even then
> Thou shalt not go the way of aged men;
> But live and wither, cripple and still breathe
> Ten hundred years.   (III, 578–579, 595–598)

The prolonged suffering without mitigation to which Glaucus is condemned resembles Moneta's fate; and his shroudlike blue cloak, which like the book he reads symbolizes knowledge (the one of nature, the other of prophecy), is a first sketch of the universal knowledge Moneta gains through suffering:

> Ample as the largest winding sheet,
> A cloak of blue wrapp'd up his aged bones,
> O'erwrought with symbols by the deepest groans
> Of ambitious magic: every ocean-form
> Was woven in with black distinctness; storm,
> And calm, and whispering, and hideous roar,
> Quicksand and whirlpool, and deserted shore
> Were emblem'd in the woof; with every shape
> That skims, or dives, or sleeps, 'twixt cape and cape.
>   (III, 196–204)

Keats's persistent combining of knowledge and suffering is for the most part forced to remain separated in *Endymion* from the image of Cynthia. She chiefly appears as the Moon, sister to Apollo the Sun, conferring idealized benediction, life to the dead, dreams to the animals, pleasure to all, and relief to the "poor patient oyster."

> Thou dost bless every where, with silver lip
> Kissing dead things to life. The sleeping kine,
> Couched in thy brightness, dream of fields divine:
> Innumerable mountains rise, and rise,
> Ambitious for the hallowing of thine eyes;
> And yet thy benediction passeth not
> One obscure hiding place, one little spot
> Where pleasure may be sent: the nested wren
> Has thy fair face within its tranquil ken,
> And from beneath a sheltering ivy leaf
> Takes glimpses of thee; thou art a relief
> To the poor patient oyster, where it sleeps
> Within its pearly house.   (III, 56–69)

But even Cynthia's benignity has been shadowed and made pallid and wan by her love for Endymion, himself as sorrowful as she. The narrator cries to Cynthia,

> Alas, thou dost pine
> For one as sorrowful: thy cheek is pale
> For one whose cheek is pale: thou dost bewail
> His tears, who weeps for thee. Where dost thou sigh? . . .
> . . . 'Tis She, but lo!
> How chang'd, how full of ache, how gone in woe!
> She dies at the thinnest cloud; her loveliness
> Is wan on Neptune's blue.   (III, 74–77, 79–82)

If this is, as I believe, the first sketch for Moneta—the immortal Moon-goddess made wan with love-watching, and later fading, and fading away, as Endymion transfers his love to the Indian Maid (who in her turn fades as the Moon rises) we can see—though Keats is not yet in full imaginative command of his materials—the cluster which he feels he must make cohere. It consists of the moon, waning, wanness, pallor, the female, love-melancholy, benign light shed by eyes ("thine eyelids fine" as he calls them in *Endymion*), a fair face, brightness, silver light, and, prophetically, relief for "the poor patient oyster"—surely Keats's most extraordinary attribution of the word "patient," which always appears in his work as a signal of attentive, solicitous vigil. Cynthia is carefully kept aloof from knowledge; but when the intellectual and cosmic knowledge of Glaucus is joined to the melancholy and pallor of Cynthia's silver light, and both are combined with the maternal anxiety of Cybele and Niobe, the result, we might say, is the countenance of Moneta. Endymion's repudiation of "cloudy phantasms" and "the monstrous swell / Of visionary seas" cannot long endure. His cry "No, never more / Shall airy voices cheat me to the shore / Of tangled wonder" will be belied in the *Ode to a Nightingale*—as indeed it is belied by the course of *Endymion* itself. But Endymion's prediction—"There never liv'd a mortal man, who bent / His appetite beyond his natural sphere / But starv'd and died"—is fulfilled, not in himself, but in the deathward progress of Moneta—a more sophisticated version of the simple death Endymion foretells.

The Moon is the mythological symbol for change, because of its waxing and waning; and by taking the Moon as his goddess in *The Fall*, Keats makes Change itself the object of his worship. But he sees Change here as theater, tragic theater. Keats chooses to think of art as dynamic, not static (having learned from the *Urn* that even if it is static our minds force it into a dynamism of origins and ends); and the model for art in Moneta's mind becomes representational tragedy, or (we might say) Shakespeare. *The Fall* is finally not a Miltonic or a Dantesque poem so much as an homage to Shakespeare, not the Shakespeare of the plays as we have them, but the Shakespeare who preceded the plays, the Shakespearean mind-in-creation.[13] In the image of Moneta, Keats affirms the intellectuality and mentality of art, but not the propositional nature of that intellectuality. It is not propositional, because it is presentational. The concept (as we might call it) or the idea demanding articulation in a work of art does not arrive in the author's brain in propositional form; it arrives in dramatic or presentational form, but is not on that account any the less conceptual or intellectual. It is her inner tragedy that fills with light Moneta's planetary eyes: she too is wed to things of light, and to enlightenment. It is perhaps too harsh of Keats to deprive her of all senses, but he is intense in the point he is making (to himself, far more than to any putative reader) — that art, in its making, requires a deep inward-turning of the imagination which repudiates, at least temporarily, the senses. And yet the point is more severe even than that: there is no anterior time, one feels, when Moneta had ever been solely a sensual being: she exists not in a cyclic relation to the senses (as though, after an imaginative inwardness, she should return to a sensuous externality) but in a parallel relation to them.[14] She only wanes; she does not wax. Her mind does not hark back nostalgically to some time of primitive health; all the contrastive force of the first *Hyperion* has gone. There has been a fall, but there will be no restoration. There is only the constant progressive burden of consciousness, and its transmutation into inner theater. The burden increases with each hour, and the elements which must be combined and harmonized into tragedy increase in number and complexity with every new experience. The import of her deathly face would be despairing (and some commentators have found it so) were it not for the light diffused from that face as a by-product, one feels, of the theater in the brain. Keats had felt a terror of her veils: the lack of knowledge is the lack of light. With the unveiling of knowledge comes the divine comfort of radiance, a radiance as cold as the urn's pastoral, but a riveting force: Keats is held back from flight by it.

Moneta's power is primarily the power of memory: Apollo is her "dear foster child," as the urn was the foster-child of silence and slow time. She is "the hierophant Omega, / Of dense investiture," as Stevens wrote in *An Ordinary Evening in New Haven*, remembering Keats's calling her "The pale Omega of a wither'd race" (288). As the single pregnant container of all time and space, her brain nullifies the hierarchical debate of the odes about the relative superiority of temporal and spatial genres of art. In both *Melancholy* and *The Fall* the quest-hero of the poem is allowed sensation and taste (of grapes, of transparent juice), but the goddess, by contrast, is ensconced in a lofty mental purity. Power seems reserved to the asensual and unpartnered goddess; the dependent hero is her trophy or her ephebe. He is enlightened philosophically by her "to see as a God sees, and take the depth / Of things as nimbly as the outward eye / Can size and shape pervade"; the philosophical power of

Moneta's race-memory is thus strictly parallel, in its comprehensiveness, to the power of the eye over the phenomenal shapes of the world of the senses. But the result of the poet's depth-vision is that he is stricken by Moneta's own illness: "Every day by day methought I grew / More gaunt and ghostly" (395-396). Just as Hyperion's reaction to the fall of his brother-Titans was to become sick at heart, so Moneta and Keats, by taking on "the philosophic mind," take on the burden of anxiety—which, more than stoic endurance, or desire for revenge, or Oceanus' optimism, or Clymene's rejoicing, is the burden of this book. From his solutions here—a symbolic final sacrifice, the immortal sickness of anxious sorrow, and a total prescinding from sense experience in his homage to the power of burdened Memory and tragic theater—Keats will turn, in *Autumn*, to a real final sacrifice of physical being. The powers of sense will be restored in that ode, and so will sensual pregnancy; but the eventual destruction of physical being will be a self-destruction initiated by a voluntary ritual inevitability, not a fall precipitated, like that of the Titans, by an insurgent generation trampling their elders down. In the first *Hyperion*, Keats had represented Change as programmatically narrative and directed only toward linear doom; he had been unable to describe positive change in the rise of the Olympians; his invention failed him as he attempted the deifying of Apollo. In *The Fall of Hyperion*, similarly, no theater of beneficent change is invented to counteract the internalized high tragedy visible in Moneta's face. But in the ode *To Autumn*, change becomes multiple: as some things fall, others rise, or disappear, or expand, or change substantial form, or remain steadily available. Instead of examining only two reciprocal movements—the Titans falling, the Olympians rising—Keats in *Autumn* turns his scrutiny on the potentially infinite movements of the natural world. Forsaking his poem of art-Thought, circumscribed within Moneta's skull, Keats turns his sensual vision—refined by perpetual waking consciousness, like that of the North Star—to the Winchester meadows in September. Forsaking the Dantesque and Miltonic model of homiletic advice and painful religious initiation into wisdom, forsaking as well the dynastic allegorical narrative of Spenserian Mutability, Keats reaches out gratefully once again for his most congenial form — the ode — and for his instinctual language of the senses. The miracle, as we shall see, is what, for Keats, the language of the senses had now become — a potentially infinite vehicle for intellectual order and ethical reflection.

In describing Moneta's face, Keats takes up again the question of the pathetic fallacy, which Saturn had earlier raised in his rage that Pan continued to make the earth be fruitful, indifferent to the Titans' fall. In the radiance streaming from Moneta's face, Keats sees a parallel to the light of the moon, who comforts those she knows not. And yet this indifference of Moneta's blank beams is belied by her solicitude for the poet. The poem remains uncertain here not only whether art has any intent to enlighten its audience with its tragic radiance, but also whether nature (insofar as Moneta is the nature-goddess Hecate-Diana-Cynthia) carries on its diffusions regardless of our presence in its universe. If, as Keats is beginning to hope, the beings of nature offer to the poet, when they are properly assembled and stationed with respect to each other, a flexible and sumptuous language of thought, then he must come to some conclusions about the relation in which we stand to nature, and about the degree to which our creations may resemble the "natural" art of organic fertility, creaturely song, and planetary light.[15]

Keats had suspected natural indifference before, in writing about the nightingale who sings but to her love, and cares nothing for the listening Night; and he sustains that suspicion here in the moon's indifferent, if comforting, beams. And, in addition, Moneta's creation of tragedy seems, as I have said, utterly independent of nature and the senses. What has been called the autonomy of the creative imagination — that is, its independence of nature — is visible in Moneta, as is, in Keats's description of her visionless eyes, his austere refusal of the pathetic fallacy.

And yet the poem does not enact the intellectual insights which it embodies. Moneta's actions are not those of an indifferent being, whether solipsistic tragic artist or unsympathetic natural moon: the iconic form she most nearly resembles at last, with the imploring poet at her feet, is Charity. Moreover, although she is, as Mutability, theoretically independent of time and space (both being contained in her skull), the past-tense narrative required by the epic framework gives this "forlorn divinity" a fixed place in vanished dynastic time. Various incorporated vignettes, however, use other tenses as Keats attempts to reproduce the everliving quality of Moneta's suffering and creating:

> Then saw I a wan face,
> Not pin'd by human sorrows, but bright-blanch'd
> By an immortal sickness which *kills* not;
> It *works* a constant change, which happy death
> *Can put* no end to; deathwards *progressing*
> To no death was that visage . . .
>
> [Her eyes] beamed like the mild moon,
> Who *comforts* those she *sees* not, who *knows* not
> What eyes *are* upward *cast* . . .
>
> [I ached to see . . .] what high tragedy
> In the dark secret chambers of her skull
> Was *acting*, that *could give* so dread a stress
> To her cold lips, and *fill* with such a light
> Her planetary eyes; and *touch* her voice
> With such a sorrow.

Intrusions of the present tense such as those referring to the immortal sickness and the mild moon in the first two examples; the use of the present participles "progressing" and "acting" (even though they serve as part of past-progressive verbs with "was"); and finally the use of the deceptive "give," "fill," and "touch" used with the modal "could," all remove the illusion of historic pastness, and betray a powerful wish that the writing should keep Moneta's perpetual presentness before our eyes. She is, after all, the goddess of continual present change, and should be so incarnated.

In *Autumn*, Keats will again raise the question of the relation between the art of nature's creation and his own art, the question of the pathetic fallacy, and the question of art's ultimate indifference to man. He will also seek a language proper not only to the immortality of nature but also to her perpetual change. He will once again worship a goddess of continual change, but he finds a better image for his goddess than the moon (who, though she waxes and wanes, does not do so in the person of Moneta, who, as I have said, stands in a perpetual waning). In deciding to worship a season, Keats finds a Platonic absolute which is, in its very concept, temporary, an eternal Idea paradoxically incorporating its own transience. Yet, unlike Mutability (a conceptual, not natural form), Autumn has a full sensual being.

Moneta is as much the goddess of death as of the Moon, just as Diana, in her underworld incarnation, is Hecate, often conflated with Proserpine. In fact, it may have been the link through Proserpine[16] which turned Keats's mind from the chaste Moneta to the fruitful and maternal Ceres—though it always took very little to make him think of Ceres. Leaving his goddess of Death, Keats chooses to venerate the goddess of Life. He forsakes cloudy Melancholy and wan Moneta, both forlorn divinities, for Autumn, a goddess who is the close bosom-friend of the Apollo-Sun. It is inconceivable that Melancholy or Moneta could have been a bosom-friend to anyone. And yet what true vision of life, invented by Keats, could help but include love and friendship? Nor could such a vision remain restricted to man-made objects—to urns (even if the urn is a friend), to sanctuaries, and to shrines. It is with a great sense of relief that we see Keats return from artifacts and monuments to natural landscape. But he no longer flees to the protected shelter of a bower or eliminates human presence; the landscape of the ode *To Autumn* opens out generously to the whole extent of the earth, bounded only by the horizon and the sky; and in this shrine made up of the entire human agricultural world, abundantly present, we find the goddess of Mutability in one of her four seasonal forms. In the Spenserian figure of Autumn, Keats, whose first extant poem was an imitation of Spenser, returns to his literary origins.

VII

Peaceful Sway above
Man's Harvesting:
To Autumn

Peaceful sway above man's harvesting,
And all those acts which Deity supreme
Doth ease its heart of love in.

  Hyperion, I, 110–112

I have fears that I may cease to be
Before my pen has glean'd my teeming brain,
Before high-piled books, in charactry,
  Hold like rich garners the full ripen'd grain.

  When I have fears that I may cease to be, 1–4

The sacred seasons might not be disturb'd.

  Hyperion, I, 293

                  The ripe hour came,
And with it Light, and Light, engendering
Upon its own producer, forthwith touch'd
The whole enormous matter into life.
Upon that very hour, our parentage,
The Heavens and the Earth, were manifest.

  Hyperion, II, 194–199

[Powers] who with gorgeous pageantry enrobe
Our piece of heaven—whose benevolence
Shakes hands with our own Ceres; every sense
Filling with spiritual sweets to plenitude,
As bees gorge full their cells.

    Endymion, III, 36–40

The squirrel's granary is full
    And the harvest's done.

    La Belle Dame sans Merci, 7–8

Life's self is nourish'd by its proper pith,
And we are nurtured like a pelican brood.

    Endymion, I, 814–815

When last the sun his autumn tresses shook,
And the tann'd harvesters rich armfuls took.

    Endymion, I, 440–441

Speak, stubborn earth, and tell me where, O where
Hast thou a symbol of her golden hair?
Not oat-sheaves drooping in the western sun.

    Endymion, I, 608–610

Our gold and ripe-ear'd hopes.

    Endymion, III, 8

    Which of the fairest three
    To-day will ride with me
Across the gold autumn's whole kingdoms of corn?

    Apollo to the Graces, 4–6

Apollo is once more the golden theme!

    Hyperion, III, 28

The sun of poesy is set.

    Endymion, II, 729

A full harvest whence to reap high feeling.

    To Kosciusko, 2

                                 Ah, ripe sheaves
Of happiness! ye on the stubble droop,
But never may be garner'd.

    Endymion, III, 272–274

To summon all the downiest clouds together
For the sun's purple couch.

    Endymion, I, 364–365

    We listen here on earth:
The dying tones that fill the air,
And charm the ear of evening fair,
From thee, great God of Bards, receive their heavenly birth.

    Ode to Apollo, 44–47

A long day may be a short year.

    Letters, I, 151: 4 September 1817

O may these joys be ripe before I die.

    Sleep and Poetry, 269

                             'Tis clear
As any thing most true; as that the year
Is made of the four seasons.

    Sleep and Poetry, 293–295

O may no wintry season, bare and hoary,
See it half finished: but let autumn bold,
With universal tinge of sober gold,
Be all about me when I make an end.

    Endymion, I, 54–57

    The great deity, for earth too ripe,
Let his divinity o'er-flowing die
In music.

    Endymion, I, 142–144

Who hath not seen thee oft amid thy store?
   Sometimes whoever seeks abroad may find
Thee.
                    — *To Autumn*, 12-14

To Autumn

Season of mists and mellow fruitfulness,
   Close bosom-friend of the maturing sun;
Conspiring with him how to load and bless
   With fruit the vines that round the thatch-eves run;
To bend with apples the moss'd cottage-trees,
   And fill all fruit with ripeness to the core;
      To swell the gourd, and plump the hazel shells
   With a sweet kernel; to set budding more,
And still more, later flowers for the bees,
Until they think warm days will never cease,
      For summer has o'er-brimm'd their clammy cells.

Who hath not seen thee oft amid thy store?
   Sometimes whoever seeks abroad may find
Thee sitting careless on a granary floor,
   Thy hair soft-lifted by the winnowing wind;
Or on a half-reap'd furrow sound asleep,
   Drows'd with the fume of poppies, while thy hook
      Spares the next swath and all its twined flowers:
And sometimes like a gleaner thou dost keep
   Steady thy laden head across a brook;
   Or by a cyder-press, with patient look,
      Thou watchest the last oozings hours by hours.

Where are the songs of spring? Ay, where are they?
   Think not of them, thou hast thy music too,—
While barred clouds bloom the soft-dying day,
   And touch the stubble-plains with rosy hue;
Then in a wailful choir the small gnats mourn
   Among the river sallows, borne aloft
      Or sinking as the light wind lives or dies;
And full-grown lambs loud bleat from hilly bourn;
   Hedge-crickets sing; and now with treble soft
   The red-breast whistles from a garden-croft;
      And gathering swallows twitter in the skies.[1]

*W*E arrive at the ode *To Autumn* with the other odes (and the interlude of *The Fall of Hyperion*) in mind. Once again Keats must find a female divinity to worship, and we ask whether it will be a classical goddess like Psyche, or allegorized motives like Fame, Ambition, and Poesy, or an artwork like the unravished bride-urn, or an allegorized emotion like Melancholy, or a tragic Muse like Moneta, or a figure from nature like the nightingale. He must find a constitutive trope: will he once again be ethical and homiletic, and turn to admonition, as he did in *Melancholy*; or will he be engaged in a fruitless and inconclusive dialectic, as he was in *Indolence*? Will he choose reduplication, as in *Psyche*, or reiteration, as in *Nightingale*? Will he be propositional and interrogatory, as he was in the *Urn*? Or will he be the visionary, as he was in *The Fall of Hyperion*, organized by its "Then saw I . . . "? Will he speak confessionally in the first person ("My heart aches") or address himself in the second person ("No, no, go not to Lethe") or will he be narrative ("One morn before me were three figures seen")? Will he begin with a vision (as in *Indolence* and *Psyche*) or with an apostrophe to an artifact or a natural creature (as in the *Urn* and *Nightingale*)? And now that he has written about music and the visual arts and the working brain of inner Fancy and dramatic tragedy, can he find a way of writing about his own art, poetry? And will he once again offer the sense of entrance and exit—rapture followed by the journey homeward to habitual self? Or will he urge himself again, as in *Melancholy*, outward into heroism and strenuous experience? After the deathly visions of Melancholy and Moneta, how will he incorporate death once more? What new combination can he try of the mythological, the allegorical, the propositional, and the metaphorical, to make a more seamless joining than he had hitherto formed? What language will he find to embody the indistinguishability of Truth and Beauty, that truth he had so far been able only to assert, not to enact?

In his autumn sonnet, *When I have fears that I may cease to be*, Keats had compared his fertile brain to a field of corn; after eighteen months of meditation on that symbol (Keats's mind was never far from Ceres), Keats returned to it for his finest ode, *To Autumn*. In the sonnet, Keats is, paradoxically, himself the field of grain and its reaper-gleaner. As the act of conceiving poems is paralleled to natural fruitfulness, his books are the garners into which his grain is gathered. A teeming brain becomes a ripe field; the act of writing is the reaping of that field; to have written all the poems one has been born to write is to have gleaned the full harvest from that teeming brain; and to have compiled one's poems in books is to have stored away riches. Keats, apprehensive that he would not live long enough to continue his youthful reaping into a final gleaning, wrote his sonnet, fearing

> that I may cease to be
> Before my pen has glean'd my teeming brain,
> Before high-piled books, in charactry,
> Hold like rich garners the full ripen'd grain.

In the sonnet, the implications of the symbol are not worked out: Keats nowhere confronts the fact that a high pile of books will leave a field entirely bare, the last gleanings gone, the teeming brain empty and stripped. The ode *To Autumn* continues the metaphor onward to the sacrificial base of harvest, and does not avert its eyes. It contains Keats's most reflective view of creativity and art, not least because it is a poem springing from so many anterior poems, both those of Keats and those of his predecessors.

The essential antecedents of *To Autumn* include, besides *When I have fears*, Shakespeare's sonnets "That time of year" and "How like a winter"; Spenser's Mutability Cantos; Milton's *Il Penseroso* and the Eve and Eden of *Paradise Lost*; Wordsworth's Intimations Ode; Coleridge's *Frost at Midnight*; and Keats's own *La Belle Dame sans Merci*, as well as his sonnets on the human seasons and the poetry of the earth. From these poems and others,[2] several strands which enter the "mingled yarn" of *To Autumn* are borrowed. These include the poet's own fear of dissolution (connected in his mind with sexuality, as we can see from *La Belle Dame* above all); the connection between natural creation and the naming which is the proper work of poetry (Milton's concern in retelling the Creation); the relation of mutability to inception and growth; the assertion that all aspects of the world are equally beautiful (borrowed from *Il Penseroso* and *Frost at Midnight*); the notion that the mind projects its own mood on the essentially neutral world ("How like a winter"); and the perennial parallel—which Keats found and marked recurrently in Shakespeare—between the seasons of man's life and the seasons of the earth.

In Keats's own account of the mid-September walk near Winchester after which he composed the ode, the defense of autumn's chaste warmth over the more conventional beauties of the chilly, if erotic, spring, takes preeminence:

> How beautiful the season is now—How fine the air. A temperate sharpness about it. Really, without joking, chaste weather—Dian skies—I never liked stubble fields so much as now—Aye better than the chilly green of the spring. Somehow a stubble plain looks warm—in the same way that some pictures look warm—this struck me so much in my Sunday's walk that I composed upon it.
>
> (*Letters*, II, 167)

Keats must have remembered, in composing his ode, the closing lines of *Frost at Midnight*, lines which assert that to the soul not raised in the city but rather nurtured in nature the most adverse season is as beautiful as the most clement one:

> Therefore all seasons shall be sweet to thee,
> Whether the summer clothe the general earth
> With greenness, or the redbreast sit and sing
> Betwixt the tufts of snow on the bare branch
> Of mossy apple tree, while the nigh thatch
> Smokes in the sun-thaw; whether the eave-drops fall
> Heard only in the trances of the blast,
> Or if the secret ministry of frost
> Shall hang them up in silent icicles,
> Quietly shining to the quiet moon.

Keats borrowed the redbreast, the mossy apple tree, the thatched roof, and the eaves from this poem, just as Coleridge himself had borrowed his eave-drops from *Il Penseroso*. *Il Penseroso*, like *Frost at Midnight*, claims that night, shade, storm, and rain are at least as beautiful, rightly considered, as the gayer charms of day and sunlight; indeed, for the reflective man, melancholy weather, or at least a shaded covert, is more beautiful than more conventionally lovely scenes. The debate about the proper response to a change (in the direction of shade or sharpness) in season or climate gives rise to the central question of Keats's poem, and Keats's response is the compensatory one he inherited from Milton, from Wordsworth (through the Intimations Ode), and from Coleridge:

> Where are the songs of spring? Ay, where are they?
> Think not of them, thou hast thy music too.

Generically, then, the autumn ode belongs with poems which debate the value of melancholy, of suffering, or at least of a harsher change, poems which use as their central metaphor the realm of nature.

Keats had entered this debate before, in the sonnets on the poetry of earth and the human seasons (*The poetry of earth is never dead* and *Four seasons fill the measure of the year*). There he had asserted the continuing presence of music in nature, as the winter "cricket on the hearth" (remembered from *Il Penseroso*) continues, almost exactly, the grasshopper's summer music; and he had argued, through the seasonal metaphor, for mortality as a constitutive part of human nature: "[Man] has his winter too of pale misfeature, / Or else he would forget his mortal nature." However, these theoretical justifications for winter, and the concurrent claim for the perpetuity of nature's music, are based on the cyclicity of nature. There is something false in the metaphor: human life reaches, as seasons do not, an utmost verge; human music ends. In his sonnets Keats's own fears prohibited both the deathly vision beyond the last gleaning and the reassuring cyclicity of the spring; the last vision allowed in *When I have fears* is that of a teeming field of ripening grain, or at most that of some partial harvest, of fields not yet entirely gleaned.

If it may be said, however glancingly, that the sonnet *When I have fears* is the first sketch for the harvest scenes of the autumn

ode; that the sonnet on the human seasons made the analogy of a
natural autumn to a human autumn more explicit; that the sonnet
on the poetry of earth gave rise, by its cricket, to the chorus of the
creatures closing the ode; that *Frost at Midnight* offered some of the
imagery (cottage, eaves, trees, and redbreast) for the first and third
stanzas; and that *Il Penseroso*, the Intimations Ode, and *Frost at Midnight* were all in Keats's mind as he debated a compensatory value to
set against the claims of spring, we are still missing several other
poems that entered into the making of the ode, notably three of
Shakespeare's sonnets (*That time of year, When I do count the clock,*
and *How like a winter*), Milton's Creation in *Paradise Lost*, and
Spenser's Mutability Cantos. *That time of year* postulates, in its first
two quatrains, a villain ("the cold," "black night") responsible for
the decay of nature; but it recovers, in its third quatrain, a sanity of
view which declares that nature is itself its own consumer as it is its
own nourisher; there is no villain, and the glowing fire of vital life
is at the same time the fire of fatal extinction:

> In me thou see'st the glowing of such fire
> As on the ashes of his youth doth lie,
> As the death bed wheron it must expire
> Consumed with that which it was nourished by.

Keats will take this absolution of life to heart, making his Autumn
the voluntary agent of her own dissolution in harvest; as she win-
nows, so is she winnowed, her hair, the tresses of wheat, soft-lifted
by the winnowing wind. In thinking of possibilities for imagery of
harvest, Keats would have recalled Shakespeare's lines from sonnet 12 which he had quoted (*Letters*, 1, 188–189) as something not
to be borne—the lines describing "summer's green all girded up
in sheaves, / Borne on the bier" of the aged corn. Keats follows
Shakespeare here in refusing a harvest thanksgiving, but declines to
show the harvest as the decay of vegetation into a "white and
bristly beard." In *How like a winter*, Keats found a poem central to
his imagining of Autumn: Shakespeare's sonnet on an autumn of
undeniable plenitude projects a bareness on the season, making it
into an image of the bereaved mind pining for its absent lover:

How like a winter hath my absence been
From thee, the pleasure of the fleeting year!
What freezings have I felt, what dark days seen!
What old December's bareness everywhere!
And yet this time removed was summer's time,
The teeming autumn big with rich increase,
Bearing the wanton burthen of the prime,
Like widowed wombs after their lords' decease;
Yet this abundant issue seemed to me
But hope of orphans and unfathered fruit;
For summer and his pleasures wait on thee,
And, thou away, the very birds are mute;
Or, if they sing, 'tis with so dull a cheer
That leaves look pale, dreading the winter's near.

From this sonnet come various Keatsian details: the "teeming autumn" yielded the "teeming brain" of *When I have fears*, which became the kernel of the autumn ode; the imagery of pregnancy and fruitfulness suggested the first stanza of the ode; the mention of three seasons in an autumn poem is repeated by Keats (but while Shakespeare moves back to summer and forward to winter, Keats moves back to summer and back further to spring, and suppresses the forward motion to winter); and, finally, Keats borrowed from Shakespeare the orphans and the diminished birdsong he used to close the ode.

The ode also depends on Milton, and on his Eve. She is a natural fertility goddess: Adam smiles on Eve "as Jupiter / On Juno smiles, when he impregns the clouds, / That shed May flowers" (IV, 500–502). Keats's initial myth of the sun impregnating the earth, who conspires with him to set budding flowers, is mediated through Milton.[3] In the book of Creation, even the devil's spears cannot escape being caught by the Miltonic net of fruition: they appear

> As thick as when a field
> Of Ceres ripe for harvest waving bends
> Her bearded grove of ears, which way the wind
> Sways them; the careful ploughman doubting stands,
> Lest on the threshing-floor his hopeful sheaves
> Prove chaff.   (IV, 980–985, Keats's italics)

Milton's wind swaying the corn this way and that may have con-
tributed something to the gnats rising and sinking on the variable
wind. In Milton, agriculture stands for the natural work of man, as
though to bend in rhythm with the seasons is part of man's essence.
According to Milton, there are changes of ambience in Eden "for
change delectable, not need," and to provide "grateful vicissitude"
(V, 629; VI, 6). Though Milton speaks only of alternation of evening and morn, Keats seems to extend the idea of grateful vicissitude to seasonal change as well, as though we would be the poorer
without it (a reflection continued by Wallace Stevens: "Does ripe
fruit never fall?"). In Milton's Eden, Adam and Eve address, in
their morning prayer, the morning "Mists and Exhalations" that
rise "dusky or grey, / Till the sun paint your fleecy skirts with
gold" (V, 185–186) — that sun is a near kin, we realize, to the
painter-sun who, through the clouds, touches the stubble-plains
with rosy hue, and makes them look warm. In Milton's Creation,
Keats found his clustering vines and swelling gourd and tree
branches hung with fruit:

> Forth flourish'd thick the clustering vine, forth crept
> The swelling gourd . . .
>   Last
> Rose, as in dance, the stately trees, and spread
> Their branches hung with copious fruit.
>   (VII, 320–324)

As Eve gardens, she is to Milton like Ceres "yet virgin of Proserpina"; she must tend her garden after planting it, she says, because

>   What we by day
> Lop overgrown, or prune, or prop, or bind
> One night or two with wanton growth derides
> *Tending to wild.*   (IX, 209–212, Keats's italics)

In Eden what we see is nature tamed, not nature wild; agriculture
and gardening, not indolence. Even after the Fall, Michael recommends temperance to Adam, so that his life may resemble in its span
the ideal model of vegetative life, fruit gathered in due season:

> So may thou live; till like ripe fruit thou drop
> Into thy mother's lap; or be with ease
> Gather'd, not harshly plucked; for death mature.
>
> (XI, 535-537)

Keats chooses to take up not the first alternative — the ripe fruit
dropping to the lap of earth — but rather the second, the fruit
gathered with ease at its maturity. (His swallows were originally
"gather'd," not "gathering.") Milton proposes his "natural" ends
(of dropping or being gathered) after a long passage on diseases
marked, like all the passages I have been quoting, by Keats in his
copy of *Paradise Lost*. Moneta, we may say, incarnates postlapsarian
fate as disease; Autumn incarnates it as a temperate and ripe harvest,
once the progeny of the sun and the earth have become "for death
mature." Otherwise, the sun itself would be useless and barren; only
in the perishable fruits of the earth does the sun find its purpose:

> The earth,
> Though, in comparison of heaven, so small,
> Not glistening, may of solid good contain
> More plenty than the sun that *barren shines*
> Whose virtue on itself works no effect,
> But in the fruitful Earth; there first received
> His beams, inactive else, their vigour find.
>
> (VIII, 91-97, Keats's italics)

Though there is agriculture in Eden, there is no fanciful alteration
of nature: there are

> Flowers worthy of Paradise which not nice Art
> In beds and curious knots, but Nature boon
> Pour'd forth profuse.   (IV, 241-243)

The landscape of *Psyche*, too, is influenced by Milton's Eden; but
Keats had been unwilling, in his earlier ode, to do without the beds
and curious knots of Fancy and "nice Art." In the ode *To Autumn*,
however, there are no wreathed trellises; form arises from function
and its incidental beauties alone. And yet there are resemblances between the gardener Fancy, in his creative power, and the season

Autumn, in hers; but Keats has decided that the untrammeled power to invent ever new flowers (and equivocal "bells" and "stars")[4] with which he had endowed his gardener Fancy is really unnecessary: the earth is beautiful enough in itself. His season is like the Miltonic Fancy (a faculty conceived of as female), being faithful to the accuracy of the senses' perceivings:

> Of all external things,
> Which the five watchful senses represent,
> She forms imaginations, airy shapes.
>
> (V, 103–105)

All the imaginations and airy shapes of the ode *To Autumn* have arisen from the "external things" absorbed by Keats's five watchful senses, on the walk to St. Cross and all through his life. It is no accident that all five senses come into play in the ode: Keats deliberately crossed out the "white" kernel of the hazel shell in his draft and made it "sweet," so that the strenuous tongue, made peaceful here, should not lack its requiting. The spirit of Milton's Paradise so breathes over the autumn ode, and the figure of Milton's Eve in her solicitude for her fruits so melts into the figure of Keats's Autumn (who is part Spenserian season, part Eve, part Ceres) that we should not be surprised to find in *Paradise Lost* the aesthetic which gives Keats the confidence to trust that in a description of earth he may achieve a description of everything else:

> *Though what if Earth*
> *Be but the shadow of Heaven,* and things therein
> Each to the other like, more than on Earth is thought?
>
> (V, 575–577, Keats's italics)

The motto of the ode might be taken from another passage, not forgotten by Keats, on the creation of the birds. After God creates them,

> Part loosely wing the region, part more wise
> In common, ranged in figure wedge their way
> Intelligent of seasons. (VII, 425–427)

Keats, like Milton's birds and his own swallows, is "intelligent of seasons." He imitates the birds' wisdom in claiming some society; his final creatures sing their song in common: the isolation of the earlier odes (*Indolence, Psyche, Nightingale*) has been left behind.

Finally, Keats's autumn ode, like *The Fall of Hyperion*, derives centrally from Spenser's Mutability Cantos. There, the terrible but beautiful Titaness who (because of the fall of her dynasty) is the classical symbol of change, presents, to Dame Nature and the assembled Olympians, a masque of seasons and months and hours. The months appear in the (comic) zodiacal order (from March through February); this is the cyclical order which brings all the universe into the "happy ending" of renewed vegetative fertility:

> For all that from [Earth] springs, and is ybredde,
> How-ever faire it flourish for a time,
> Yet see we soone decay; and, being dead,
> To turne again unto their earthly slime:
> Yet, out of their decay and mortall crime,
> We daily see new creatures to arize,
> And of their winter spring another prime.

This passage is concerned solely with vegetative decay and regeneration. But Spenser decides to include in his cantos not only natural decay but violent corporeal death as well, first in the symbol of beasts massacred by men:

> The beasts we daily see massacred dy
> As thralls and vassals unto mens beheasts.

In the subsequent masque of seasons and months, Spenser turns from the cycle of vegetative decay and resurrection to the agricultural intervention in that cycle by man. Several of his personages appear with their appropriate agricultural implements: Autumn bears a sickle, March a spade, June plough-irons, July a scythe and sickle, September a knife-hook, October a ploughshare and coulter, January a pruning hatchet, and February a plough and pruning-tools. These implements harrow the ground and cut down its produce, aborting the natural cycle of decay and self-reseeding in favor of the agricultural cycle of human planting, reaping, and gathering into garners. Keats's concentrated imagination reduces all the Spenserian agricultural masque-figures to one—the season Autumn—who is not, as in Spenser, a masculine figure, but rather a corn-goddess derived from pagan myth but filled with Spenserian reminiscence. Spenser's masculine Autumn appears

> As though he joyed in his plentious *store*,
> *Laden with fruits* . . .
> Upon his head a wreath, that was enrold
> With ears of corne of every sort, he bore;
> And in his hand a sickle he did holde,
> To *reap* the *ripened fruits* the which the earth had yold.
>
> (italics mine)

Keats combines elements of this figure of Autumn with details taken from other masque-figures—Spring, with "flowres / That freshly budded and new blooms did beare"; March, who strews the earth with seed, "And fild her womb with fruitfull hope"; August, who leads "a lovely Mayd / Forth by the lilly hand, the which was cround / With ears of corne, and full her hand was found" (Spenser identifies this virginal Proserpina-figure with Astraea). Keats deliberately suppresses aspects of Autumn that Spenser includes—September, "heavy laden with the spoyle / Of harvests riches," and October, drunken with the "must" or foam of the grape harvest's wine vats and with the oil of the olive harvest. In creating his paradoxical figure of Autumn, accessible to all, moving but still, Keats borrowed from Spenser's description of great Dame Nature herself:

> Great Nature, ever young, yet full of eld;
> Still moving, yet unmoved from her sted;
> Unseene of any, yet of all beheld.

These eloquent mythical figures, presented by Spenser's copious syncretism in a form half-allegorical, half-mythological, are such a rich repository of conceptual mystery and emotional depth that Keats could have found no more comprehensive symbols on which to depend for the natural and classical impulses of his ode. (Its Christian impulses, as we shall see, are drawn from other sources.)

This long excursus on some of the poems that lie behind the ode is a digression in appearance only, since the claims that can be made for the ode depend intimately on the weight of meaning its words are made to bear; the proximate contexts of the ode create the meaning the words have in the poem. I will return to the question of language in the ode at the close of this chapter; but it is time now to turn to the ode itself, to establish, first of all, its various structural movements, often described in general terms, but not looked at closely enough, I think, by previous commentators.[5] This ode, unlike its predecessors, exhibits several great organizing motions at once, engaged in mute interplay.

The first great motion is the temporal one. We see as the poem opens the ripening fruits of the earth; next (in a flashback) the flowers that preceded them; and then the proto-harvest of nectar from the flowers, accomplished by the bees, the first harvesters. In the second stanza we view the second harvest of grain and fruit (the cider-making is the result of the fruit harvest); and finally in the third stanza we come to the stubble-plains. From budding flowers to denuded fields we go in one motion, but with incidental oddities to which we shall return.

The second great organizing motion of the ode occurs in space. The poem rises in a wide haze of mists and maturing sun, an overview or panorama not to be returned to until the final stanza of the ode. Within the body of the ode, there is a remarkably meticulous topography, beginning with the human dwelling, the thatched cottage and the grape vines encircling its eaves—the first and closest of many concentric plottings of space. Beyond the cottage we pass to the apple orchard, the kitchen garden with its gourds and nut tree, and the beehives (commonly under the cottage-trees)—all the immediate surroundings of the central house. In the next stanza we go "abroad"—to the outbuildings, the granary, the threshing floor, the building housing the cider press, and to the cornfields full of wheat and poppies. We also learn that the gleaner must cross a brook to get from cornfield to granary. (Keats was by this time intensely conscious, as his notes to *Paradise Lost* show, of the gains to be won by careful "stationing" of all details.) In the third stanza we see or conjecture spaces farther afield. We may look to the horizon where we see barred clouds,[6] and we may reach in thought beyond the stubble-plains (and their incorporated tributary brook) to the river (one natural boundary of the farm), to the hilly bourn[7] of sheep pasturage (another natural boundary), to the hedgerows (planted where river or hill did not separate one farm from another), and finally to a croft (perhaps a far corner of the farm). In the last line, after this careful situating of the perimeter on a plane, the space of the poem becomes three dimensional, and, in a sudden expansion of direction, we lift our eyes up to the skies, the upper "boundary" of the farm.

Besides the temporal passage from flowering and fruition to cider-making and stubble-plains, besides the spatial expansion of perspective from the central thatched cottage to the perimeter of the farm and its upper bounding by the sky, the poem seems to sketch, though lightly, a passage through a season-spanning day—from the mists of dawn, through the noon heat in which the reaper drowses, to a sunset.

There is also a movement in field of imagery. Though descriptions of what sort of imagery animates the first two stanzas have differed (with emphasis given to kinesthetic imagery in the first, and visual imagery in the second), everyone agrees that in the last stanza it is the ear, rather than the eye, which is the chief receptive agent.

Finally, and most interestingly, it has always been noticed that the figure of Autumn, shadowy at best in the first and third stanzas, rises to a visible presence in the second stanza. This rising and subsequent effacement, probably the most beautiful motion of the poem, has inevitably asked for explanation.

The orchestration of these five large effects—the successive seasonal blooming and harvesting over time, the spatial expansion from cottage to horizon, the sequence of the single prototypical day, the change in field of imagery, and the disappearance of the personified figure of the season—is itself accomplished with remarkably little strain and with no announcement. Imperceptibly the poem moves on in seasonal time, earthly space, diurnal progress, imagery, and "population"—for if the second stanza is "inhabited" by the allegorical figure, the first is equally "inhabited" by fruits and the third by creatures, to speak in approximations. Within each of these large movements, there are puzzling submotions, which must be noticed before any "reading" of the ode is possible. In one sense, almost nothing I have so far said is "true," if by true we mean adequate to the lines of the poem. I have said, for instance, that we see as the poem opens the ripening fruits of the earth—roughly true if we think of what the first stanza of the poem chooses to display most amply. But as the poem opens we "see" first a goddess and a god (as I will soon recount); and yet this is not strictly true, because the speaker enters rather into the intent of the Season, and we are made privy not only to her relation with her Miltonic paramour the sun but also to her conspiring, which remains, as Geoffrey Hartman has made us see, in the realm of what he calls surmise rather than accomplishment.[8] In yet another sense we see nothing; the position of the reader vis-à-vis this poem is a strange one. The poet is so unconscious of his reader that we have only the choice of becoming him in his apostrophe and losing our own identity. There is no social dimension to this voice, none of the comfortable assumption of a shared social language after the manner of Thomson, nothing of the communal language of Latin invocation. If we see at all, it is through the eyes of Keats that we see, not through our own. The colloquy with Autumn is so close that when the poet says to her, "Think not of them," there is no society but himself and his goddess present. It was from this poem that Stevens learned of the existence of the interior paramour, in the intensest rendezvous, "within its vital boundary, in the mind." Keats, like Stevens, has made "a dwelling in the evening air, / In which being there together is enough." The public diction of the *Ode to Psyche* belied that poem's claim that it was sung only into the goddess's own soft-conchèd ear. But the autumn ode is private, and flows between poet and Season, and we are absorbed into the flow.

I return, then, to my approximations, each of them provisional, as one aspect of the ode at a time is held to the light. As I have said, in each of the five great motions of the ode, all simultaneous, there are puzzling submotions. In the first stanza, the puzzling anomaly is the chronologically late appearance of the proto-harvest from the flowers, undertaken by the bees. In this earliest of harvests, the harvest of nectar, the landscape remains undespoiled: the bees do not pluck the flowers but rather extract from them the nectar which in the form of honey is stored in the bees' granaries, the "clammy cells" of their hives.⁹ This is an Edenic harvest, a harvest belonging to summer. Not only is there no visible damage to the landscape, but rather, in the manner proper to paradisal fruitfulness, the earth continues to produce of its own volition more and more offerings. The bees, our surrogates, live in a prelapsarian dream, thinking that "warm days will never cease." (We may notice in passing that the birds of the earthly paradise, who sing their spring songs of true love, are missing in Keats's adaptation of the paradisal topos in the first stanza, but are later remembered in the backward glance to the "songs of spring.") In the appearance, out of sequence (since it arrives after the appearance of fruit), of the flower harvest, we can see the undertow of nostalgia at work in the ode, an undertow which, while the ode moves steadily forward in time, itself moves in reverse, till it brings us to the Shakespearean backward glance to the sweet birds of spring at the beginning of the last stanza, and to the equal backward glance to spring lambs in speaking of the autumnal full-grown sheep; it also summons up the rosy bloom of the close. For the moment, we can leave this countercurrent of nostalgic reversal of time remarked, and pass on.

A competing submotion in the first stanza, however, reveals why it is necessary that the bees and their harvest of overbrimming cells be placed last. Many of Keats's verbs representing the actions of autumn are verbs having, if allowed to progress, a natural terminus: loading ends in overloading, bending ends in breaking, filling ends in overflowing, swelling ends in bursting, plumping ends in splitting.¹⁰ If the fruits of the earth are not harvested when they are ripe, natural process dictates a continuing into overripeness, bursting of skin, rottenness, and death. More than one poet has let the first stanza of Keats's ode continue uninterrupted in his imagination — has let the apples fall from the trees "and bruise themselves an exit from themselves" (Lawrence), or has let the gourds swell to streaking and bursting:

> Our bloom is gone. We are the fruit thereof.
> Two golden gourds distended on our vines,
> Into the autumn weather, splashed with frost,

Distorted by hale fatness, turned grotesque.
We hang like warty squashes, streaked and rayed,
The laughing sky will see the two of us
Washed into rinds by rotting winter rains.
                    (Stevens, *Le Monocle de Mon Oncle*)

In deciding to make his ode not a poem about nature alone but rather a poem about all that happens in a given season, emphasizing intervention (by bees, human beings, and a goddess) in natural processes, Keats has to warn us of the road he chooses not to take — of those termini which nature, left to herself, would attain. Strained as we are by his verbs of loading, bending, filling, swelling, and plumping, we need to be relieved by one action brought to its natural end, and Keats gives it to us: summer has "o'er-brimm'd" the honeycombs. The cup that runs over is not only a hallowed image of harvest, but also the only agreeable choice among the termini. One long trajectory of ripening, then, comes to an end in the bursting of bounds symbolized by the overflowing honey; the other trajectories (of fruits and vegetables) are not allowed their natural termini, however, because their growth is interrupted by the harvest of full-ripened apples, grapes, nuts, and gourds. There is no seed here left to fall back to the ground (another road not taken, but one which occurred to Keats in the letter where he lies awake "listening to the Rain with a sense of being drown'd and rotted like a grain of wheat" — *Letters*, I, 273). There is no implication in the ode of a cyclical process which would, left to its own devices, produce the fruits of a following spring. There is no fruit which falls to the earth and dies. Not natural process alone, but the interaction of natural process and human harvest, is the central topic of the poem, linking it to the georgic tradition.

It is time to glance at the opening of the first stanza, where the mythological framework of the poem is introduced. The myth invoked, inherited directly from *Paradise Lost* but indirectly from classical mythology, is that of the sky-god impregnating the earth so that she may bear fruit. Heaven and earth embrace, "and forth the particulars of rapture come," in Stevens' words. But in Keats's version, the sky-god is Apollo the sun, the earth-goddess is Autumn, and their mutual relation is euphemized as one between "bosom-friends." She, all mists and mellow fruitfulness, and he, the maturing agent, conspire together, he breathing warmth, she moisture. In this allowing of the "lower sense" of sexuality into his poem, Keats gives full credence to the sexual origins of all "teemings" — those of art as well as those of nature — and permits, at least in the natural and mythological order, a "peaceable and healthy spirit" to replace the hectic sexuality of *La Belle Dame sans Merci* and the *Ode on Melancholy*.

After the brief allusion to the sun, Keats removes him from the landscape. In view of Keats's almost inevitable association of Apollo with sun and harvest, the disappearance needs explaining. Earlier, Apollo had cried to the Graces, "[Who] will ride with me / Across the gold autumn's whole kingdoms of corn?" (*Apollo to the Graces*), and we might have expected him to ride with the Season through the poem. But here he disappears. In spite of the fact that the activities of the stanza are logically governed by the verb phrase "conspiring with him how to," the activities seem in fact to be those of the Season alone as, once impregnated, she brings forth fruits. (Though the form may be that of surmise, the impression is one of steady action.) Keats is certainly influenced, in leaving Autumn alone in her work, by Eve's gardening; but he is also remembering, I think, Shakespeare's image of Autumn as pregnant but widowed — "The teeming autumn big with rich increase, / Bearing the wanton burthen of the prime, / Like widowed wombs after their lords' decease." But in Shakespeare this invention — the decease of the impregnating lord — is a back-formation from the young man's absence: the virtual disappearance of the sun in Keats must find another explanation. The sun's participation in the action of the first stanza seems to extend chiefly to blessing, as the first verbs after the conspiring of season and sun are a pair combining practical and spiritual activity — "load and bless" — whereas after this pair the verbs occur singly and are only practical ones, as the Season goes about her work of bending, filling, and so on. We are perhaps justified, then, in seeing the "blessing" as the work of the sun who, having bestowed his sexual blessing (else he would "barren shine"), can withdraw his active presence. Keats was tempted to reinsert the sun in the second stanza, but bravely resisted, striking out a beautiful line ("While bright the Sun slants through the husky barn") in order to keep Apollo occluded. And even at the end, to which I will recur, the sun remains hidden, though active, behind the barred clouds.

Some of the pathos of the ode arises, in fact, from the unaccompanied nature of the divine Season as she appears in the second stanza (there are no other reapers in the field, no threshers in the barn), though that pathos is not fully evident until the vigil at the cider press. And yet she is not, in one sense, alone: she is generously present, like Spenser's Dame Nature, to all beholders. Seek and ye shall find, says Keats in a Christian echo. It is not a question, as Hartman reminds us, of the remote goddess who is seen briefly if at all;[11] "Who hath *not* seen thee" is the more proper question here than who has, and the proper remark about her accessibility is "Sometimes whoever seeks abroad may find / Thee." Autumn is lonely only in her difference from her company of votaries; hers is an ontological, not a social, loneliness. In the second stanza she is no longer the active and purposeful creator that she had been at first glimpse; now she is seen, framed in the habitual present tense, as a harvester, disposed in any number of characteristic stationings in the landscape.

The second stanza is divided like the first (with its fruits and bees) into two unequal portions, the first concerned with the grain harvest, the second with the fruit harvest. We recognize the underlying convention of the two autumn harvests, normally resulting in bread and wine, but we must explain (especially since grapes on vines are present in the first stanza) the choice of apple juice (we see it newly pressed, as yet unfermented into cider) rather than wine as the liquor of this ode. (Though England is not a wine-making country, the ode could easily accommodate wine in its unspecified geography.) We recall of course Keats's characteristic sobriety, inherited from Milton's *L'Allegro*, which refuses Venus and Bacchus as progenitors of mirth; in Keats this becomes the refusal of "Bacchus and his pards." It is inconceivable that the autumn ode, which originated in Keats's praise of temperate air and Dian skies, could admit wine and intoxication to its harvest scene—though we see the return of the repressed in the fume of poppies, a phrase also allowing the "lower sense" of smell to appear in the poem.

We must still inquire why the harvest scenes take the form they do, a question that has been frequently put. We see in this poem a thresher who does not thresh, a reaper who does not reap, a gleaner who does not glean, a cider-maker who does not turn her press. Though determined on his agricultural harvest, rather than on natural process, Keats forbears to show us the Season undoing her own activities of fruition. Instead, he shows her insensibly matured and then depleted through the harvest. She sits careless first, like a girl caressed by the wind;[12] next, she is seen drowsy, fulfilled, in a maturer sensuality, in an involuntary intoxication from poppies (Keats replaces his habitual cultic incense with a nonreligious word as he chooses "fume," at once recalling the smoke of incense, the vapors of wine, and the perfume of flowers);[13] third, she takes care in the bearing of a gleaned burden on her laden head; and last, she sits patient in a long vigil, watching "the last oozings hours by hours." In this stanza, the flowers of the proto-harvest appear again, inextricably twined with the grain in an image of total sexual maturity, masculine and feminine. Autumn acquiesces in but does not enact her own dissolution. Her tresses are the winnowed grain, her life-blood the last oozings. But these intimations of a staying-of-harvest do not explain Keats's rearrangement of the normal order of the grain harvest. Where we would expect (in this minutely conscious poem) first reaping, then gleaning, then threshing, we find instead first threshing, then reaping, then gleaning, a sequence invented, I believe, to show the difficulties of presenting an inactive harvest, and one imbued with pathos. Though the archetypal image of harvest is that of reaping, the most energetic single harvest image is that of threshing: when "the stars shall be threshed, and the souls threshed from their husks," then, as Yeats and Blake knew, would come the trampling out of the vintage where the grapes of wrath are stored. Keats wishes to avoid any appearance of apocalypse, and so the season, far from herself wielding the flail, becomes in the threshing scene entirely passive, and is herself, in her metamorphosis into grain, "winnowed" by the soft wind. Gleaning must occur last in the series of scenes from the grain-harvest because it is by definition the most pathetic of harvest-phases, associated as it is in Keats's mind with the image of Ruth, in tears amid the alien corn. And yet, refusing to succumb to the pathos inherent in the image of gleaning (present by indirection in old age's "few, sad, last gray hairs" or Shakespeare's "yellow leaves, or few, or none"), Keats permits himself to show the gleaner only as a careful tributary presence on her way to the granary, a presence steady and skillful, not homesick and estranged. In the arrested motion of this stanza, the thresher sits, the reaper drowses, the gleaner balances her laden head, and the cider-maker watches in vigil. Spenserian "store" yields gradually to store undone: the soft-lifted hair of the intact wheat gives way to the half-reaped furrow of poppies and corn, which in turn is re-placed, imaginatively, by the cut spears borne in the basket (no bier) burdening the gleaner,[14] and all disappear in favor of the crushed and no longer recognizable apples, obliterated into drops of essence.

At this progressive diminution and extirpation, the mind rebels, and yields powerfully to its nostalgia for its springtime. The natural question for it to voice in its yearning, given the imagery of fruits and flowers hitherto marking the season, would be "Where are the flowers of spring?" ("The simple flowers of our spring," as Keats called them two weeks after his first hemorrhage — Letters, II, 260). The apparent illogicality of "Where are the songs of spring?" can be explained on various grounds — Keats's recollection of Shakespeare's autumnal tree with its ruined choirs, his association of the gleaner with Ruth and the nightingale, and his intent to end the poem with music. These all summon up the backward glance to the songs of spring, those birdsongs of love (his own song of the nightingale among them) not mentioned in the first stanza of the ode, though belonging by decorum to any picture of the earthly paradise. In the antiphonal exchange of question-and-echo which opens the last stanza, the season herself seems to be revoicing the question of her poet: he asks "Where are the songs of spring?" and "Ay, where are they?" she sighs back (if only in his conjecture — a conjecture we do not see until his reply to her, "Think not of them, thou hast thy music too," since until that reply he might be thought to be en-gaged only in a rewording of his own question, a dialogue of the mind with itself). In the fiction of the poem, the poet is touched by the Season's grief, which he has, by his question, unwittingly caused; he bends to reassure her and comfort her lack, rather than his own:

"Thou hast thy music too." In this, the central debate-exchange of the ode, the poem becomes most self-reflexive (and therefore, as Bridges saw, comes close, given its presentational aesthetic, to unsettling its poise). I shall return to the ode's meditation on itself. But here, we must pass to the main intent of this closing stanza which, like the two preceding it, is divided into two apparent parts (but with the briefer preceding, rather than following, the longer part, a reversal of proportion which is itself a chiastic closure). As we saw the fruits chiefly in the first stanza (but with a brief final glimpse of the bees and the later flowers), and as we saw the corn harvest chiefly in the second stanza (but with a brief final tableau of the cider harvest), so here we focus chiefly on the music of the creatures (but with some brief initial attention to the landscape).

The landscape initiates the grand syntactic balance of this stanza: "*While* this, *then* that, *and now* the other." The landscape is presented in terms of agent and effect: the "barred clouds bloom the soft-dying day, / And touch the stubble-plains with rosy hue." But of course the barrèd clouds are not the actual agent of this rosy light: it is the setting sun, obscured by the level clouds on the horizon, who is the real agent; and the "bloom" of the sun's present work echoes, phonetically, the "bless" of his earlier appearance at the opening of the poem. The sun, creator of life, can at this moment no longer work his maturing inward power; now he can be only a painter, capable simply of external effect, setting a bloom on the day to make the stubble-plains look warm as some pictures look warm — Keats borrowing from his letter on the autumn walk the image of the sun as painter (using a "rosy hue" from his palette). Keats rejected the impulse to borrow from Shakespeare and Chatterton: his earlier alternative, "While a gold cloud gilds the soft-dying day," though preserving the aura of Apollo — "once more the golden theme" — was at once too derivative, too artificial, and too chilly. In his decline, the sun keeps the same mystery he presented at his most powerful; veiled by mists at the beginning, by cloud at the end, he remains faintly removed from the visible landscape, though intrinsic to its early fruitfulness and to the late, if external, bloom on its dying countenance.

During this brief moment, while the sun's transient color warms the stubble-fields, gnats, lambs, and crickets utter their sounds; in the appended period, introduced by the inceptive "and now," the whistle of the red-breast and the twitter of swallows conclude the poem. In this stanza of the creatures, the most discreet and yet most constitutive element is the unmoving center from which all is seen and heard. The listener, who had admired the universal motions of Autumn's intent in the first stanza, and who had sought abroad to find her in her various manifestations in the second stanza, here stands rooted to one spot, noting the directions from which the sounds of his small society come to him. He hears the gnats mourning *among* the river sallows, the lambs bleating *from* hilly bourn, the red-breast whistling *from* a croft, and swallows twittering *in* the skies. The listener does not himself wander from river to hill to hedge to croft; rather, the sounds converge toward him, creating a centripetal submotion opposing the powerful centrifugal motion of the stanza as it goes about its work of establishing the outlying boundaries—river, hill, hedge, and croft—of the farm.

In the description of the creatures, Keats engages in a testing of his own feelings toward his social closing scene. At first, in the passage on the gnats, all is pure pathos: the "small" gnats, those ephemeral insects, are assembled in a "wailful" choir, singing an infantine dirge as they "mourn"; in their helplessness they are wholly in the erratic power of the air, "borne aloft / Or sinking as the light wind lives or dies."[15] The next passage, too, yields to pathos, as sheep are represented as "full-grown lambs" (the equivalent of calling human beings in some context "full-grown infants"). The so-called lambs have a verb resembling their title: in a construction which is parallel, in its rapid diminution, to "full-grown lambs," they are said to "loud bleat"; and since we associate bleating, when predicated of lambs, with the young seeking their mothers, this is rather like calling human speech "loud babytalk." The modifiers ("full-grown" and "loud") raise to "adult" status the central noun and verb ("lambs . . . bleat") which nonetheless are the essential descriptive words of the kernel-sentence, and retain their infantile connotations.

However, after these two tender-hearted descriptions, of the gnats and the lambs, Keats pulls himself up short with an enormous effort of will, refusing pathos. (In fact the effort toward stoicism had begun with the invention of the lambs, as I hope to show, but tonally the presence of the lambs is clothed in pathos.) In a chastened realization that music, even if not that of the nightingale, is nonetheless music, Keats announces that crickets—plain hedge-crickets, unmodified by adjective or adverb of pathos—"sing." It is a verb wholly unlike "mourn" or "bleat," and is of course for Keats the perfected verb of music. After this stiffening of courage and bestowal of the honorific word "sing," retrospect ends, and the speaker and his utterance converge in the present: "and now" red-breast and swallow join the choir. The verbs at the end are neither pathetic nor honorific, but instead acoustically exact: the red-breast whistles, the swallows twitter.[16] However, to banish pathos entirely is as untrue as to yield to it utterly, and so the modifiers of these two admirably neutral verbs are allowed some fleeting measure (introduced more by reader than by writer) of pathos. The red-breast is said to whistle "with treble soft," and though this can be taken simply as a musical notation, still the context urges us to associate the modifier (as in the phrase "childish treble") with that soft high voice we associate with child singers; and the swallows (in the most gently touched of these phrases) are "gathering" in a mutual cluster—whether for their night-wheeling or for migration is deliberately left unspecified, but the steady onward progress of the season in the poem urges us to think of winter.

IF, NOW, having rapidly glanced at the sources of the ode, and at its chief motions and submotions,[17] we attempt to arrive at a thematic reading of the whole, we must pass to more spacious questions of sequence, disposition, myth, tone, and logic. Since I see no reason to ignore information when we possess it, I would begin with the originating image of the entire poem, the stubble-plains. The whole poem, to my mind, is uttered from the stubble-plains; and its tones, even of greatest celebration, are, I think, intelligible only when they are heard as notes issuing from deprivation.[18] It would seem that in spite of his somewhat forced approval of the stubble-fields, as it is voiced in his letter ("Aye better than the chilly green of the spring"), Keats's first imaginative act, on seeing the bare plains, was a reparatory one, comparable to the act which prompted the *Ode to Psyche*. He wished to fill up the empty canvas of the landscape, to replenish its denuded volume, to repopulate its boundaries. And so, like his own Autumn, he begins to "load" the empty autumn space with a thatched cottage, grapevines, an apple orchard, a kitchen garden, a nut tree, beehives, and flowering meadows. The Miltonic espousal of Earth and Sun fills the scene, too, with a benevolent pair, even if they are felt rather than seen.[19] This reparatory effort is a literal evisceration of self. The autumn bounty that pours onto the page represents a fantasy of recreating the depleted landscape out of one's own rebellious conspiring against death.

If Keats cannot, in restitutive fantasy, resurrect "the teeming autumn, big with rich increase," his imagination will, in a second attempt, rise to another response in an effort to deny the obdurate blankness of the stubble-plains from which the spirit of the corn has fled. The fantasy embodied in the second stanza of the ode is a providential one: a figure of care, enhancement, and concern will be made to hover in the landscape, even if the fruits of the earth prove fugitive. (The "Dian skies" of the letter perhaps awakened the wish to incorporate a goddess into the panorama, and, as we know from the sonnet *To Homer*, Keats thought of Diana as triple Hecate, "Queen of Earth, and Heaven, and Hell," a goddess possessed of that triple sight that Homer possessed and that every poet desires to find on the shores of darkness. The female goddess of the second stanza also brings to mind, as I have said, Spenser's Nature and Milton's Eve; and Ceres, Pomona, and Proserpina seem also present in Keats's imagination.) The girl sitting careless on a granary floor or asleep amid the poppies is like Proserpina before her abduction (Milton's Eve-Proserpina is "herself a gathered flower"); the more burdened and careworn figures of the gleaner and the watcher by the cider-press resemble the sadder figure of Ceres after Proserpina's disappearance. Whatever the exact correspondence, this shape-changing female figure in the landscape bears unmistakable resemblances to classical goddesses. On the other hand, goddesses do not reap furrows or carry burdens or press apples; and in spite of the arrested motion here, it is certainly the figure in the landscape who has reaped the half-furrow, and it is her hook, as she sleeps, that spares the next swath. At most, goddesses of the harvest hold a symbolic scythe, or bear, motionless, a basket-cornucopia; they do not do work, or sleep in the midst of work, or walk with laden head. This female in the landscape is, then, closer in her actions to Milton's Eve, as I have said earlier. But Eve only gardens and gathers; she is never pictured as one reaping, with the power to spare or end the life of the corn (lopping and pruning enhance the life of the plant, they do not end it), nor is she pictured as changing the substance of any of her gathered plenty by force (as the cider-press crushes the apples). Keats's female in the landscape is Spenserian and postlapsarian—a human figure who also looks divine, or a divine figure who has taken on the labor and mortality of the human.

If Keats's poem is not about natural process left to itself but about human harvest interrupting that process, we touch, in the appearance of this figure, Keats's most intimate conviction that nature herself would assent, if with reluctance, to the harvesting of her beauties and her amplitudes, rather than see their abandonment to the wind and the weather and their natural fate. But her will to harvest meets her knowledge, expressed in the scene in the granary, that it is she herself who is winnowed; and so her scythe stops in mid-motion. By awakening his figure; by returning her, laden, across the brook; by stationing her, in her own passion, next to the last drops of harvest pressing, Keats makes her the participant in, and witness to, her own willed death. Her life—her swaths of corn, her apples—is, by her own action, transubstantiated into that "store" which, in the altered and "essential" form of grain and cider, will fill her granaries and urns. But in the process the original form has disappeared—there are no more plains of wheat and poppies, only an expanse of stubble. The goddess's form has vanished; the transubstantiation is complete. The poppies, untransubstantiated, are the sacrifice absolute.

In what is the most ascetic choice of the poet, there is no view of the usual conceptual harvest-counterpoise—those "rich garners" full of grain. Even *La Belle Dame sans Merci* had allowed them: "The squirrel's granary is full, / And the harvest's done"; it is the one plenitude in the birds' silence and withered sedge. At the end of harvest, two generic motions offer themselves to the harvest-poet. One is the harvest celebration—the hock-cart, the bringing in of the sheaves, songs of thanks, a banquet, and intoxication from the vintage. The other is the cyclical return to spring, always (in the human case) magical, since it contravenes death: "Spring come to you at the farthest / In the very end of harvest." There are no stubble-plains in *The Tempest*. But Keats will not invoke either a banquet-celebration or a resurrective Spenserian Garden of Adonis. He will write a different kind of post-harvest coda. The loss of the female figure from the landscape precludes any ritual celebration of the ingathered harvest. When she is gone, there is nothing left remarkable—or so he first feels. The eyes see only a *nachschein*, external, on the soft-dying day; there seems no inner vitality in the landscape as the eyes take in the scene.

Keats's two initial reparatory motions of replenishing the landscape, whether with fruit or with figure, have exhausted themselves—the one in the o'er-brimming of the clammy cells (a proto-image of "rich garners," but deliberately not a beautiful one, else it would subvert the intent *not* to celebrate "store"), the other in the vigil over the oozings of the cider-press, which drained his season's life-blood. His third effort, at this point in the poem, since he will refuse both conventional harvest rejoicing and magical vernal return, must be to find something to write about in the bare landscape from which he has now twice averted his eyes—that landscape left after flowers, corn, fruit, and the vegetation goddess who was their spiritual embodiment have all been cut down, threshed to grain, and pressed to oozings. Or, to put it more exactly, it is the landscape left after the vegetation goddess has, by self-immolation, transubstantiated her earlier growing forms into essential "store," insofar as that is possible: those that cannot be transubstantiated are forever, like the poppies, lost. It is not fanciful, I think, to see in this transubstantiation and loss by self-immolation Keats's parable of the work of the poet. The store of poetry is not similar in any visible way to its source in growing life; and not all of growing life can be transubstantiated into the kernel and juice of the preserved "store." Untransmuted, life drops back into the earth and into the endless biological cycle. Jesus' parable recommends that the grain of wheat die into the earth; Keats's parable recommends that it be taken away from nature and transmuted into "store." And yet Keats claims for his transubstantiation-by-execution (what else are the scythe and cider-press but machines of painful execution?) a result—not earthly bread and wine in garners, still less sacramental wafer and cup, but a further transubstantiation, the subject of his last stanza.

The desolation of the visible scene, once the female sculptural figure vanishes, is the desolation of the little town robbed by the urn of its inhabitants; the absence at the heart of things brings us again into the shrine of Melancholy in the very temple of Delight. The goddess has dwindled in direct proportion to the stored harvest, as the grapes, so to speak, have burst or as the apple juice has oozed. Motive has been transformed into product, energy into essence, life into art. The consolation following on the synecdoche "Where are the songs of spring?" must of course itself be musical, but by his deliberate invoking of gnats (small and wailful and helpless in the wind, however light), and by his infantilizing of sheep (as bleating lambs), as well as by his attributing a "treble soft" to the red-breast, Keats suggests that the post-sacrificial autumn music issues from a choir of orphans. Earlier, in *La Belle Dame sans Merci*, he had said that in desolation no birds sing, an exaggeration he had shared with Shakespeare, whose sonnet (and whose recantation of the exaggeration) he now recalls, using its constellation of orphans and diminished birdsong:

> Yet this abundant issue seem'd to me
> But hope of Orphans, and un-fathered fruit,
> For Summer and his pleasures wait on thee,
> And thou away, the very birds are mute.
>   Or if they sing, 'tis with so dull a cheer,
>   That leaves look pale, dreading the Winter's near.

If Keats's creatures in the last stanza are orphans, they are in mourning for a dead mother. The figurative clinging together of the orphan choir, as they converge in centripetal sound toward the listener, suggests their precariousness and insecurity. "We were left," says Wordsworth of himself and his orphaned siblings, "trooping together as we might." If we follow one drift of the poem, we hear in Keats's final lines the weak voices of orphaned children, blown helplessly by the winds of circumstance, but yet, "spite of despondence, of the inhuman dearth," uttering their soft sounds of life over the soft-dying day. If we follow another drift of the poem, the more neutral one refusing pathos, we hear the music of the season's choir.

If we pause, now, to ask the largest thematic questions, those prompted by the totality of the ode, and answerable only insofar as we can combine into one perspective the manifold offered by the poem, we are inevitably drawn into some comparisons. In many of his poems, Keats is prompted to responses other than the ones he here adopts when he discovers an absence at the center of the world. *La Belle Dame sans Merci* entertains the void; Keats feels no stir of any compensatory energies, since he has been, in the person of the knight-at-arms, helplessly enthralled and disenthralled, and his own will, in his self-doubling as narrator, is powerless in the outcome.[20] In the *Ode to Psyche*, to turn to the opposite extreme, he engages energetically in a reparatory mimetic fiction, and ends his poem once the point-for-point reparatory shrine is constructed, though he can fill its center only prospectively, hoping that Psyche will come to the bower and that its casement, open wide, will let the warm Love in. In *Nightingale*, art can temporarily fill the void with the intense paralleled song in the artist and reverie in the audience, but is rudely insufficient as a permanent device to fill the vacuum of passing life. The *Urn* for the first time acquiesces in the deathliness of art by admitting that the folk on the urn can neither leave the urn (as they can do in *Indolence*) nor return to the town. But that ode requires that the livingness and deathliness of art be seen alternatively rather than simultaneously: nothing in its fiction escapes its propositional duality of Yes/No, Alive/Dead, nor its conceptual duality of Beauty and Truth.

The ode *To Autumn* begins, like *Psyche*, in a mimetic reparatory effort; unlike *Psyche* it does not first articulate the lack toward which the reparation is directed, but conceals those originating stubble-plains in their function as origin until the last stanza. The fact that they are the origin, however, explains the peculiar non-narration of the first two stanzas, which makes the first a "surmise" in Hartman's sense, and the second a recounting of a habitual mode. The only "now" is the "now" of the song over the stubble-fields. Nonetheless, we recognize in the figure of Autumn in the first stanza a lineal descendant of Fancy in the *Ode to Psyche;* each touches creation into bloom, each is the imagination-as-repairer of actual lack.

But *Autumn*, once its reparatory efforts at vegetative and providential plenitude are abandoned, subsides at first into an attempt at balance. While the nostalgic note of rosy bloom over the land is sounded, *sostenuto*, in the syntax, the creatures are allowed, in sound, their independent possession of the air. Had the memorial gleam been allowed to remain fixed on the fields for the entire duration of the last stanza—had the syntactic frame, that is, been simply "While this, then that"—we might say that the sense of loss which had stimulated the energies of the imagination had remained unobliterated, for all the poet's best efforts at presentational objectivity. But such is not the case. In the last moment of the ode, both loss and its compensatory projections (whether in ripening fruit, in peopled landscape, or in rosy bloom) are forgotten in an annihilation of subjectivity and a pure immersion in the actual:

> And now with treble soft
> The red-breast whistles from a garden-croft;
> And gathering swallows twitter in the skies.

These sounds are detached, syntactically, from the sunset warmth bathing the earlier orphaned songs. The glance that rises to the skies in the last line (the swallows twitter "in," not "from," the skies) has lifted itself away from the panorama of the land and its missing riches, and is purged of self-referential pathos and nostalgia for the past. The ode has floated free of its occasion, and ends poised in the sound of song, sufficient unto itself.

The restorative hopes of the first two stanzas have been abandoned. The extraordinary mimetic power of poetic description, its gift of *trompe l'oeil*, however consoling a fiction, is a fiction nonetheless. A poem, Keats realizes, is not a "picture"; it cannot "reproduce" either the stubble-fields it contemplates or the richer produce of an earlier season; it is no urn, no frieze. And a poem is not a conjuration; it cannot reincarnate an unravished bride, a neglected heathen goddess, a dead mother, or a Ceres hypostasized from the life of the fertile earth. A completed poem — so Keats seems to be insisting in leaving his pictures and his figures behind and in choosing sound (recalling the abstract art of *Nightingale*) as his last resort — is nothing but a thin thread of sound, rising and falling in obedience to its governing rhythms. Though it possesses, seemingly, all the expressive power of human speech, the music of poetry is in fact not ordinary speech but rather sound lifted and sinking as the metrical law governing it rises and falls. Faced with the stubble-plains, the poet can only, after his first denials of deprivation in his radiant illusionist effects, subside into his own oscillatory utterance. It is an utterance that can expand or contract, as the need arises — shrinking, in its smallest dimension, to the briefest of notations in phrases like "to swell the gourd" or "hedge-crickets sing," and swelling, in its widest expansion, to the small incorporated narratives of the bees, the sleeping reaper, and the choir of gnats. It is for this reason that Keats's "perfected" word for poetic utterance, for which he has been seeking throughout the last stanza (trying, in sequence, "songs," "music," "wail," "mourn," "bleat," "sing," and "whistle" — and even, perhaps, "touch" and "bloom"),[21] is "twitter," a verb which preserves the association of a neutral fluttering sound, rising and falling, though within the smallest of gamuts.

We find, I think, an ampler solace than that offered by reparatory and mimetic fictions in this return, by Keats, to the human norm, a return in which expansive imaginative gestures of replenishment are stilled in favor of the sobriety of the actual. Still, the poem as a whole has other dimensions besides this self-reflexive one which has affirmed that a poet has no recourse — in the face of all he knows of creation, flowering, and fruition, of disappearance, denudation, transmutation, and extinction — except to utter a tenuous and rhythmic rising and sinking of sound.

In mythological terms, the poem retells the story of the fertility and death of the mother, which, otherwise considered, is the story of the origins and growth to adulthood of the child. In this poem the mother, after the sexual beginning, is a chaste single mother (if not quite the virgin-mother of Christian myth). It is perhaps not too fanciful, remembering triple Hecate, to see the season as a creative heavenly goddess at the opening of the ode, as an incarnate earth-goddess in the center, and as a disembodied goddess of Hades in the close. The orphaned creatures of the last stanza are not far from Proserpina in Hades pining for her lost mother.[22] The poem remembers, with perfect fidelity, every phase of the mother's presence, from her active energy in animating all things to her relaxation and fatigue in her accomplished maternity, followed by her gradual decline into patient vigil. This poem spares us the vision of the mother's face "bright blanch'd / By an immortal sickness which kills not," but the mother's deathwards progress is both intimated in the second stanza and confirmed in the third as she, the soft-dying day, is attended by her grieving children just as she herself attended the last drops from the cider-press. The love which Keats has shown for the goddess during the first two stanzas threatens, in his deathbed watch, to turn into pity and grief alone, though it is only by her death that he has been prompted to call her back to life in verse. For a moment, resolve and art falter, and, forgetting his independent poetic energy, Keats feels like a gnat blown hither and thither, like a lamb, however full-grown, bleating for the ewe. The poem, in this mythological construct, gives full credence to the child who remains within every adult, and to the infant crying in the night at the mother's death. The great effort of will required to convert grief into something that can legitimately be called not wailing or mourning or bleating but song is at once the effort to rise from childhood to adulthood and the effort to assume the musical objectivity of the Orphic voice. To leave a group converging downward to the deathbed and join a group in the skies is to make that same growth in stature and expansion of view.

One is not exempt, however, while lifting one's vision above temporal ravage and lifting one's voice in song absolved of grief, from conveying some metaphysical sense of the lived import of existence and death. Keats borrows, as I have said above, the Shakespearean absolution of nature from villainy, and sees life, as Shakespeare does, "Consum'd with that which it was nourished by." I think that Shakespeare's abandonment of the external agency of cold and black night taught Keats, too, to abandon his personification of Autumn. In letting the creatures (who seem, since Autumn here is exclusively a vegetation and harvest goddess, to be as independent of her agency as of her death) possess the final stanza, he permits the day to expire without causation, to die simply out of its own dissolution. Most of all, Keats learned from "Consum'd with that which it was nourished by" to make his poem one not of natural process alone, nor one of a vegetative season alone, but rather one in which harvest, the means of the human consumption of fruit, is necessarily linked with nourishment, the earth's fruition.[23] And once the great paradox has been played out, with all inevitable reluctance, Keats can find a music worthy of "the death bed whereon it must expire."

The leisureliness and spaciousness with which the paradox of life's nourishment and consumption is enacted in the ode gives, however, a very different sense of life from that conveyed by Shakespeare's fiercely concentrated epigram. Keats's deployment of suspended time and expanded space, above all, forbids all conception of life as cramped, hurried, cut short, or incomplete. We are persuaded to think of it as thinning out into gleanings, oozings, and twitterings before it finally becomes invisible. In the ode, we have followed a multiplicity of rhythms at once so seasonal and so human that the nearly invisible last choir seems to suggest the participation of life in the rhythms of a third realm, an aesthetic one—more elusive than the natural vegetative realm of the opening or the human agricultural realm of the center, but standing over them and independent of them in a vibration of the ether, a polyphony in the skies. The gathering swallows were earlier called "gathered" swallows; but Keats, even in this ultimate moment, refuses agency, changes the modifier to "gathering," and permits the last motion of the poem to remain spontaneous and uncaused. He was perhaps tempted to make his last choir one solely of winged creatures, diminished nightingales; but as he had said in a July letter, he had of late been moulting, and hoped to acquire not new wings but a pair of patient sublunary legs (*Letters*, ii, 128). Into his flock of winged creatures (the last line originally began "And new flock still") Keats introduces a true georgic flock—the full-grown lambs, whose patient sublunary legs tether the final chorus to the ground. These are not pet-lambs of the sentimental farce that Keats feared to be made part of but lambs of the authentic georgic pastoral,[24] keeping the poem mindful of the earth's bourn while its sounds are borne aloft (Keats would have been conscious of the echoing "bourn"-"borne" of earth and heaven).

Just as the human figure in the second stanza rises almost imperceptibly from among the fruits of the earth, so the voices of the last stanza rise invisibly above the extent of the stubble-plain, and form that suspiration of organic life paralleled by the light wind, itself the symbolic respiration of the inorganic world. If there is an "ideology" expressed by this ode, it is not only the Hesperian one described by Hartman,[25] but also a georgic one which perceives the harmony among the varied rhythms which have evolved in man's long life in nature. Vegetative growth and human harvest combine to form a new sort of goddess, one who is available to all of us because she is ourself in our labor, as well as being the goddess of all that grows. Perhaps without Milton's Eve and the Christian doctrine of the Incarnation, Keats's goddess, so clearly human, engaged in the work of life, patient in vigil, and eventually transubstantiated into an essence different from her human form, could not have been imagined. But this goddess embodies a reproof to Christian incarnational myth and Christian sacrificial suffering. She arises from no external necessity: Keats's universe contains no offended God exacting atonement. She incarnates herself, in fruition and habitation, simply out of that divine affinity between man and nature of which Keats was so sure, that mutual greeting of the spirit between "things real" and the senses. The rhythm of incarnation, growth, and self-sacrifice that permeates the poem is wholly self-generated, prompted by no debt, motivated by no agency, demanded by no doctrine. The poem represents a radical secularization of the Christian myth of the divine which incarnates itself in the human figure, a secularization prompted in part by Wordsworth's secularization of Milton, but reaching to an unforced union of the natural, the human, and the divine envisaged but not, I think, accomplished in the spousal verse of the *Prelude*. In Keats's ode, that union of the gods, the earth, and human labor has become, as Wordsworth had hoped it would, "a simple produce of the common day."

The constitutive trope of the ode *To Autumn* is enumeration, the trope of plenitude. In Keats's three lists—of flowers and fruit, of apparitions of the goddess, and of autumn songs—we see that each phase of the season is blessed by its own plural being. Keats needs the whole of the natural world—earth, vegetation, population, architecture, and sky—for his metaphor. Like his sun-inspired Season, the poet, Keats implies, powerfully touches all things into life, but his wand is the wand of Fancy; he too in creative energy loads and blesses the bareness of the world with his working brain. Just as surely, in sacrificial self-immolation, he gleans with his pen what his fertile brain has conceived; as being passes into art, it loses its "natural" shape and turns from "drooping oats" to grain, from apples to oozing drops, without however losing its truthful origin in life. The beauty of poetry does not resemble mimetically the beauty of life—how could it, consisting as it does of a light polyphony of sound? The Gordian knot of representational verisimilitude—which had perplexed Keats from *Psyche* through *Nightingale* to *Urn*—is finally cut. Verisimilitude (or representational "Truth") is dismissed as a criterion for poetic art. Two others are implicitly substituted: the first, Keats suggests, is that poetry should derive from life (as juice and grain derive from apples and corn); the second is a criterion of appropriateness (the songs of the gnats and crickets are appropriate to autumn as the song of the nightingale was appropriate to spring).

Within the trope of plenitude, which is his symbolic form for the season, Keats, in a powerful claim for the sensual power of poetry vis-à-vis music and sculpture, satisfies each of the senses, higher and lower alike, in a relaxation of censorship that dissolves the ethical strenuousness of both *Indolence* (in its guilt) and *Melancholy* (in its admonitions). The plenitude takes various syntactic forms, varying from the simplest doublings ("mists and mellow fruitfulness," "load and bless," "more, / And still more") to the amplest distributiveness, seen most clearly in the frequent apparitions of the goddess—found sitting, *or* asleep, *and sometimes* crossing a brook, *or* by a cider-press. (These sights are not alternatives but additives, as there seems scarcely a place where the goddess might not be sought and equally found.) We see the plenitude of one instrument after another being added to the choir: the gnats, and full-grown lambs; hedge-crickets; the red-breast; and gathering swallows. For the plenitude of multiple nouns, we find multiple verbs—mourn, and bleat, and sing, and whistle, and twitter. Keats offers the plenitude not only of lists but of generous (and seemingly incidental) detail, as we learn that the trees are "moss'd" and the cells are "clammy" and the flowers are "twined" and the lambs are "full-grown." Though all these details are functional, they read as gratuitous in their sensual pleasure. We encounter the plenitude of particular succeeded by generalization: "To bend with *apples* the moss'd cottage-trees, / And fill *all fruit* with ripeness to the core." We find as well the plenitude of repetition: "mellow *fruit*fulness," "to load and bless / With *fruit* . . . / And fill all *fruit* with ripeness"; "the winnowing *wind*," "the light *wind*"; "later *flowers*" and "twined *flowers*"; the "*soft*-lifted" hair and "the *soft*-dying day" and the "treble *soft*"; the soft-*dying* day and the wind that *dies*; the *bourn* and the gnats *borne* aloft; the *songs* of spring and the hedge-crickets that *sing*; the delighted infinitives "to load," "to bend," "to swell," "to set budding." The multiplication of instances, as Keats extends his lists (and seems never hurried, spinning out his stationing and his details), gives the exquisite variety of proportion a charm of waywardness that makes plenitude feel like profusion—a spray of flowers here, a garland there, a single blossom elsewhere, as one instance is lengthy (the bees), another terse (the gourd). While so much else is taken, the plenitude abides, never faltering in its invention, its variety, and its loveliness of disposition.

Keats, at the end of the poem, is the listener to his own music. It is not being used, as the nightingale's song was, to distract him from death: he listens intently while gazing at the full spectacle of a world vegetatively bare, if still offering something to the eye; he knows the day is dying. Beauty now includes as intrinsic components "absence, darkness, death—things which are not," as

Donne called them. Keats too is re-begot of these, but finds them present in coexistence with music—a dissonant and muted polyphony, but music nonetheless. Keats adopts many roles in this poem: he is, by way of his goddess and his creatures, successively a creator, the things created, a harvester, a seeker, a finder, a singer, and a listener to his own music. These roles permit him to exhibit the grand movements of profusion, decline, progressive expansion of view, sadness, and equanimity which coexist in the poem. Life, with its human seasons, and art, with its teeming, its gleaning, its transubstantiation, and its music, seem coterminous, and even indistinguishable, in this richest of the odes.

THE LANGUAGE of the ode *To Autumn* is scarcely to be examined apart from the structure of the ode, since the structure is so actively constituted by the language, which is here less ornamental, and more entirely "necessary," than in any of the earlier odes. The other odes tend to give signposts and signals, discursive and propositional, indicating which direction they are about to take; *To Autumn*, as I have said, takes implication to its furthest reaches, announcing almost nothing in propositional or conceptual terms, bringing symbol as close to mimetic appearance as possible. We must read the poem with Keats's own mind—where "sun" equals "Apollo," where "corn" equals "hopes," where "mist" (as in the letter on "dark passages," *Letters*, I, 281) summons up "mystery," where "the setting sun will always set me to rights" (*Letters*, I, 186); where the dying tones that fill the air of evening receive their heavenly birth from Apollo, the god of bards; where the cells of bees equal "spiritual sweets"; and where Deity eases its heart of love by keeping peaceful sway above man's harvesting. For Keats, it is certain, all these implications were in the poem. Its ethical basis he had discovered in *Hyperion*—that "the sacred seasons might not be disturb'd," not even by the gods. Already in *Endymion* he had known the solution to the too simple trajectory of decline as a model of life: it could be more truly said that "life's self is nourished by its proper pith, / And we are nurtured like a pelican brood." The mother, Autumn, depletes herself as she gives up to us the fruits of the earth and her life's blood; but how differently from *En-dymion* the ode embodies the process, departing from the recollection in the pelican of Christian iconography, and correcting it into a harmonious transubstantiation from the sensual to the aesthetic. Nothing in the ode, to take another instance, seems more organic than the gnats; but if we read with the Keatsian mind we recall the passage they most derive from, occurring in the same letter as the passage "We are in a Mist—*We* are now in that state—We feel the 'burden of the Mystery.' " The gnats, it turns out, come from a passage in which Keats is worrying yet once more the relation between sensation and thought, and says that if we have (as he did) a temperament radically volatile, then sensations send us vertiginously up and down, out of control; but if sensations are accompanied by knowledge, we have wings to balance our risings and our fallings:

> The difference of high Sensations with and without knowledge appears to me this—in the latter case we are falling continually ten thousand fathoms deep and being blown up again without wings and with all the horror of a bare shouldered Creature—in the former case, our shoulders are fledged, and we go thro' the same air and space without fear. (*Letters*, I, 277)

The melodrama of "falling continually ten thousand fathoms deep and being blown up again without wings and with . . . horror . . ." has been chastened in the ode to the purity of "borne aloft / Or sinking as the light wind lives or dies"—and the gnats are partway between the security of knowledge (they have wings) and the helplessness of sensation (the wind is more powerful than they). Horror is mitigated to resignation; a youthful fearlessness in the possession of knowledge has been taught its limits. But without this passage, would we have felt confident in allegorizing the gnats? To read with the mind of Keats, insofar as that is possible, is to read the poem as it is right that it should be read, as though it were written, not in "English," but in "poetic," that language which each poet invents anew. The autumn ode, to continue in this vein, is the only one of the odes which does not contain the word "Adieu," and yet we take it, with some reason, as one long adieu, Keats's valediction to the sensual world. We have warrant for that interpretation, once again, if we read with his mind, and recall the end of the epistle to his brother:

> Now I direct my eyes into the west,
> Which at this moment is in sunbeams drest:
> Why westward turn? 'Twas but to say adieu!

For Keats to turn westward was to see Apollo and the laurelled peers, to venerate the golden lyre, and to say adieu: this sort of shorthand is everywhere his practice in the ode. It makes for a poetry of immense suggestiveness; this symbolic weight, when joined to the principle of concatenation (which might, along with enumeration, be called the constitutive trope of this ode), makes continual "statements" without seeming to do so, and without having to use propositional form. There is no form (whether syntactic, grammatical, rhetorical, or descriptive) in the ode which is not symbolic, formally meaningful. Keats no longer needs to say, "The sacred seasons might not be disturb'd," because his fluidly moving concatenation of seasonal phase-motion says it for him. He has reproduced "th'inaudible and noiseless foot of time" (*All's Well*, v.iii; Keats marked the line). With respect to the debate on whether the swallows are migrating or not, whether their migration means they "join a warm south" to the end of the poem (Hartman) or not, one can only cite Keats's quasi-proverbial use of the phrase "they all vanish like Swallows in October" (*Letters*, I, 154), and say he thought of October swallows as annihilated beings. Though there are dangers in such associations as in any contextual readings, when there is a Keatsian context it seems folly to neglect it.

What I have said earlier about Keats's language in the ode had chiefly to do with the paradigmatic chains of linked significance — as the practical verbs *load, bend, fill, swell, plump, set budding*, and *o'erbrim* are one chain; and *sitting, asleep, drowsed, keep steady*, and *watch* (the verbs of habitual state) are another; and *mourn, bleat, sing, whistle*, and *twitter* are another; and *fruit, vines, apples, gourd, hazel shells*, and *flowers* are another (the creations); and *granary, winnowing,*

reaped, hook, gleaner, cyder-press, and *gathering* (the harvest words)
are another; and *mists, clammy, oozings, clouds* (heavenly and earthly
moisture) are another; and *dying, wailful, mourn, dies* are another.
We usually refer to such groups as "image clusters": but Keats's are
not, in the usual sense, decorative "imagery," but rather thought-
bearers. These chains organize the poem so closely (loading every
rift with ore) that there is scarcely a word in the poem not straitly
bound to other words, hardly a chink not filled. The syntax, too,
being organized by the double parallelism of enumeration and concatenation, exists in a network full of redundancy—not a syntactic
form but echoes, and is echoed by, another phrase. Where there is
X, there will be Y; nothing, it seems, is to go lonely or unpartnered, syntactically speaking. If autumn is a season of *mists* it will
also be a season of *mellow fruitfulness.* Or, if we take the larger
apostrophic unit "X of Y" ("Season of mists and mellow fruitfulness"), it will be partnered by the next line, also an apostrophic
"X of Y" ("Close bosom-friend of the maturing sun"). It is not
necessary to insist on the way the syntactic parallels throughout are
reinforced by the closely worked patterns of sound in the poem,
where Keats is more careful than ever before to "weigh the
stress / Of every chord" (*Poems*, p. 368). His ear has never been
more industrious, his attention never more meet, his lyre never
more closely inspected. He is here at once a "miser of sound and
syllable" and profligate of both. The extreme parallelism in syntax
creates a grand underlying simplicity which harmonizes the semantic variety of the poem. If, in the last stanza, we have five songs and
differing vignettes, they are nonetheless presented in kernels which
are syntactically almost identical:

> the small gnats mourn
> full-grown lambs bleat
> hedge-crickets sing
> the red-breast whistles
> gathering swallows twitter

All the odes, of course, exhibit some parallelism in syntax, but
Autumn is the only one that organizes each of its stanzas by multiple
syntactic parallels—the infinitives of the first stanza, the views of

Autumn (all objects of the verb "find") in the second stanza, and the kernel-sentences of song in the third stanza. Within this grand design of syntactic simplicity, variety has mimetic force, as in the long and playful phrase about the running vines, or the excursus on the rising and falling gnats. All through the poem, the strict procession of everything in parallel is a symbolic form standing for order, measure, necessity; while the internal variations stand for multiplicity, changefulness, and idiosyncrasy. All the creatures, in parallel, are compelled by their being to evening utterance—but while one mourns, another bleats, another sings, another whistles, another twitters. All the vegetation, in parallel, is compelled by the season to increase; but one is a fruit-loaded vine, another an apple-bent tree, another a swollen gourd, another a plumped shell, another a budding flower. The outlines differ, the verbs differ, but the principle of growth presses through each instance. No earlier ode so perfectly allows for unison and diversity.[26]

We see, of course, links with the language of the other odes. As I have said, Autumn herself is in part a descendant of the Spenserian Fancy of Psyche, but in Psyche nature is poor by comparison to the unbounded inventions of Fancy, while in Autumn no plenitude can be imagined that would outdo nature's own. And yet, Keats wrote to his brother just after composing this ode that Byron "describes what he sees—I describe what I imagine—Mine is the hardest task. You see the immense difference" (Letters, II, 200). This remark, coming on the heels of the ode, ought to remind us how wrong it would be to see the poem entirely in mimetic terms. Paul de Man has made us see that the poems of Yeats are most allegorical when seeming most natural, and has also, perhaps too emphatically, insisted that Keats's "naturalistic" description of America in What can I do to drive away is a self-portrait, of the mind starved and at bay.[27] In reminding ourselves that Keats's Season is another version of the gardener Fancy touching all into bloom, not least (via Apollo) the stubble-plains, we link this ode to the other meditations on poetry. But if we continue to compare this ode with others, we are struck by the palpable absence here of the liturgical language present above all in Psyche and Melancholy. The clear religion of heaven will not here borrow its languages from the religions of earth. Only the "choir" of gnats echoes the "virgin-choir" of *Psyche*; of rosy sanctuary and sovereign shrine, anthem or requiem, censer or altar, priest or priestess, there is no trace; and the speaker is neither consecrated votary, initiate of the *penetralia*, nor pale-mouthed prophet. The soul—the central figure in *Psyche*, itself alternately "idle spright" and dreaming lawn in *Indolence*, a property transferred to the nightingale who pours her soul abroad, the "spirit" which is opposed to the sensual ear in *Urn*, and the cloudy trophy of *Melancholy*—that "soul" has here vanished, as word and as entity. We might say that Autumn is all body; and when she is not body, she is grain and cider, transubstantiated body. She is not a deity engaged in peaceful sway above man's harvesting; she is the harvester and the harvested. Keats had discovered, in *Melancholy*, that the experience of the spirit can be narrated in the vocabulary of the body—that to experience joy intensely is to burst a grape against a fine palate with a strenuous tongue. For a moment in that ode he is sure that by describing a tongue and a bursting grape and a fine palate, he is writing the history of intellect and emotion. It is in that conviction—that not propositions but images are the language of the philosophic mind—that *To Autumn* is composed.

In the language of the autumn ode there is no sublimity of the sort that Keats had found necessary in *Psyche* and the two *Hyperions*. Here there are no untrodden regions, no mountains, no fledged steeps, no ascent to a perilous altar. The plane of the poem is, until the end, a horizontal one. There are no pinnacles of imagined hardship; the Elgin marbles have come to drowse on the half-reaped furrow. The georgic vocabulary had of course appeared before in Keats (notably in *Endymion*), but in that poem whenever Keats wished the language to take on spiritual meaning, he had tended to make the analogy an explicit one, as when he spoke of the religious Powers

> whose benevolence
> Shakes hands with our own Ceres; every sense
> Filling with spiritual sweets to plenitude,
> As bees gorge full their cells.
>
> (*Endymion*, III, 37–40)

There is, in this passage, a hanging back from severity of thought, an easy mingling of sense and spirit, which Keats had found possible before writing the last of the odes. In harshly separating sense from spirit in the *Urn*, Keats was repudiating this facile amalgam of senses and spiritual sweets; and yet the ascetic separation proved as artificial as the amalgam was thoughtless. *Autumn* uses sense to speak of spirit, but does so not by the means of emblem and gloss but rather by means of its own articulation of sensory elements. In the articulation itself (whether by lists, or by parallelism, or by choice of items) lies the spiritual import.

It is because he has chosen things and the articulation of things as the vehicle of spirituality—thereby depending on denotation and syntax for symbolic meaning—that Keats can here afford to be silent, mythologically speaking, and never once mention Ceres, or Proserpina, or Flora, or Pomona, or Arcady, or the Olympians, or Bacchus, or Apollo. The classical world is explicitly present in every other ode, and it was Keats's boast, in *Psyche*, that if Milton had banished the classical deities from English poetry he would reinstate them: "I am more orthodox than to let a hethen Goddess be so neglected" (*Letters*, II, 106). *Autumn* gives up the gods, at least by name. As a legacy (even if by contrast) from Milton they represented to Keats a self-destroying entanglement with Milton. A poetry self-consciously English, of the sort he is attempting in *Autumn*, can include no Greek names. Nor can it include classical artifacts and artists: there is no mention of urns, Phidias, Homer, or Attic shapes. Equally, it refuses European romance motifs: there is no Provençal song, no demon Poesy, no faery lands forlorn, no elves. History and human social forms are excluded: there is no emperor, no clown, no Ruth. And though Shakespeare, Spenser, Milton, and Wordsworth are still the great Presiders here, there are no echoes so overt as to be outright allusions (like the allusions elsewhere in the odes to *Hamlet* or Milton or the *Excursion*).

As Keats determines to do without mythology, history, and literary allusion, so he also determines to do without the personal pronoun and without introspection—to do without a hero, we might say (the hero he had glorified in *Melancholy*). He also relinquishes natural and human architectural space: there will be no bower or sanctuary; there will be no casement opening from a shelter onto a vista (almost a necessity in art, as in life, for Keats). We are never within the central cottage—the poem moves from its thatch-eaves outwards. It sounds perhaps odd to say that the mists and the generous fields outside the cottage are in fact transmuted forms of the foam and perilous seas of *Nightingale*, but I think the statement is nonetheless true. Keats has realized that there is only one expanse, not two; he will no longer invoke the contrast of the elfin grot with the cold hillside, of the fruits of the earth with the manna-dew. The links we can trace between *La Belle Dame sans Merci* and *Autumn* make the Belle Dame an early figure for the reaper: when the Belle Dame has finished her work the sedge has withered, the birds have fallen silent, the roses of the lover's cheeks have withered, the squirrel's granary is full, and the harvest is done. In putting the rosy hue back on the land's countenance, in reinvesting the cold hillside with warmth, and in releasing the birds once again into song, Keats is undoing, in *Autumn*, the charm he had wound up in *La Belle Dame*, reinstating an internal vitality of song in the landscape of deprivation. He is undoing at the same time, by giving human dimensions to the female Season, the various mythologically altered dimensions—from subhuman (Medusa) to superhuman (Melancholy and Moneta)—that he had attributed to female goddesses in the past. By making his goddess bride, mother, and dying earth-spirit, he goes beyond the brides Psyche and Urn, the demon Poesy, the virginal maiden on the urn, the elusive Dryad-Nightingale, and the purely tragic Moneta or the simply dualistic Melancholy.

It goes without saying that since Keats's central effort in the language of *To Autumn* is to have thoughts and emotions embodied by sensuous things, he suppresses all the abstract language of allegory—of the warm Love, of Fame and the demon Poesy, of Youth and Beauty and Phantoms and cold Pastoral and Melancholy and aching Pleasure and Delight and Joy. This abstract vocabulary is so supremely important in the other odes that its sacrifice is as great, for Keats, as the sacrifice of mythology. We might say that allegory and mythology had been the two symbolic systems—Spenserian and Miltonic—in which Keats had been nursed. The silent, nameless concrete symbolic system of *Autumn* springs direct, as I have said, from Shakespeare's "intensity of working out conceits," which proved to be a way of "saying fine things unintentionally" (*Letters*, I, 188). Keats's study of Shakespeare's images in the sonnets led him to see that "intention" could be left unsaid, that he no longer had to draw explicit parallels, as he had in *When I have fears*, between his pen and a gleaner, between rich garners and high-pilèd books, between feelings and full-ripened grain. As late as the July before the September in which he wrote the ode, he was still feeling obliged to draw the personal comparison: "The very corn which is now so beautiful, as if it had only taken to ripening yesterday, is for the market: So, why shoᵈ I be delicate" (*Letters*, II, 129). The conceit of the ripening corn is the richest in all of Keats, constantly in his mind. When Ruth stands amid the alien corn, it is the only time in Keats that corn is alien, and it is a mark of his extreme anguish at the demands of his own vocation at the time of Tom's death that he could see the corn in that way, at the moment when he saw the faery land of imagination as forlorn. Both nature and art seemed to him, after his brother's anguish, equally comfortless.

If I emphasize the linguistic asceticism of the ode *To Autumn*, its willing sacrifice of mythology, allegory, history, literary allusion, and personal reference, it is because it is so commonly celebrated as a poem of linguistic wealth. We can better judge the wealth that is there for seeing the wealth—common to the other odes—that is not, seeing the everything that is not there as well as the everything that is.

It is not that Keats, perceiving Shakespeare's method of intensely working out a conceit, had not done something in this vein before. He had—in the shrine of *Psyche* and in the scherzo on wine in *Nightingale*, to give only two celebrated instances. But, unlike Shakespeare, he had offered a gloss ("in some untrodden region of my mind" to locate the shrine or, negatively, "not charioted by Bacchus and his pards" to explain the remarks on wine). What Keats was daring enough to do in *Autumn* was to take the Shakespearean example to its limit, and let the working out of the conceit speak entirely for itself. He thus forsakes, in his last asceticism, that propositional language of "Truth" which he had thought necessary for running his flag up the admiral-staff—the language of explanation, justification, and philosophizing. For a poet aiming at "Thought" and "Truth," this was the riskiest asceticism of all. It meant the assertion that propositional language was not the only language in which Truth could dwell; and it meant that Sensation and Thought were not two things but one, providing one wrote of articulated sensation; that Beauty and Truth were not two things but one, providing one had stationed Beauty truly.

WE HAVE SEEN in part what the language of *Autumn* is: linked things, linked apparitions, linked actions, linked syntax—all not arbitrarily linked, but linked by minutest design. And we have seen what it is not: not mythological, nor liturgical, nor allegorical, nor romance-derived, nor historical, nor "literary," nor introspective, nor propositional. It remains true, however, that we sense a mythology (in the conspiring of sun and season, and in the central opulence of the harvest-figure), that we perceive a hymn of worship (in spite of the emphasis on description), that we derive from the poem allegorical meanings, that we sense in it a profound literary allusiveness, that we read it as a lyric and introspective poem, and that we take its own single proposition—"Thou hast thy music too"—to stand, implicitly, for many others. When we attempt to account for the indubitable presence in the poem of so much that it has renounced, we are driven in part, as I was in my first descriptions of the poem, to make explicit its delicate hints. We point out the sky-god and earth-goddess and bring into mythological literalness the euphemisms "bosom-friend" and "conspiring"; we expose the buried logic of the sequence ending in "o'er-brimm'd"; we call attention to the stasis in the midst of harvest; we indicate the absence of things we might expect to find (such as the harvest feast or the vintage); we bring consciously to the surface the silent lapsing of time and the gentle expansion in space; we place the ode in its subgenres (the cult-hymn, the georgic, the valediction, the pastoral elegy); we see its conceit-subjectivity after the manner of the Shakespearean sonnet; we even see its lingering-out homage to the sonnet form.

But having done all this, we need to let the ode subside once again into its low relief. It never announces or insists on any of its lapses and expansions and changes of focus. Not a breath of insistence or announcement will it give. We scarcely notice that one sense has been touched into responsiveness and then allowed to relax as another is brought into play. The severe and controlled examinations of one sense at a time in the preceding odes have borne their fruit: as the autumn ode opens, we are ready to indulge all the tactility and taste learned in *Melancholy*; in the center of the poem, we call on all the visual disposition of classical figures learned in *Indolence* and *Urn*; and as the ode draws to a close, we invoke all the fineness of ear learned in *Nightingale*. The more strenuous actions of earlier odes reappear here in a gentler form: the intense cultic vows of *Psyche* and *Melancholy* and *The Fall of Hyperion* have modulated into a habitual love; Keats's quests—the desperate pursuit on the urn, and the aching for wings to follow the allegorical figures in *Indolence* and the bird in *Nightingale*, together with the wild voyage in the draft of *Melancholy*—yield to the generous and frequent finding of the goddess in the fields; the bursting of Joy's grape is slowed to the o'er-brimming of the honeycomb and the oozing of the cider-press; the "for ever" of the *Urn* is modestly restricted to the "sometimes" and "oft" of the rewarded quest and to the "now" of the dispersed creatures.

In all of these mitigations, easings, and softenings we sense Keats's less combative attitude. His native pugnacity and ardor give the earlier odes their vivid energies; but in moulting, and substituting for his wings a pair of patient sublunary legs, he slowed his pace; in becoming a chrysalis again, he watched, and waited, and took notes through his two loopholes of vision. A year earlier, when he had felt "blind in mist" on Ben Nevis, he had been in despair:

> I look into the chasms, and a shroud
> Vaprous doth hide them; just so much I wist

Mankind do know of hell: I look o'erhead,
  And there is sullen mist; even so much
Mankind can tell of heaven: mist is spread
  Before the earth beneath me; even such,
Even so vague is man's sight of himself . . .
                  . . . All my eye doth meet
Is mist and crag — not only on this height,
But in the world of thought and mental might.
                  (*Read me a lesson, Muse*, 3–14)

Now, between the mists of dawn and the clouds of sunset, Apollo is still obscured; but the rage has gone.

If, then, the language of the ode can best be seen to be what it is — a language ascetic, scaled down, softened in tone, and wonderfully consistent — by comparison with the other odes in their multiple "languages," their more "imaginative" scope, their higher pitch, their more ambitious range — then the ode is best read as the end of a sequence of experiments in the recording of thought and feeling and language, its values and hues seen accurately only in the company of its peers. But then one can also separate it from them, and look at it alone. Once its own level is taken for granted, and its intimacy of tone and delicacy of progress are seen not contrastively but absolutely, we can ask, within this special language of insensible change and reflective praise, what distinguishes one stanza from another, besides the obvious differences in the senses appealed to, the putative stanza "topic" (fruits, harvest figure, and music), and "focus" (broadening out, lapsing down). Here we come to the central question: what, here, has Keats "imagined"? ("I describe what I imagine.") He has imagined, first of all, what John Bayley has called the domestic but what I would prefer to call the inseparability of the domestic and the wild, the agricultural and the natural, as the wild (notably the closing choir) is the context for the domestic, and the agricultural the counterpart of the natural. The very vagueness of "all fruit" and "later flowers" enlarges the early domestic cottage garden to a natural realm outdoing, as I have said, even the gardener Fancy's. In the second stanza, wind and winnowing intertwine like the natural poppies and the cultivated corn, much as the man-made hook lies on a natural furrow and the laden head is seen in conjunction with a brook; finally, a machine of force, a press, is juxtaposed with the natural, "voluntary" action of oozing (not spurting, not involuntary).

In the third stanza the clouds (by transferred action) are imagined as (human) painters and the gnats are a (human) choir and the wind, like an animate being, lives and dies; the crickets have a song and the red-breast a musical "treble" and the swallows are said to be "gathering" (the most elusive transfer of an agricultural word). Art (in painting of hues, in song, in treble, and in choir), nature, cultivation, and the domestic (the lambs) are here all "imagined" as inseparable in conjoined action. If they were not so "imagined" we should be reading Thomsonian description; and we know we are not.

Keats's "imaginings" bear and sustain inquiry into their most minute parts. As he "imagines" what ripeness is, he imagines first its bearers (the vines, the trees). Here, fruit is an ornamentation, an enhancement, a blessing; it is vines that are loaded and blessed with grapes, it is the trees that are bent with apples. Ripeness is here a possession, a solace, and a welcome burden. Next, ripeness is repletion, being filled to the core; Keats's empathy now is for the emptiness that has been longing to be filled, and that feels now what fullness is, to the very center of its being. Next, ripeness is expansion into amplitude of outline (the swelling of the gourd); next, it is the introduction of a new interior, glandlike swelling — almost, one might say, the adolescence of fruit, as it is plumped with a sweet kernel; next, it is simple multiplicity ("more, and still more later flowers"); next, it is teleological ("flowers *for the bees*"); next, it is production beyond containment, as the cells are o'er-brimmed. This is the imagining of all possible definitions of ripeness. It is in this sense that Keats, we may say, has begun to "philosophize." He philosophizes by finding, for every analytic relation of ripeness that he perceives, an appropriate synthesis of verbs and nouns, and their appropriate syntactic relation. In the fine discriminations of this stanza we can see an advance over the simpler "intensities" of the figure of reiteration in the nightingale ode.

We may see the same careful degree of analysis in the description of the harvest figure. She is first defined by her attributes (mists and fruitfulness), next by her sexual relationship (as bosom-friend and co-conspirer with the sun), next by her agency ("to load and bless" and so on). These are all conventional ways of defining a divinity; the missing one is the definition by genealogy (Autumn is, like the urn, a bride, in this case a bride of the sun, not of quietness, but she is no one's child, foster or otherwise, because she is, like Spenser's Dame Nature, the Magna Mater). Seasons have no parents, only antecedents (each other); the link to antecedence is made here with the mention of Autumn's two antecedents, summer and spring. Seasons have no progeny of their own ilk, only conse-quents—again, each other. The only item suppressed in the ode is winter. We may wonder whether it is out of pain or out of discre-tion that Keats decides against mentioning it. He did not flinch from it in the sonnet on the human seasons; and I think he does not flinch from it now, especially since the open mentions of death (in the wind and the day) show his willingness to bring all closures for-ward to inspection. I think that he has realized, like Wittgenstein (in Robert Lowell's formulation), that "Death's not an event in life, it's not lived through." We cannot either describe or "imagine" winter.

Keats will end his analysis of the seasonal figure as he began, with one of her attributes: besides mists, she has music (if not mel-odies).[28] But in between beginning and ending comes his second philosophical analysis of the figure, this time not by her agency but by the disposition of her figure. In the first vignette, the balance of figure and ground is, so to speak, equal: Autumn sits careless on the floor, her hair is soft-lifted by the wind. There is a balance of forces, and they suggest equanimity and tranquillity and stability. In the second vignette, the forces of nature have overbalanced, momentarily, the forces of cultivation; the half-reaped furrow, the fume of poppies, the swath and its flowers, briefly maintain themselves during the sleep, the drowse, and the hook-in-abeyance of the harvest figure; but then the balance shifts decisively again as she rises in dominance, all laden head and steadiness, over the sub-ject brook. Lastly, she is poised in statuesque patience, her tool, the cider-press, having ended its work of subduing the apples. The resistances of nature to harvest are given their due, as they vary from powerful (the fume) to obstructive (the brook) to pathetic (the slowness of the last oozings); but all resistance is in vain. After the careless repose, the threshing will be completed; after the noonday rest, the latter half of the furrow will be reaped, and the last basket will be taken across the brook; and the last oozing will be "pent in walls of glass" as summer's distillation.[29] Cultivation, in its agricultural victory, means the end of nature—fields of corn, poppies, apples, all; the last steps across the fields and beyond the brook close the imagined history of harvest and resistance.

I have said enough earlier about the autumnal music to show how fully it too is "imagined," how analytic it is of attitudes toward the cutting down of nature by the introduction of cultivation. This is a poem about nature, and civilization, and the consequent discontents and blessings. If the ode inherited its compensatory sunset rhetoric from Wordsworth, it does not give his answer, that our capacity to make metaphor is our reward in adulthood for our loss of original intensity of sense. Keats felt, so far as we can see, no diminution of sensual intensity in adulthood; on the contrary. His grief here is for change and death, metaphorical and actual, for the absolute certainty of the reaped furrow, the crushed apples, and the vanished poppies. He declares— silently, by his poem's sequence—that song can occur only after harvest, in the stubble-plains. For the work of every swath reaped, a soft treble; for the work of every grain winnowed, a wailful choir. For the singing, there has to have been reaping and pressing; for reaping and pressing,, there must have been ripening and budding. Keats takes, in the fullest scanning perspective, the measure of his art and its cost in teeming and sacrificing, realizing that the gardener Fancy and the scything Autumn and the spectral singers at the close are all manifestations of triple Hecate, maiden, mother, and tragic Muse. Keats had not been able to write music for *Melancholy* (the only ode without some music, since even *Indolence* has the throstle's lay) because he made his soul, in that poem, into a cloudy trophy; here, by releasing the soul after its suffering into the canonical psychic form of a singing creature, he can replace the throstle of *Indolence*, the virgin-choir of *Psyche*, the bird of

Nightingale, and the pipes and timbrels of *Urn* with melodies uttered by nature, heard by the sensual ear but attributed (as "thy music") to a divinity herself in mourning for the nightingale.

This divinity—the season—is the first of Keats's allegorical figures to incorporate effortlessly into itself, in its very concept, the notion of transiency. In *Nightingale* and *Melancholy* transiency was attributed *post hoc*, as I have said, to figures (Youth, Beauty, Love, Joy, Pleasure, Delight) not in themselves intrinsically, by their iconic name, possessing it. It was Keats's genius to light on the one expansive natural symbol which, if it were not transient, would not be itself—a season. In singing a hymn to a season, he is worshiping Beauty-incorporating-its-own-ending. He had first conceived of this possibility under the rubric of action in *Melancholy*, as to taste the grape is *de facto* to destroy it. But one cannot worship an action as one can worship a divinity. Keats's search for a divinity fully adequate to what he knew to be true of life had taken him from Poesy, Fame, and Love through the eternal Soul (*Psyche*), the art of Music, and the art of Sculpture, to the figure of Paradox (*Melancholy*'s inextricable joy and grief), to the figure of Mutability itself in Moneta. But Moneta's changes are exclusively tragic, a one-directional progress toward a death that never comes. And since Moneta does no labor, but is only a cultic priestess and visionary, this image, too, must finally have seemed inadequate to Keats. He stops, in the last ode, at Change, but it is a change that mercifully, unlike Moneta's theater, comes to an end. The day dies, the season ends, the vistas end in horizons and skies, the fruits end in oozings. The end is not exclusively tragic. If there is decline in the landscape, there is also expansion of view; if there is blankness to the eye, there remains memory, the source of art. The change of *Autumn* occurs between a *terminus a quo* (the late summer blooming) and a *terminus ad quem* (the last days of the season). In that sense the ode continues the processional sense of life evident in *Urn*, with the town as the nostalgic limit of origin, and the sacrificial altar the limit of envisaged end. In one philosophical analysis of life (as a determinate span) and art (as a self-contained product), this metaphor (of a procession that occasionally arranges itself on an artwork in a beautiful stasis) is defensible. But Keats's sense of life cannot be contained within the high decorum of the processional *Urn*: in the last analysis he thinks of the poet as a worker, one who does socially productive labor. The leaf-fringed legend swells into leaves of reality, the figure detaches herself from the urn and moves into the fields, the altar turns to a threshing floor, and the sacrificial heifer suffers an earth-change into corn and apples. Between the terminus of summer and the end of autumn Keats creates a world of beauty, labor, and nourishment that seems the only possible one in which to live.

Keats's last ode turns away from that meditation on the art of tragic drama which generated the inner globe-theater of Moneta's skull. Keats's Shakespearean ambitions, and his own attempt at historical drama in *Otho the Great*, had led him to make history and memory the principles of Moneta's omniscient dramatic art. But *The Fall of Hyperion* is at odds with itself, offering, within epic narrative, an aesthetic of theater, as Keats's admiration of Milton and Shakespeare conflates their genres. *The Fall of Hyperion* itself, deflected somewhat from Spenser and Milton by Dante, has in fact no consistent aesthetic of its own: the didactic concerns of the induction on the poet's role, the lyric vision of Moneta's perpetual theater, and the epic history of the Titans have not found a common aesthetic territory, or a theoretical base in Keats's letters.

Against the unsteadiness of the *Hyperions* we can set the coherence of *Autumn*, where Keats's sense of what his art is and what it can do is unshakably secure. If we draw out the implications of the ode with respect to creation, we see first Keats's extreme relief and even happiness. The work of creation, he tells himself, if he is to take his example from the work of the Season, is illimitable: there are always more boughs to bless, more honeycombs to fill, more flowers to be brought to bud. The principle of inspiration—Apollo, the sun—is eternal; the principle of conspiration—the earth's receptivity— can never fail. These represent in this poem the "things real" and the "greeting spirit"; and both are here affirmed perpetual, and—an immense source of relief—rather maintained by mystery than obstructed by it. Growth in knowledge comes not by striving; it comes when the poet, in his negative capability, is "content to look / On mists in idleness," without any irritable reaching through the mists or the barrèd clouds to try to

see the face of Apollo plain. The tolerance of mist as mystery ex-
culpates indolence and renames it the openness of the flower: the
"spiritual Cottager" (*Letters*, I, 255) allows himself in this ode the
time for the "innumerable compositions and decompositions which
take place between the intellect and its thousand materials before it
arrives at that trembling delicate and snail-horn perception of
Beauty" (*Letters*, I, 265).

The renaming of indolence as receptivity enables Keats (as his
simile of the flower and the bee suggests—*Letters*, I, 232) to in-
tegrate the "feminine" (or the languorous or the drowsy) into
himself, and dismiss the too strenuous, masculine heroic image of
self and art recommended in *Melancholy*. In consequence, the receptive sexual basis of creativity is gratefully admitted, and Thought
(as Apollo) and Sensation (as Earth) are now conceived of as a
golden pair, inseparable. The mutual vivifying breath that issues in
their conspiring is both creative spirit and sensual exhalation; and
the production of the physical artifact—a grape, an apple—is at the
same time a loading (in the physical world) and a blessing (as the
embodiment of a divine idea). In this ode, art has no single favored
shape (a bird, an urn, a shrine); the homely gourd is as paradisal as
the apple. Nor is there any hierarchy of genres; the goddess of the
cult hymn has come among the laborers and the insects; sublime art
and folk art insensibly join. Autumn, the season-artist, though at
times solitary in her work of embodiment and harvest alike, is not
alone: the originating impulse which set her to work was her conjunction with Apollo, and her audience comes abroad to seek and
find her in the fields (a "finding" impossible to imagine between
Ruth and the nightingale, though the song "found" Ruth). The art
of lyric, in Keats's homage to it, is shown to combine the powers of
music and the powers of plastic art (the creatures, the sculptural
goddess), and is proved to range from the decorative (the adornment of the earth) to the concentrated (the distillation of summer
in the honey) to the elusive (in the last choirs). It is an art both
male, in idea and blessing, and female, in creative engendering and
work and contemplation. It benefits the world, and delights in its
own creation. It also is the harvester—and a conscious undoing
harvester—of its own fruits. It does not only (like Robert Frost)

gather apples; it crushes them. It does not only (like Shakespeare) bear in the sheaves; it threshes the corn. It is less interested in the store which such processes produce (the poet has in fact no interest in the store—there are no rich garners here except those of the bees, no full granary) than in the process by which the transubstantiation takes place, in which both the fruit and the harvester are disembodied. A poet does not read his past poems, nor look for himself in them; he has been placed by his new access of knowledge into a new state of ignorance (*Letters*, 1, 288) and is once more busy with his compositions and decompositions.

There is, the autumn ode tells us, a lyric music appropriate to every hour and to every season; an endless succession of lyric tones are generated by the spirit's greeting of the earth, by dreaming taking its colors from something of material sublime. The musical art of the nightingale and the sculptural art of the urn are both triumphantly enclosed within the art of verbal lyric, which can, if the autumn ode is to be believed, express a flowery tale of Ceres more sweetly than the urn itself, and can rival, in its heard melodies of breath, the melodies of natural music. Lyric—to Keats's supreme joy—admits guiltlessly all five senses, and pleases all five senses, not directly (as he had mistakenly thought in the "glutting" of *Melancholy*), but with "spiritual sweets."

Keats's perplexed mind has come to the great discovery that lyric makes sense by giving a natural sensual topography to the algebra of thought. Into every presented equation of stationed objects, we can read an analogical "meaning": though no two readers will formulate the embodied idea identically, Keats's stationing (let us say of the sequence of the goddess sitting careless, asleep, steadying her head, crossing a brook, and watching with patient look) governs quite closely the range of meanings which are possible under the rubric of the lyric equation (carelessness followed by drowsiness, followed by a wakened alert care, closed by a patient vigil "hours by hours"). Keats's notion of lyric allows for dreaming ("conspiring"), for a drugged intoxication during the work of transubstantiation ("the fume of poppies" halfway through the reaping), for the reluctance ("sparing the swath") to continue the intellectual creative work which undoes the beautiful appearances of sense, and for the will to garner represented by the burdened but steady traversing of the brook. The wakeful anguish of the soul, purified into a vigil over essence in its slow disappearance, is equally given its due. The poet's lawful ambition to deck the whole world and to be sought out from afar amid his store is not repudiated; the effortlessness of access to art is taken for granted, since everyone who seeks the goddess may find her. Keats's art has never wished to be hermetic; the nightingale poured forth her soul and anyone could listen; the figures on the urn are finally proved to need no explanatory legend. "[These poems] will explain themselves—as all poems should do without any comment," said Keats, sending George his rondeaus (*Letters*, II, 21). The single most important discovery of the poem is that the passing from dreaming to waking is the moment not of void, but of store and of utterance; without the scythe and the cider-press, there would be no grain and no oozings and no impetus to listen to the autumn voices. The poem does not go inward (to a shrine, to a bower, to the *penetralia*); it moves outward to engirdle the earth. It both stations the self in the center of the world, watching and listening, and dissolves the same self into music. The poem is sometimes prospective (in its conspiring) and sometimes nostalgic; it can bring itself equally well to think of the present sensual moment and of its own subsequent thread of sound. It can remember the songs of spring and it can forget that warm days will ever cease. It can move with time in organic process or it can oscillate up and down like the gnats in thought. It is mimetic; it is (in its antiphony) dialectical; it is (in recounting the day and the season) parabolic in its rise and fall; it is (here, by not disturbing the sacred season) ethically admonitory in its rhythms of passage, its concatenations and articulations. It is propositional (after its algebraic fashion); and most of all, it is multiple.

This ode is multiple in the roles it allows the lyric self (as worshiper, appreciator, painter, consoler, and elegist); but chiefly it is multiple in the number of polyphonic effects, each pointing in a slightly different—or even contradictory—direction, which it can simultaneously sustain. Here, there are so many vectors—those several organizing motions, each one of them kept going till the end, Keats's great discovery for depth in lyric—that, depending on the weight one gives to each in summing up the result of their interacting forces, one feels differently about the poem. Sometimes the vector of decline governs, sometimes that of expansion, sometimes creativity, sometimes sacrifice, sometimes plenitude, sometimes necessity. The absolute economy of the organization can, finally, make the ode seem to have the pure aspect of a geometric theorem; its "proof" is as austere as its symbols are luxuriant. Those abstractions into which Keats lapsed, which were his only life, here take their own life, as he wished them to, from the material sublime. The anguish and struggle of all the other odes are not forgotten (we scarcely know whether to name the autumn figure Indolence, Poesy, Psyche, Delight, Melancholy, or Moneta). The other odes are remembered with homage through the lightest of allusions to their subjects, their rhetorical shapes, their constitutive tropes, their goddesses, and their explorations of sense and thought—we see a reminiscent cloud here, a grape there, a Greek figure, a question and a proposition, a drowsiness, a song, a creating gardener-fancy, a quest for a divinity, a fragrance of flowers, a replication of earthly scene, an embracing couple. The adieu of the poem is so widely faithful it need not be spoken aloud.

In an early sonnet, beset by dark vapors on the plains, Keats wished for a time when the vapors would disappear and he could see "Autumn suns / Smiling at eve upon the quiet sheaves" (*Poems*, p. 89). It is clear that he now knows it to be impossible to keep the sheaves, or to see the sun without obscuring clouds. In that sense, *Autumn* is tragic, but it is not tragic as the other odes are. *The Fall of Hyperion* had been the occasion for the revisiting of all the tragic places of the previous odes—especially *Nightingale* and *Melancholy*. Keats's tragic, lurid, guilty, and fevered recollections were drawn off there, leaving a clear pastoral middle ground as the ample terrain of the last ode—or so we would say if the stern perfection of its structure did not tempt us to see in it the extracting genius of essence itself at work, where the tragedy of necessity cannot tell itself apart from the fluid current of desire.

Conclusion

If he utterly

Scans all the depths of magic, and expounds
The meanings of all motions, shapes, and sounds;
If he explores all forms and substances
Straight homeward to their symbol-essences;
He shall not die.

> *Endymion*, III, 696–701

I have lov'd the principle of beauty in all things.

> *Letters*, II, 263

I am pick'd up and sorted to a pip.

> *Letters*, II, 323

THE odes of John Keats, considered all together, make up a system of inexhaustible internal relations. Each one, when taken as a vantage point, casts light on Keats's authorial choices in the others; and only by grouping them as a sequence can a reader see what Keats decides to use, and what he decides to suppress or discard, in each. His choices are not arbitrary, but they can seem so if the development of each ode from its predecessors is not taken into account. Arranged as I have arranged them here—*Indolence, Psyche, Nightingale, Urn, Melancholy,* and *Autumn*—they tell an eloquent tale of Keats's intent to devote himself, like Milton, rather to the ardors than to the pleasures of song. After the silent, songless, purgatorial severity of *The Fall of Hyperion* Keats regains Spenserian luxury, but of a spiritual as well as a sensual sort, in the ode *To Autumn* (which itself is a poem about sacrifice and self-immolation, and is, for all its luxury, ascetic).

"A complex mind," said Keats, "is one that is imaginative and at the same time careful of its fruits" (*Letters*, I, 186). Keats's complex mind, in the odes, is pondering complex questions. What, for the religious unbeliever, should be the "system of salvation"? Are there objects or processes worthy of worship by the human mind? What is the modern poet's relation to classical myth and allegorical language? Is the dualistic description of man as composed of senses and spirit in conflict a true one? Does art originate in nature or is it opposed to nature? Can poetry be goaded by ambition or is it conceived in indolent reverie? Is art a process wholly conceptual or must it, to be called art, be embodied in a medium? Is abstract art to be preferred to representational art? Is there a hierarchy of arts, according to their medium, and if so, where does poetry rank in this hierarchy? Is the aesthetic act one in which we "lose ourselves" in a better world, or one in which we actively work to represent and reproduce the entire world in which we live? Is it possible to attend to "medium" and "message" at one and the same time in confronting a work of art? Can aesthetic emotions be mixed as well as pure, and if so, which is the higher form? What is aesthetic temperance, and what is its relation to aesthetic and emotional intensity? Is the artist, or the artwork, a benefactor to man?

These and other general questions were preoccupying Keats as he composed the odes. At the same time he was working out in these great poems questions of a more private nature. These have to do with his feelings about women as brides, elusive objects of fancy, goddesses whose due was religious veneration, helpless beings needing rescue, patient mothers, and Muses. They also have to do with his feelings about sexuality—the irreconcilability of "mad pursuit" and romantic love, the wish for an unravished bride, the paradoxical nature of human passion that left him both cloyed and parched, the tragic necessity that the grape of intensity be burst so that joy could be tasted, the presence of melancholy in the ultimate recesses of delight, the terror of a mistress's anger, the comparison of the mind to a womb, and the assertion of the possibility of a creative "pregnancy" within the womb of the brain.

These religious, philosophical, aesthetic, and sexual problems were joined in Keats's mind, as he wrote the odes, by problems about expression in language. He is evidently engaged, throughout the odes, in experiments on his own linguistic and figurative resources, as he begins to work more consciously and sedulously the treasuries of language he had poured out in a fine profusion (and uneven coherence) in the relatively structureless *Endymion*. We see him in the odes pondering the relative value of various lyric structures, from the simplest to the most complex; we find him concentrating not only on one symbol at a time (a bird, an urn) but on one trope at a time, as a governing device for a poem. (He also chose a governing trope for the whole sequence, the trope of apostrophe, which is the figure for what is to be venerated.) We see him growing in power, until he learns to orchestrate the relations of theme, symbol, trope, syntax, and register of diction in ever more powerful ways.

Philosophically speaking, the most interesting of Keats's conclusions, as he comes to the end of his sequence, is his view that art is both absolutely dependent on, and at the same time absolutely sacrificial of, nature. Given the "disagreeables" of nature, Keats felt (in *Nightingale*) the intense appeal of a non-natural abstract art like music, but his appetite for truth and completion did not permit him, finally, to choose either abstraction or fantasy as his form of art. He bravely tried to think (in the *Urn*) that verisimilitude should be the criterion for art, and that art should include the *thanatos* of sacrifice as well as the *eros* of sexual pursuit. This was an ethical decision for Keats, as was his choice of the "communicative" solace of a public and social art (one embodied in a medium and consequently, like the urn, a friend to man) over a private art such as the inner mental construction of Psyche's shrine or the unheeding and fugitive self-expressive art of the nightingale. In giving himself the dramatic role not of creator but of audience to the birdsong, the urn, and the theater in Moneta's brain, Keats found a way of asking himself what he as a poet should be to his audience. He decided to be not the indolent dreamer, not even the active "internal" artist of Psyche's bower, not the heedless self-expressive nightingale, but rather an artist who, like the sculptor of the urn, left behind an artifact for the centuries. But his own art could not be representational as the visual arts could be; some criterion other than verisimilitude had to be his guide.

It is at this point that Keats's thinking about a "system of salvation," his speculations about this world as a vale of soul-making, and his aesthetic explorations begin to coincide. The theory of soul-making proposed a transubstantiation of an "intelligence" into a "soul" by its encountering, recognizing, and incorporating into its progressively formed identity "a world of pains and troubles." This self-transubstantiation, through labor and pain, from intelligence to soul formed the new basis of Keats's aesthetic. Nature would be, in a parallel process, transubstantiated into art. The final product, though dependent on the initial base, would not resemble it: an identity is impossible without an intelligence as base, but the final identity "looks" very different from the original blank "intelligence." In taking the most ancient act of man's life in nature —the harvest—as his symbol of the meaning of civilization, Keats chose an image which was Christian as well as classical and agricultural. Identity and art alike are constructed from the ground of nature, but what results after labor and pain (grain, apple juice) is entirely different in appearance and substance from its natural base (corn, fruit). In seeing the obliteration of natural form as the prerequisite for the construction of spiritual or aesthetic form, Keats is unsparingly faithful to his own sense of the artifice necessary to creation; but he remains as well the greatest celebrant, in English, of the natural base without which no art and no identity would be possible. He admires without stint both nature and intelligence, but he admires even more culture's teleological aim toward "store," and the soul's aim toward identity.[1] His reaper-Muse is always seen "amid [her] store," and she is finally absorbed wholly into "store": her hymns are sung in her absence.

Keats's final conclusions about woman and sexual experience are no less seriously considered. His first preference for the youthful, the virginal, and the bridal yields eventually to more "adult" and severe goddesses like Melancholy and Moneta. But in *Autumn*, we see the season in all her phases—initially as a bride, then as a goddess of fertility, as a careless dreamer, as a tired worker, as a patient vigil-keeper, and finally as a dying mother, mourned by her children. The issue of male sexuality, its parching and cloying, is resolved, insofar as it can be, not only by the recognition of the necessary bursting of Joy's grape, but also by Keats's forsaking, in *Autumn*, his old rhythm of intensity followed by desolation; he chooses, rather, the rhythm of a steady rising and setting, concomitant with rhythms of expansion and etherealization. The generous acceptance of all the senses into his final ode argues for the disappearance of the sense of sexual guilt which provoked the image of mad pursuit of maidens loth. The transmutation of Milton's Christmas remark about the earth—"It was no season then for her / To wanton with the sun, her lusty Paramour"—into the guiltless autumn "conspiring" of earth with her "bosom-friend" the sun suggests that Keats now envisaged a sexual relation that made the couple "bosom-friends" as well as lovers (a relation he had found with Fanny Brawne, the first woman admitted to his inmost thoughts, and the first to whom he would send books of poetry). Philosophically, aesthetically, linguistically, and privately, the odes tell a compressed story, in their successive dissatisfactions with each previous "solution," of Keats's strenuous development as a man and as a poet. They seem, as they succeed each other, an exemplification of Schelling's prescription for artistic process that "art, to be art, must first withdraw from nature and only return to it in a final consummation."[2]

We are warned by the art historian Henri Focillon that structural forms, of the sort I have abstracted from the odes, "are not their own pattern, their own mere naked representation. Their life develops in a space that is not the abstract frame of geometry; . . . it assumes substance in a given material . . . A form without support is not form, and the support itself is form."[3] I hope that my singling out various linguistic, rhetorical, constructive, or thematic forms in the odes will be followed, in the minds of my readers, by a replacement of these forms in their original material matrix in the poem, which is itself, as Focillon rightly says, a form. In *The Archaeology of Knowledge*, Foucault says that "whatever the techniques employed, commentary's only role is to say *finally*, what has silently been articulated *deep down*":

> It must—and the paradox is ever-changing yet inescapable—say, for the first time, what has already been said, and repeat tirelessly what was, nevertheless, never said. The infinite rippling of commentary is agitated from within by the dream of masked repetition: in the distance there is, perhaps, nothing other than what was there at the point of departure: simple recitation. Commentary averts the chance element of discourse by giving it its due: it gives us the opportunity to say something other than the text itself, but on condition that it is the text itself which is uttered and, in some ways, finalised. The open multiplicity, the fortuitousness, is transferred, by the principle of commentary, from what is liable to be said to the number, the form, the masks and the circumstances of repetition. The novelty lies no longer in what is said, but in its reappearance.[4]

The end of commentary is, then, to recite the poem anew, but with a sense of the multiple choices made from all possible language-events in order that this text be produced. I will be content if a reader leaves this book convinced that Keats's structural forms have meaning, that his tropes bear independent significance, that his divinities are not randomly chosen, and, above all, that his meditations on art are systematic and progressive in complexity.

In speaking of the composing of music in his 1940 Norton Lectures, Stravinsky says of the artist:

> Step by step, link by link, it will be granted to him to discover the work. It is this chain of discoveries, as well as each individual discovery, that gives rise to the emotion . . . which invariably follows closely the phases of the creative process.
>
> All creation presupposes at its origin a sort of appetite that is brought on by the foretaste of discovery. This foretaste of the creative act accompanies the intuitive grasp of an unknown entity already possessed but not yet intelligible, an entity that will not take a definite shape except by the action of a constantly vigilant technique.[5]

It is a process of discovery of this sort that I have wanted to reveal in Keats's work as he composed the sequence of the odes. By reflecting on his "constantly vigilant technique," and by specifying for each poem the "foretaste of discovery" which anticipates the next, I have hoped to render more intelligible these great poems, which remain "forever warm and still to be enjoyed."

Notes

Index

Notes

Introduction

1. "Variations on the Eclogues," *The Art of Poetry* (New York: Pantheon, 1958), p. 307.
2. "Poetry and Abstract Thought," *The Art of Poetry,* p. 81.
3. Paul Valéry, "In Praise of Virtuosity," *Aesthetics* (New York: Pantheon, 1965), p. 195.
4. I have suggested some relations between Stevens and Keats in "Stevens and Keats' 'To Autumn,' " in *Wallace Stevens: A Celebration,* ed. Frank Doggett and Robert Buttel (Princeton: Princeton University Press, 1980), pp. 171–195.
5. "Concerning 'Adonis,' " *The Art of Poetry,* pp. 11–12.
6. Gillian Beer, "Aesthetic Debate in Keats's Odes," *Modern Language Review* 64 (1969), 742–748. See also Joseph Kestner's argument relating *Nightingale* and *Urn* to temporal and spatial arts, in "Keats, The Solace of Space," *Illinois Quarterly* 35 (1972), 59–64.
7. Valéry, *The Art of Poetry,* pp. 148 ("It was the intention of making, which *wanted* what I *said*") and 192.
8. See "Spectral Symbolism and Authorial Self in Keats's *Hyperion*" (pp. 57–73) and "Poem and Ideology: A Study of Keats's 'To Autumn' " (pp. 124–146) in *The Fate of Reading* (Chicago: University of Chicago Press, 1975).
9. "The Creation of Art," *Aesthetics,* p. 132.
10. In an unpublished paper delivered at the MLA, 1980, entitled "Processes of Imagination and Growth in Keats's Odes," and in essays to be part of a book on Keats.
11. "A Reading of Keats," in *Essays of Four Decades* (Chicago: Swallow Press, 1968), p. 264.

I.   Stirring Shades and Baffled Beams: The *Ode on Indolence*

1. [Stillinger's notes.] Text (including heading and epigraph) from Brown's transcript (*CB*)   11 ye] *made out of* you *CB.*

2. *The Consecrated Urn*, pp. 313–335: "The point of real importance is the early date of the conception, and not of the composition" (p. 314n). The *Ode on Indolence* has been variously considered the first, the second, or the last of the odes. Like Holloway (*The Charted Mirror*, p. 41) and Blackstone I take it up first, as first imagined (on or about 19 March 1819, as retold in *Letters*, 11, 78–79), as "seminal" to the rest (Blackstone), and as the "baldest and simplest" of the odes in its language (Holloway). Its prosody seems to prove, being metrically regular, that it was written after the *Ode to Psyche*, and probably after the *Ode to a Nightingale* (though it is not inconceivable that Keats invented the ten-line stanza found in *Indolence*, was dissatisfied with the poem, had recourse to a slightly different stanza—with one line shortened— for *Nightingale*, and then returned to the regular ten-line stanza for *Urn*). It is certain that it shows more confusion of focus (in its past narration, its subsequent introspective reverie, and its interspersed addresses to the figures) than any of the subsequent odes, all of which have a single vocative focus. It is also certain that its lethargy preceded (on the evidence of the letters) the active engagement in creation that produced the other odes. Its structure of stalemate—of solicitation and refusal—seems logically to precede the active efforts of construction, pursuit, interrogation, quest, and seeking that motivate the other odes. I think it is not true that "Keats's mood . . . does not develop in the course of the poem" (Holloway, p. 42). On the contrary, the all-but-irrepressible stirring, budding, and singing in Keats's lawn-soul in the fifth stanza are very different from the benumbed sense, the lessened pulse, and the drowsiness of the second stanza, just as the aching for wings to follow the figures is different from the defiance of them at the close. As W. J. Bate says (*John Keats*, p. 528), "What had started as a mere rendering of a mood of passivity begins to betray a divided attitude crossed by inconsistent attempts at self-persuasion." Nor can I agree with Walter Evert that the poem tallies with Keats's statement, in the letter containing the "germ" of the ode, that his languor "is a rare instance of advantage in the body overpowering the Mind" (*Letters*, 11, 79), and is consistent with what Evert calls "Keats's general movement away from intellectualized conceptualization in his reaction to the external world" (*Aesthetic and Myth in the Poetry of Keats*, p. 306). Keats wished to resist conceptualization, it is true, in the state of "weakened . . . animal fibre," as he called it, as he recovered from his black eye after being hit by a cricket ball; but the ode recounts just how impossible he found it to "move away from intellectualized conception," since those intellectualized concepts Love, Ambition, and Poesy will not leave him alone, and he is powerless to banish them. That the concepts are still bald and simple (to borrow Holloway's vocabulary) only means that

Keats has further to go before he arrives at rich conceptualizations like that of Autumn.

3. *Poems*, p. 655.

4. "If I think of fame of poetry it seems a crime to me, and yet I must do so or suffer," he wrote from Tom's sickbed (*Letters*, 1, 369). Rollins accurately prints "fame of poetry" but I suspect that the "of" is a slip of the pen for "or."

5. See Geoffrey Hartman, "False Themes and Gentle Minds," in *Beyond Formalism* (New Haven: Yale University Press, 1970), pp. 283-297.

II. Tuneless Numbers: The *Ode to Psyche*

1. [Stillinger's notes.] Text (including heading) from *1820*. Variants and other readings from Keats's draft (*D*), his letter to George and Georgiana Keats, 14 February-3 May 1819 (*L*), and transcripts by Brown (*CB*) and Woodhouse (*W²*).   *Heading* Ode to] Ode To (Ode *added afterward*) *D*   4 into] < to > into *L*   5 dreamt] dreamt *altered to* dream'd *W²*   6 awaken'd] awaked *L*   9 couched] < cl > couched *L*   10 roof] fan *D*, *L*, *W²*, *and originally CB*; fan *altered to* roof *by Keats in CB*   13 'Mid] *interlined above* < In > *D*; Near *W²*   14 silver-white] freckle pink *in the margin* (*but* silver-white *undeleted in the text*) *in D*; freckle-pink *L*; freckled, pink *W²*   14 Tyrian] syrian *D*, *L*, *CB*, *W²*   15 calm] soft *CB*   17 bade] bid *D*, *L*, *W²*   20 eye] < dawning > eye *D*   22 O happy] O < p > happy *L*   23 true!] ~ ? *L*   24 latest] lastest *L*   26 Phoebe's] *successively* (*a*) Night's < wide > full, (*b*) Night's orb'd (*c*) Phoebe's *D*   28 hast] hadst *L*   30 delicious] melodious *D*, *CB*, *W²*   32-34 No *and* no] No< r > *and* no< r > *in all eight places in D*   36 brightest] Bloomiest *D*, *L*, *CB*, *W²*   42 among] *interlined above* < above > *D*   43 by my] by (*corrected by Keats to* by my) *CB*   43 own] *interlined above* < clear > *D*   44 So] O *D*, *L*, *CB*, *W²*   45/46 < Thy Altar heap'd with flowers, > (*written vertically in the margin with a mark for insertion after 45, the line and the mark then deleted*) *D*   47 From] *interlined above* < Thy > *D*   57 lull'd] *interlined above* < charmd > *L*   57 to sleep] asleep *altered to* to sleep *CB*   62 feign] *interlined above* < frame > *L*   63 breeding . . . breed] *successively* (*a*) plucks a thousand flower and never plucks (*b*) plucking flowers will never pluck (*c*) breeding flowers will < never > breed pluck (never *deleted by mistake instead of* pluck *in the third version*) *D*   63/64 < So bower'd Goddess will I worship thee > *D*   67 the . . . Love] warm Love glide *altered to* the warm Love *D*; Love *W²*.

2. Psyche is "restored," not "resurrected": she was forgotten, not dead. The opening tableau shows she is ever immortal. She is not a "dying immortal" or "immortal but also fading," as Leon Waldoff would have it ("The Theme

of Mutability in the 'Ode to Psyche,' " *PMLA* [1977], 412). Psyche is, as Keats said, "neglected." On the other hand, Waldoff's psychoanalytic reading of the ode as a "rescue fantasy" (p. 410), a "defense against irrevocable loss" (p. 415), and, finally, an "adaptation" (p. 417) are intelligent insights into the ode as a psychological document. His concluding emphasis on will and resolution is far truer to the poem than readings which emphasize only irony or an empty center. The long and sometimes fanciful discussion of the ode by Homer Brown (*Diacritics* 6 [1976], 49-56) considers, following Harold Bloom in the *Map of Misreading* (p. 153), that "Milton's Satan as the artist of deceit at Eve's ear becomes the 'gardener Fancy' and the speaker of Keats's Ode" (p. 54). Brown urges too strongly that "the mortality of all the gods, including art, including the Psyche of this Ode, the mortality of all cultures" is Keats's concern (p. 56). But the poem is a restoration poem (however qualified). It is a poem about substitution, as Brown says, but *not* about endless substitution around and over a Derridean absence: such is not its tone. Leslie Brisman argues ("Keats, Milton, and What One May 'Very Naturally Suppose' ") that Keats is engaging in the creation of a "countermyth" against the decay of nature, a countermyth asserting that "inspiration [is] renewed as faithfully as are plants and seasons" (p. 4). (See *Milton and the Romantics* 6 [1975], 4-7.)

3. I am not unaware by how much the poem falls short of its claim of restitution, nor of the ironies (discussed most recently by Sperry and Fry) that it encounters on its way to the final fane. But these difficulties in the path—culminating in the vacancy of the final tableau—do not defeat the passionate tone of the poem. Bloom, not insensitive to the ironies, yet speaks of the poem's "rhapsodical climax," and sees the open casement emphasizing "the openness of the imagination toward the heart's affections" (*Visionary Company*, pp. 395, 397). It should not be forgotten that for Keats, especially in his moments of prizing verisimilitude, it was important to speak the truth about his life; one of the truths behind the *Ode to Psyche* was that he was not yet embowered with Fanny Brawne. That he still hoped and longed for her is evident from the final entreaty, and it goes counter to the current of the poem to prize its uncertainties over its hopes, still ardent and as yet undefeated.

4. Commentators have expended a good deal of effort on making an allegorical identification of Psyche. She is "the soul of human love" (G. Wilson Knight, *The Starlit Dome*, p. 302); the mind rescued by Love (Bate, *John Keats*, p. 490); the visionary imagination (Perkins, *The Quest for Permanence*, p. 222 ff.); the human-soul-in-love (Bloom, *The Visionary Company*, p. 390); "the simple consciousness of Being" (Fry, *The Poet's Calling in the English Ode*, p. 226); "the goddess of the poetic soul, the Muse" (Sperry, *Keats the Poet*, p. 254); the *moth-goddess*, who symbolized melancholic love" (Garrod, *Keats*, pp. 98-99); "the intelligent 'Spark' struggling to become a soul . . . a love-

goddess with an understanding of troubled human experience . . . a personification of human nature subjected to an inevitable and cruel process of growing up and growing old" (Allott, "The 'Ode to Psyche,' " in Muir, *John Keats*, pp. 84, 86); "Love itself, the poetic-butterfly-moth idea" (Jones, *John Keats's Dream of Truth*, p. 206); and so on. Probably some such identification is necessary if one is to write about the poem at all; but surely the point to be made is that Keats is engaged in one of his recurrent recoils against emblematic allegory; such recoils always took him in the direction of mythology. Mythology was suggestive, emblematic allegory bald. Mythology, capable of motion, hovered; emblematic allegory was frozen in a single gesture. Mythology derived from narrative and came bearing, even if lightly, the aura of its narrative around it; allegory, originating in conceptualization, had no richness of story about it. The fluidity of concept associated here with Psyche comes precisely from her mythological origins; the ode marks Keats's resistance to the "fair Maid, and Love her name" sort of writing, to which he had resorted in *Indolence*.

5. I discuss this art of wounds and cures at length in "Lionel Trilling and the Immortality Ode," *Salmagundi* 41 (1978), 66–86.

6. Though critics mention the derivation of this passage from Milton, they have failed to see that Keats draws only on the passage about the more acceptable pagan gods, and they have not seen Keats's anti-Miltonic aim — to put the gods back into English poetry, when Milton had banished them as unfit and false subjects for the Christian poet.

7. Allott (p. 87) and Sperry after her (p. 254) mention that Keats recalls the banning of pagan gods in Milton, but they do not see that Keats saw the ban as a loss *to poetry*, or that he is defying Miltonic truth-categories. Douglas Bush's assumption that Keats adopted echoes from Milton "simply because they fitted his idea of providing [Psyche] with proper rites" seems to take too lightly Keats's indignation that anyone should think it possible to do without "the beautiful mythology of Greece." See "The Milton of Keats and Arnold," *Milton Studies* 11 (1978), 103.

8. She in fact is the only one of the "faded Olympians" not to have declined; she is still properly addressed as "brightest." It therefore seems no part of Keats's intent to show her as careworn and acquainted with grief, as Allott would have it (Muir, pp. 84, 86).

9. I owe this formulation to Professor Patrick Keane of Le Moyne College.

10. I cannot therefore share Fry's conviction that the couple represent "the bisexual and at least partly daylit scene of creation that chaster poets, notably Collins, had tried to represent euphemistically" (*The Poet's Calling*, p. 223). Nothing is being "created" by Cupid and Psyche, whether in the myth or in Keats's poem; they are figures for sexuality, but not for procreation. (Keats's departure from *Comus*, where Milton envisages twins born from the union

of Cupid and Psyche, is explicit.) Nor can the forest scene be legitimately called a "primal scene" (Fry, p. 225) if those words are to carry the shock and dismay which Freud predicated in the mind of the child witnessing such a scene. Keats does not stand to his scene as a child witnessing a parental act; the scene is a projection of his own desire, and he cannot therefore be said to be, as Fry says he is, following Bloom, "the poet as voyeur" (p. 225). If Fry means that Cupid and Psyche are to be taken as figures drawn from Adam and Eve, then there is no reason to call the scene "bisexual," at least not in the usual sense of that word.

11. He speaks of his "half-fledged brain" in a letter of July 1819 (*Letters*, II, 130).

12. The chiastic structural pattern of bower-cult-cult-bower (what I have called the mirror-image shape of the ode) seems to me clear enough to bring into question Fry's notion that the shape of the ode is one of "rondure" — "The whole poem is the shrine, couched and soft-conched. It is a shell, rounded as the mind" (*The Poet's Calling*, p. 227).

13. Homer Brown notes the defiance of Milton ("blind and blindly superstitious") in these lines. But he thinks of Psyche as too exclusively one with Keats, contrasting Keats's ode to the traditional ode "of worship to an otherness." Keats is not writing a hymn to himself; Psyche is, not least, Fanny Brawne. See Brown, "Creations and Destroyings: Keats's Protestant Hymn, The 'Ode to Psyche,' " *Diacritics* 6 (1976), 49–56.

14. Leon Waldoff, also making the point that Keats's divinities are female (in a paper delivered at the MLA, 1980, and entitled "Processes of Imagination and Growth in Keats's Odes"), argues psychoanalytically that all are attempts at the (impossible) restoring of a maternal image.

15. Lawrence Kramer in "The Return of the Gods: Keats to Rilke," *Studies in Romanticism* 17 (Fall 1978), 483–500, places the ode into a tradition of the theophanic poem, "the genre in which the return of the gods takes place" (p. 484), and writes very interestingly on "the riddle ritual" (p. 494) of the naming of Psyche, and the subsequent withholding of her name.

16. Sperry voices the same criticism (p. 259); but he is wrong in saying (p. 257) that the "buds . . . burst into thought 'with pleasant pain.' " They do not — only thoughts, in the form of trees on the steep, do. Fancy is not painful; thought is. Keats allows in his earthly paradise in this poem only flowers, not fruits, thus restricting his gardener to the single season of spring.

III. Wild Warblings from the Aeolian Lyre: The *Ode to a Nightingale*

1. [Stillinger's notes.] Text (including heading) from *1820*. Variants and other readings from Keats's draft (*D*), transcripts by Woodhouse (*W²*), Dilke

(*CWD*), and George Keats (*GK*), and the version published in *Annals of the Fine Arts.*   *Heading* a] the *D*, *W²*, *CWD*, *GK*, *Annals*   *Before* 1 Small, winged Dryad *D* (*see Textual Note*)   1 My] *deleted in D and nothing substituted*   1 drowsy] *interlined above* <painful> *D*   1 pains] *written beneath* <falls> *D*   4 past] *interlined above* <hence> *D*   11 hath] has *D*, *W²*, *CWD*, *GK*, *Annals*   12 Cool'd a long] Cooling an *altered to* Cool'd a long *D*   14 Dance] <And> Dance *D*   16 true, the] true and *D*, *W²*, *CWD*, *GK*, *Annals*   16 blushful] blissful *GK*   17 beaded] cluster'd *D*   20 away] *not in W²*, *CWD*, *GK*, *Annals*   22 hast] have *CWD*   24 other] other's *CWD*, *GK*; other's *altered to* other *W²*   26 spectre] *added above the line* (*and a hyphen inserted before* thin) *in D*   26 and dies] *written beneath* <and old> (*another* old *is interlined and deleted before* pale *in the same line*) *D*   27 sorrow] *interlined above* <grief> *D*   30 new] *added above the line in D*   31 to] *interlined above* <with> *D*   37 Cluster'd] *deleted in D and nothing substituted*   39 heaven] *added above the line in D*   40 Through] <Sidelong> Through *D*   42 soft] <blooms> soft *D*   43/44 <With with> *D*   44 month] mouth *Annals*   49 dewy] sweetest *D*, *W²*, *CWD*, *GK*, *Annals*   50 The] *written over* <Her> *D* (*but see Textual Note*)   52 been] *added above the line in D*   54 quiet] painless *D*   57 forth] thus *D*, *W²*, *CWD*, *GK*, *Annals*   59 wouldst] would *D*   59/60 <But requiem'd> *D*   60 To] For *altered to* To (*actually producing* Fo) *D*; For *W²*, *CWD*, *GK*, *Annals*   65 song] *interlined above* <voice> *D*   66 for] from *CWD*   69 magic] *interlined above* <the wide> *D*   70 perilous] <Ruthless> perilous *D* (*but see Textual Note*)   72 me back] *interlined above* <me> <me> (*the first deleted* me *written over* {ba}) *D*   72 to my . . . self] unto myself *D*, *W²*   74 deceiving] *made out of* deceitful *D*   78 valley] vally<'s> *D*   79 vision, or a] vision real or *D*   80 music: —] ~ −*D*; ~? *W²*, *CWD*, *GK*, *Annals*.

2. Jean Hagstrom, in *The Sister Arts* (Chicago: University of Chicago Press, 1958), John Hollander, in *The Untuning of the Sky* (Princeton: Princeton University Press, 1961), and James Winn, in *Unsuspected Eloquence* (New Haven: Yale University Press, 1981), have traced the long debates about the interrelation of the several arts, and the attribution to each of specific virtues. Keats would have been aware of these debates through his acquaintance with Haydon's library.

3. Though *Annals of the Fine Arts* concerned itself above all with painting and sculpture, Keats's printing in it a poem about music was not unprecedented. In 1818, *Annals* had printed (II, 564) a letter from a reader to which he appended his own very bad poem praising music for "raising the soul on high." The letter, which attracted an indignant editorial comment, began:

> Sir, Painting, Sculpture and Architecture have been defined as the sensual, Poetry and Music, as the intellectual branches of the fine arts.

The editor starred "sensual," and replied:

> Sensual! as if Poetry has not been made infinitely more the means of corrupting the senses than even Painting or Sculpture . . . 'Our art' says Reynolds, 'like all arts which address the imagination, is applied to a somewhat lower faculty of the mind, which approaches nearer to sensuality; but through sense and fancy, it must make its way to reason; for such is the progress of thought, that we perceive by sense, we combine by fancy, and distinguish by reason: and without carrrying our art out of its natural and true character, the more we purify it from every thing that is gross in sense, in that proportion as we lower it to mere sensuality, we prevent its nature, and degrade it from the rank of a liberal art; and this is what every artist ought well to remember . . .'

The point I want to make is that Keats, in printing *Nightingale* in such a journal, defined it as a poem about one of the fine arts. The question of the sensuality of the various arts had been historically so much debated since classical times, and the hierarchy of the senses so much discussed, that Keats could not escape such problems. Keats's own inquiry in the odes has to do not only with the relative grossness of the senses but also with the relation between those intellectual distinctions proper to "reason" (in Reynolds' sense) and the progress, which Reynolds phrases with a deceptive suavity, from "sense" through "fancy" to "reason."

4. Both Longinus and Quintilian make this distinction; see Winn, pp. 32–33. The relevant passages are: "Notes . . . although in themselves they signify nothing at all, often cast a wonderful spell . . . over an audience" (*On the Sublime*, ch. 39); "Musical instruments, in spite of the fact that their sounds are inarticulate, still succeed in exciting a variety of different emotions in the hearer" (*Institutes*, ch. 9).

5. See Hartman, *The Fate of Reading* (Chicago: University of Chicago Press, 1975), pp. 57–73, "Spectral Symbolism and Authorial Self in Keats's 'Hyperion,' " on Keats's "counteridentification" with Tom, in equating a poetic fever with a tubercular one.

6. Robert Pinsky, in *The Situation of Poetry* (Princeton: Princeton University Press, 1976), p. 51, cites this passage as an example of the poetry of realist description. It is, in fact, just the opposite (since Keats is "blind"); it is an example of pure imaginative conceiving and literary allusion.

7. See, for further consideration of origins, my earlier article, "The Experiential Beginnings of Keats's Odes," *Studies in Romanticism* 12 (1973), 591–606.

8. Cf. also *Isabella* 41, ll. 1–2: "The Spirit mourn'd 'Adieu!' — dissolv'd, and left / The atom darkness." Keats marked several passages in his Shakespeare that are relevant to this ode: besides the passages from *Hamlet* (all marked by underlining, side marks, or a check) that I have cited, he underlined the following relevant lines:

From *Antony and Cleopatra* (ii.vii and iv.xiii):

> Till that the conquering wine hath steep'd our sense
> In soft and delicate Lethe.

> Then is it sin,
> To rush into the secret house of death,
> Ere death dare come to us?

From *Macbeth* (v.iv):

> Raze out the written trouble of the brain;
> And with some sweet oblivious antidote,
> Cleanse the stuff'd bosom.

Others have noted the allusion to Claudio's speech on death (also underlined by Keats) in *Measure for Measure*. Keats's Shakespeare (one of his two Shakespeares) which I have used here is not the one referred to by Caroline Spurgeon, but rather the seven-volume edition of the plays now in the Houghton Library Keats collection: William Shakespeare, *The Dramatic Works*, 7 vols., Chiswick, 1814. It passed to Joseph Severn on Keats's death.

9. Sperry (p. 244) refers to "the parabola shape of these poems." Such a phrase, appropriate to *Nightingale*, does not take account of the differences among the odes, which are very great, as I hope to show.

10. The rarely cited poem written in Scotland in July 1818 ("There is a joy in footing slow across a silent plain") contains Keats's first intimations that the journey homeward to habitual self could offer strength, familial affection, and insight (instead of disappointment and disillusion). The lines relevant to *Nightingale* are:

> Scanty the hour and few the steps beyond the bourn of care,
> Beyond the sweet and bitter world—beyond it unaware:
> Scanty the hour and few the steps, because a longer stay
> Would bar return and make a man forget his mortal way . . .
> No, no, that horror cannot be—for at the cable's length
> Man feels the gentle anchor pull and gladdens in its strength . . .
> Yet be the anchor e'er so fast, room is there for a prayer
> That man may never lose his mind on mountains bleak and bare;
> That he may stray league after league some great birthplace to find,
> And keep his vision clear from speck, his inward sight unblind.
>
> (29-32, 39-40, 45-48)

Nightingale still wants blindness and a journey "beyond the sweet and bitter world." In the *Urn*, Keats will open his eyes.

11. Earlier the line had read "where youth grows pale, and spectre thin, and old" (and originally Keats had begun "where youth grows old"). The allegorical impossibility that Youth should grow old prompted the revisions, which

themselves prove that "youth" is here allegorical, not naturalistic, in intent. Natural youth of course ages; allegorical Youth cannot. However, the allegorical youth is also subject to time here, and is to that extent nonemblematic.

12. *The Hymn to Pan* reads, in several stanzas, like a model for these "completions" and exhibits some of the same incoherence of assemblage. As the first of Keats's odes, it should perhaps have been included in this book. However, it is not linked to the later odes either by theme (it is about nature, not poetry, on the whole) or by speaker (the speaker of the later odes is a poet) or by form (it tends to Huntesque couplets, and does not derive from the sonnet forms inspiring the later odes). Its passage from the ripe pastoral to "sounds that wither drearily on barren moors" and thence to the ethereal makes it, of course, an important thematic source for *To Autumn*.

13. *Letters*, II, 260 (14 and 16 February 1820).

14. Originally Keats wrote "fairy land" in the penultimate stanza of the ode, changing it later to the "faery" land of Spenserian romance. The first spelling was probably prompted by his borrowing the flowers from Titania's bower.

15. Taking fees as a physician, says Keats in a letter, "is not worse than writing poems, & hanging them up to be flyblown on the Reviewshambles" (*Letters*, I, 70); Rollins cites *Othello*, IV.ii.66–67, "as summer flies are in the shambles, / That quicken even while blowing." The passage from *Othello* (conjoining "flies" and "blown" like the ode) seems a more likely source for the flies than the passage in Spenser (*Faerie Queene*, I.i.23) showing a shepherd brushing away gnats, cited by Douglas Bush in his edition of Keats's *Selected Poems and Letters* (Boston: Houghton Mifflin, 1959).

16. I am indebted for this reference to Irene Harris' unpublished Boston University dissertation "The Influence of Shakespeare on the Odes of Keats" (1978).

17. Some readers are wont to people the casements; but Keats's earlier casements are so clearly placed in relation to people (himself in *Indolence*, Psyche and Love in *Psyche*) that the absence of personal reference here is notable.

18. Cf. the first version of this frieze of the worship of Flora in *To Leigh Hunt, Esq.*

19. I see no warrant for interpreting "viewless" (used by Shakespeare, Milton, and Wordsworth, in passages Keats knew, to mean "invisible") as "blind," as John Bayley does (in "Intimacies of Implication," *Times Literary Supplement*, May 7, 1982, p. 500). Bayley asks, "How can *wings* be invisible?"; but of course it is Poesy which is invisible, because its action is empathic listening and self-projection.

20. "And mooned Ashtaroth / Heav'n's queen and mother both / Now sits not girt with tapers' holy shine . . . "

21. This poem, by becoming a midnight poem, belongs with Donne's *Nocturnal* and Yeats's *Byzantium*, where midnight represents the moment of the death of the sensual body.

22. "Generations" comes from *The Excursion* (IV, 760–762), lines which are alluded to earlier in the ode in the description of fading youth. The passage reads: "Man grows old, and dwindles, and decays; / And countless generations of mankind / Depart, and leave no vestige where they trod." Keats may have recalled, in thinking of the nightingale as musician, Portia's remark (*Merchant of Venice*, v.i.106) about the nightingale's being thought "no better a musician than the wren." Keats underlined the passage in his seven-volume Shakespeare in the Houghton Library.

23. In their original appearance in the epistle to Reynolds, the magic casements have elves and fays clustering around them, and the perilous seas are populated too, with a golden galley; the elves, remembered from this passage probably engendered the name of "elf" for "Fancy":

> The doors all look as if they oped themselves,
> The windows as if latched, by fays and elves . . .
> A golden galley all in silken trim!
> Towards the shade under the castle wall
> It comes in silence.
>
> (*Dear Reynolds*, 47–48, 58–60)

24. Though the art-forms of bower and shrine in *Psyche* are representational, no human beings (and no insects or fruits, as I have said) are permitted to inhabit them. Thus the challenge of representation is not faced, in terms of human sorrow, in *Psyche*.

IV. Truth the Best Music: The *Ode on a Grecian Urn*

1. [Stillinger's notes.] Text (including heading) from *1820*. Variants from Brown's transcript (*CB*) and the version published in *Annals of the Fine Arts*.   Heading Ode on] On *Annals*   1 still ∧] ~ , *Annals*   8 men or gods] Gods or Men *Annals*   9 mad pursuit] love? what dance *CB, Annals*   16 can . . . bare] bid the spring adieu *Annals*   18 yet] O *CB, Annals*   22 ever] never *Annals*   34 flanks] sides *CB*   40 e'er] ne'er *altered to* e'er *CB*   42 maidens ∧ overwrought,] ~ , ~ ∧ *CB*   47 shalt] wilt *CB, Annals*   48 a] as *CB*   49 "Beauty . . . that] ∧ Beauty is Truth, — Truth Beauty, — that *CB*; ∧ Beauty is Truth, Truth Beauty. — That *Annals*.

2. I think all commentators are now agreed with Bate that the *Urn* shows "the concentration of a second attempt" (*John Keats*, p. 510), even though we cannot date these two odes precisely. Sperry rightly insists (p. 268) on "the decisiveness of a context for reading the odes as a progression," and he and I are in agreement on the order *Psyche, Nightingale, Urn, Melancholy, Autumn*.

We differ on *Indolence*, which I put first (from its date of conception), and he, by date of appearance, puts after *Melancholy*.

3. I believe that Keats also raises, in these two odes, the question of the origins of art. In pursuit of this question, some theorists turn to "natural music" (birdsong) as the origin of human music, which is said to "imitate nature." Other theorists turn to the origins of art in Western history—for example, to the ancient world (which for Keats was the Greek world). More recently, theorists have turned to "primitive" art. In *Nightingale* and *Urn*, Keats seeks instruction from two conventional "wellsprings" of art, nature and the ancient Greek model. See the connection drawn between the sculptural and the mythic (and the opposition of both to "consciousness") in Nancy Goslee's article "Phidian Lore: Sculpture and Personification in Keats's Odes" (*Studies in Romanticism* 21 [1982], 73-86).

4. The urn represents, of course, only one visual possibility among several. The epistle to Reynolds had used a painting to similar effect. Besides Keats's wish to return to the origins of art, he simplifies his case by choosing a monochromatic object, thus restricting his observations to shape undistracted by "Titian colors touch'd into real life." He chooses sculpture over painting as closer (being "in the round") to representational "truth"—and chooses bas-relief over statuary as affording more narrative material. He chooses an urn over a frieze because it has no beginning nor end in outline, and can therefore, by its circular form, represent both eternity and the female better than a rectangular form. (All the addressed objects of veneration of the odes are female.)

5. The figures on the urn do not possess any of the identifying attributes (wingèd heels, a sheaf of wheat) which would enable us to identify them as gods; nor are they engaged in activities (fighting the Minotaur, for example) which would identify them historically or mythologically.

6. Wallace Stevens' reflection on Keats's wish to repose in the mere enjoyment of Beauty and Sensation, frustrated by his inevitable progression to Thought, Truth, and questions, is contained in *The Ultimate Poem Is Abstract*:

> One goes on asking questions. That, then, is one
> Of the categories. So said, this placid space
>
> Is changed. It is not so blue as we thought. To be blue,
> There must be no questions . . .
>
> It would be enough
> If we were ever, just once, at the middle, fixed
> In This Beautiful World Of Ours and not as now,
>
> Helplessly at the edge, enough to be
> Complete, because at the middle, if only in sense,
> And in that enormous sense, merely enjoy.

7. Keats seems to have derived the idea of the "finer tone" from *Paradise Lost* (v, 374–376):

> *. . . though what if Earth*
> *Be but the shadow of Heaven,* and things therein
> Each to other like, more than on Earth is thought?

(Italics indicate Keats's underlining in his copy of *Paradise Lost* now in the Keats Museum, Hampstead.)

8. Though the ode is often said to be speaking here about the transiency of passion, Keats insists (through the *burning* forehead and the *parching* tongue) that sensual fever persists even in sorrow and cloying; his bafflement is more evident than is any sense of the evanescence of passion.

9. Every reader has felt that the factual question "What men or gods are these?" is vastly different in tone from "Who are these coming to the sacrifice?" The second is a question of a procession in motion—"What is the nature of this group coming next?"—rather than a wish for an identifying historical reality.

10. Cf. *Paradise Lost*, VIII, 183–184: "Nor with perplexing thoughts / To interrupt *the sweet of life*" (Keats's underlining).

11. It might at first seem that the tonal "break" is a break between apostrophe (immediacy) and propositional reflection (mediated thought). If such were the case, "art" would remain purely sensational, and reflection would exclude the apostrophic surge of feeling. That this is not so is clear from the procession stanza, where apostrophe is present not only in the querying remark to the priest (part of the "sensational" content), but also in the reflective remark to the town ("thy streets . . . will silent be"). In this way the reflective portion of aesthetic reponse is shown to be as "immediate" and full of feeling as the sensory response itself is.

12. It is a matter of dispute whether one can maintain consciousness of matter and medium at once—can weep for the heroine, so to speak, while admiring the zoom shot. I side with Keats, but there is distinguished opinion on the other side. Even in repeated rereadings, one must choose; empathy of the sort an author would wish to evoke cannot be maintained unbroken while one is considering, say, Dickens' use of evolutionary vocabulary, or Stevens' use of the definite article. As soon as intellectual consideration of medium comes into play, the fiction of the construct lapses.

13. Keats here repeats the *Nightingale*-word "fade" (used of sound becoming faint) and the *Indolence*-word "fade" (used of phantoms vanishing) in yet a third sense, that of Beauty losing her lustrous eyes.

14. I see no evidence for puns here (brede/breed or overwrought maidens). However, I think it likely that the "embroider'd" of *Indolence* and the "breeding . . . breed" of *Psyche*, both used of Fancy, engendered the "brede" of the *Urn*.

15. *Letters*, I, 192; Keats is criticizing the aesthetic lifelessness of West's art, and uses the phrase by contrast.

16. For a discussion of the philosophical vocabulary of sensation, see Sperry, ch. I, *passim*.

17. It is touching that the word Keats uses for the expressivity of the urn in his close is "say'st" rather than "showest." Propositional truth can only be expressed in language, Keats's own medium. Representational truth (sensation in the eye) yields (as thought in the mind) propositional truth.

18. This crux now seems settled. See Jack Stillinger, *Twentieth Century Interpretations of Keats's Odes* (Englewood Cliffs, N.J.: Prentice-Hall, 1968), pp. 113-114, where the *consensus gentium* seems to be that the last two lines are spoken by the urn to men.

19. The whole thought structure of the *Urn* is a binary one, as though the governing polarity of Beauty and Truth insensibly worked on Keats's mind so as to make everything present itself (at least in the first instance) in binary form. Bride summons up child; the sylvan historian is better than rhyme; are the shapes deities or mortals; are we in Tempe or Arcady; are these men or gods; who are the males, who are the females; what pursuit, what struggle; what instruments, what ecstasy? "Heard" summons "unheard," the sensual ear is opposed to the spirit; the youth cannot leave his song nor can the trees be bare; the lover cannot kiss yet should not grieve; she cannot fade, he has not his bliss; he will love, she be fair. Some of the pairings are contrastive (pursuit and struggle, males and females) but others are coordinate (instruments and ecstasy, leaving the song and the trees being bare). The binary pattern is visible throughout the poem, though it becomes more graceful as it plays the folk against the priest, the heifer's lowing against her adornments. It is so surprising when the binary pattern is resisted (as in the three imagined situations for the little town) that we almost force the lines back into binary shape—in this case conflating "river" and "sea shore" as though there were an "and" between them instead of an "or," and pairing that one line with its two alternatives against the next line containing a single mountain-location. Of course the equivalency, line for line, helps us to read the phrase in a two-part way,

> What little town by river or sea shore
> Or mountain-built with peaceful citadel,

instead of hearing it as a three-part phrase,

> What little town by river
> or sea shore,
> or mountain-built with peaceful citadel.

If Keats says "Attic shape!" he seems compelled to echo it with "Fair attitude!"; if he says "men" he must say "maidens," if he says "forest branches" he must say "trodden weed." By the time he says "Beauty is Truth" we feel he *must* say "Truth Beauty" or he would be breaking an almost inflexible pattern; similarly, "all ye know on earth" would feel incomplete in this ode without its matching half, "all ye need to know." This binary pattern, so strictly maintained, is not natural to Keats in so compulsive a form. The odes are all stately, and show many parallelisms of diction and syntax; but the norm is exceeded by far in the *Urn*, and suggests a deliberate constraint on reverie.

20. Even in Keats's first poem, a Spenserian description of an enchanted isle, Keats finds himself introducing into his idyll, without any compulsion from the genre, Dido's grief and "aged Lear['s] . . . bitter teen"; the early poem to the robin (*Stay, ruby breasted warbler, stay*) envisages bleak storm and a leafless grove, "the gloom of grief and tears."

V. The Strenuous Tongue: The *Ode on Melancholy*

1. [Stillinger's notes.] Text (including heading) from *1820*. Variants and other readings from the extant holograph (arbitrarily cited as *D*) and Brown's transcript (*CB*).   *Heading* Ode on] On *D*; Ode, to *altered to* Ode, on *CB*   *Before* 1

I

Though you should build a bark of dead men's bones,
    And rear a phantom gibbet for a mast,
Stitch creeds together for a sail, with groans
    To fill it out, bloodstained and aghast;
Although your rudder be a Dragon's tail,
    Long sever'd, yet still hard with agony,
        Your cordage large uprootings from the skull
Of bald Medusa; certes you would fail
    To find the Melancholy, whether she
        Dreameth in any isle of Lethe dull.

(*the stanza crossed out in pencil*) *CB. The remaining three stanzas in CB are numbered 2–4*   2 Wolf's] <Henb> Wolfs *D*   6 nor the] or the *D*   9 drowsily] *successively* (*a*) heavily (*b*) sleepily (*c*) drowsily *D*   11 fall] *interlined above* <come> *D*   12 a] *added above the line in D*   14 hill] hills *D, CB*   15 glut] *interlined above* <feed> *D*   16 salt] <dashing> salt *D*   21 dwells with] lives in *D, CB*   27 save] but 27 him] *interlined above* <those> *D*   29 taste] *added above the line in D*   29 sadness] anguish *D*.

2. Now in the Keats Museum, Hampstead.

3. The word "phantom" allies the gibbet to the urn-"phantoms" who are commanded to "vanish . . . into the clouds" at the end of *Indolence*. The clouds

are the dwelling-place of phantoms; this links the final destiny of the hero-become-phantom (to be hung among Melancholy's "cloudy" trophies) with that of the urn-figures.

4. *Anatomy*, Part 8, Sect. 2, Memb. 1, Subs. 1. Keats's advice-giving has occasioned comment: Empson recognized the "didactic tone . . . a parody, by contradiction, of the wise advice of uncles" (p. 215) but he rather too easily slides over his perception of something parodic in the poem and assumes the advice is seriously meant by Keats, finding, like other commentators (Leavis among them) the "pathological." "There is no need for me to insist on the contrariety of the pathological splendours of this introduction," Empson continues, still speaking of the first stanza. (*Seven Types of Ambiguity* [New York: New Directions, 1947; rev. from British edition of 1930], p. 215.) Leavis, in *Revaluations*, finds it a poem of "perverse and debilitating indulgences," exhibiting one of "the most obviously decadent developments of Beauty-addiction — of the cult of 'exquisite passion' and 'finest senses'" (p. 60). This is what comes of reading a poem as if it were an undramatic sermon. But a poem has its own drama; and an evolution from two sorts of error to an equilibrium of truth is the drama in this case.

5. My attention was first called to the resemblances among these figures by my student Gerald Shepherd, in an unpublished paper on Keats's allegory.

6. The varying forms of this figure are being traced by Leon Waldoff in successive as yet unpublished essays. He includes the urn as a female form.

7. Stillinger points out in his note on the *Ode on Melancholy* that the original holograph has only three stanzas; Brown's transcript on which the canceled stanza appears is a later version of the poem than the holograph. Keats apparently began with the final three stanzas, then thought of prefacing them with a new first stanza, and finally decided against it.

8. The resemblance of this speaker to the knight-at-arms in *La Belle Dame* is evident; the poems share the paraphernalia of pallor, anguish, rose, garland, strange foods, grotto, eyes, kisses, lips. What the *Ode on Melancholy* does not include is music of any sort.

9. Keats replaced the phrase "the rainbow of the dashing wave" by the phrase "the rainbow of the salt sand-wave" in order to include the sense of taste explicitly in the categories of glut.

10. I reproduce Keats's markings in his copy of Shakespeare's poems in the Keats Museum Library:

> | *My smoothe moist hand, were it with thy hand felt,*
> | *Would in thy palm dissolve, or seem to melt.*
>
> (*Venus and Adonis*, 143–144)
>
> And when from thence he struggles to be gone,
> ||| *She locks her lily fingers, one in one.*
>
> (*Venus and Adonis*, 237–238)

> Full gently now she takes him by the hand
> A lily prison'd in a gaol of snow,
> Or ivory in an alabaster band:
> So white a friend engirts so white a foe.
>
> (*Venus and Adonis*, 361–364)
>
> Her Hand
> (In whose comparison all whites are Inke)
> Writing their own reproach; *to whose soft seizure,*
> *The Cignets Down is harsh, and spirit of Sense*
> *Hard as the palme of Plough-man.*
>
> (*Troilus and Cressida*, i.i. 57–61)

The treatment of the eyes in the ode is also drawn in part from *Venus and Adonis*; but neither of these passages was specially marked by Keats: "Look in mine eye-balls, there thy beauty lies" (119); "His glutton eye so full hath fed" (399).

11. From *Hamlet*, the ode may recall Hamlet, in "the very ecstasy of love" (II.i.103) imprisoning Ophelia's hand and feeding deep in his perusal of her face:

> He took me by the wrist and held me hard; . . .
> He falls to such perusal of my face
> As 'a would draw it. (87, 89–90)

12. For the link in Keats's mind between clouds and silence, see the draft revision of *Endymion*, II, 335: "Obstinate silence came <cloudily> heavily again."

13. It is nonetheless of interest that the vehicle for redeeming the "lower" senses is the tongue, the organ of the "mother tongue" (*The Fall of Hyperion*, I, 15) and the organ allied in Milton with music (cf. "a tongueless nightingale," 206, and "Music's golden tongue," 20, in *The Eve of St. Agnes*). The tongue, apt for relish, for kissing, for music, was the richest organ available for Keats.

14. The rainbow comes from the original presence of the weeping cloud; cf. Burton (*Anatomy* 3.4.2.6), "A blacke cloud of sin as yet obnubilates thy soul, terrifies thy conscience, but this cloud may conceive a rain-bow at the last." This passage on the cure of Despair was marked by Keats. The peony, rather oddly isolated here, may be a reminiscence of Peona; her name is probably derived, as John Barnard notes (*Complete Poems*, p. 565), from Lemprière's glossing of Paeon: "A celebrated physician who cured the wounds which the gods received during the Trojan war. From him physicians are sometimes called *Poeonii*, and herbs serviceable in medicinal processes *Poeniae herbae*." The peonies are here called to be serviceable to the medicining of melancholy, once the suicidal option has been refused.

VI. The Dark Secret Chambers: *The Fall of Hyperion*

1. [Stillinger's notes.] Text (including heading) from Woodhouse's W^2 transcript.   217 her] *made out of the* W^2 236 other] *added above the line*

in *W²*   238 lang'rous] *written (in a blank space left for the word) first in pencil and then in ink in* W²   298 what] *ed;* was *(with the penciled query* "what?" *in the margin)* W².

2. Yeats may be remembering Saturn by his voiceless stream, and rightly makes the inference that life has turned to art in turning to something quiet as a stone, when he writes "Men Improve with the Years": "I am worn out with dreams; / A weather-worn, marble triton / Among the streams." "Frozen are the channels of the blood," he says in an adjoining poem ("The Living Beauty"), recalling perhaps the deadened and voiceless stream in Keats and the cold finger of the Naiad. "The Living Beauty" certainly derives from both the indifference of the nightingale's song and the fleeting animation of the figures on the urn, as Yeats criticizes "Beauty that is cast out of a mould / In bronze, or that in dazzling marble appears, / Appears, but when we have gone is gone again, / Being more indifferent to our solitude / Than 'twere an apparition."

3. Geoffrey Hartman suggests (*Fate of Reading*, p. 72) that the Naiad's gesture is iconographically meant as a warning against the profanation of a sacred place. The idea is an apposite one, but Keats is generally more explicit when conferring sacredness on a place.

4. It must be recalled that Hyperion and Apollo are in effect one person for Keats: though Lemprière's classical dictionary declares, *s.v. Apollo*, "It may be proved by different passages in the antient writers, that Apollo, the Sun, Phoebus, and Hyperion, were all different characters and deities, though confounded together," it is clear that Keats's practice was to confound, rather than to discriminate among, these characters.

5. It is significant, I believe, that Keats wrote to Fanny Brawne from Leigh Hunt's house in the summer of 1820 to say that he had, for the past week, been "marking the most beautiful passages in Spenser, intending it for you" (*Letters*, II, 302). Spenser's influence extends beyond Keats's early poems; it is a lifelong one.

6. Cf. the resemblance of this line to the beginning of Keats's *Character of C.B.* (written just before the odes): "He was to weet a melancholy carle."

7. It must be emphasized that the statue of Saturn is a seated one, and it is intact. The speaker must ask the identity of the god represented in the colossal statue: as he stands before it, its "broad marble knees" (214) obscure his seeing its face. From afar, as he entered, he perceived it as "an image, huge of feature as a cloud, / At level of whose feet an altar slept" (88-89). Later he speaks of it as "the image pedestal'd so high / In Saturn's temple" (299-300). When Saturn fell, features of his image, till then immortally young, became in an instant old, exhibiting thereby the mimetic accuracy of authentic art. Moneta says, "this old image here, / Whose carved figures wrinkled as he fell, / Is Saturn's." Saturn's image is allowed to age as the im-

ages of the couple on the urn are not: he cannot, so to speak, keep his lustrous eyes, even in his iconic form. The reading of this passage by Anne Mellor is consequently in error: she says (*Keats-Shelley Journal* 25 [1976], 73) that the image is Moneta, and that the "fallen statue at [Moneta's] side" is Saturn. But there is no fallen statue. As Moneta tells Keats after he has ascended the steps, "Thou standest safe beneath this statue's knees," and, it is clear, the face is higher (where Keats cannot see it) than the knees. The point about the shrine is that it is *intact*—it is all that is left untouched by the rebellion. The monuments of vanished dynasties outlive them; "le buste / Survit à la cité." Art is the residue of history.

8. Hartman (*Fate of Reading*, p. 73) says of the autumn ode "The granary is full," but it is precisely the full granary that the ode purposely omits, as I hope to show.

9. *Autumn* might seem to be a poem of patient sublunary legs alone, except that it ends once more with winged creatures (crickets, gnats, birds). However, these are mixed, significantly, with the unwinged full-grown lambs, who, as the visibly deviant members of the list of creatures, tether the poem to earth. The lambs are a touch of genius: if all the creatures of the last stanza were winged, Keats's import would be quite other than it actually is.

10. Stuart Sperry has revealed the many echoes of *Paradise Lost* in *The Fall*, saving it from being thought a more Dantesque poem than it is. However, Sperry consequently sees it rather too strongly as a poem about "sin"; I prefer Hartman's ascription of "shame" to Keats. Though it is true that Moneta says that the poet is less than the nonvisionary benefactors of mankind, Keats argues (it seems to me successfully) against her condemnation. Sperry takes Moneta's as the last word on this matter; but she is only a vehicle, after all, by which Keats puts to himself a "worst case" against writers. She is not necessarily the final arbiter of the question: only the whole poem is the arbiter.

11. *Fate of Reading*, p. 63.

12. Cf. Coleridge's "Limbo."

13. By internalizing Mutability's masque of seasons and months—a cyclic comedy—into a historic or mythic "high tragedy," Keats made Moneta Shakespearean, not Spenserian.

14. I take Moneta's permanent fixity in imagination to be Keats's critique of his model for aesthetic reflection in *Urn*—that we can "forget" that the urn is an art object while we are lost in its "life," and "remember" its marble medium only intermittently. The alternation of sensuous receptivity and aesthetic reflection may well have been Keats's more youthful way of life; but Moneta's unsleeping act of imagining seems to represent his latter burden of perpetual consciousness.

15. It is perhaps worth remarking that there is no music in Moneta's temple—another mark of Keats's austere ascetic intent in envisaging the monumental shrine. Though there once had been music in the liturgical past, perhaps, the liturgies are extinct; there remains only the "mingl'd heap confus'd" of "robes, golden tongs, censer, and chafing dish, / Girdles, and chains, and holy jewelries" (78–80) These are the paraphernalia of Psyche's shrine, but the priest and virgin-choir have vanished. In reinstating music (even of a diminished sort) in *Autumn*, Keats is admitting to himself the excessive severity of vision in *The Fall*.

16. It is, I think, significant that when Mutability pleads her case before the Olympians, the "infernal Powers" are forbidden to appear, with two notable exceptions, Pluto and Proserpina:

> Onely th' infernall Powers might not appeare;
> As well for horror of their count'naunce ill,
> As for th' unruly fiends which they did feare;
> Yet Pluto and Proserpina were present there.

We see by this passage that where Mutability appears, Pluto and Proserpina (whose legend is the mythical embodiment of the allegorical idea of Mutability) cannot be absent. Keats, with his exquisite sense of myth, would have seen that the way to represent mutability mythically—if he wished to forsake allegorical images—was to turn (as he did) to the story of Ceres, Pluto, Proserpina, and the origin of seasonal change. But he leaves out the malevolent agency of Pluto, making Ceres and Proserpina the elder and younger manifestations of a single seasonal goddess, herself the agent of her own change.

VII. Peaceful Sway above Man's Harvestings: *To Autumn*

1. [Stillinger's notes.] Text (including heading) from *1820*. Variants and other readings from Keats's draft (*D*), his letter to Woodhouse, 21, 22 September 1819 (*L*), and transcripts by Brown (*CB*) and Woodhouse (*W²*).   *Heading* To Autumn] *no heading in* D, L   4 With . . . vines] The Vines with fruit D, L, CB, *W²*   6 fruits] D, CB (furuits *in* D)   6 ripeness] sweetness D, CB (sweeness *in* D)   8 sweet] white D, L, *W²*   9 still] yet *W²*   12 thee . . . store?] thee? for thy haunts are many *altered to* thee oft amid thy store<s>? D   12 store] stores L, *W²*; store<s> CB (D *also* —see preceding note)   13 abroad] *interlined above* <for thee> D   15/16

> < While bright the Sun slants through the husky barn;—
>   orr on a half reap'd furrow sound asleep
>   Dos'd with red poppies; while thy reeping hook
>   Spares form Some {slumbrous} minutes while wam slumpers creep>

(husky *added above in the first line; the second line interlined above* {Or sound asleep in a half reaped field}) D   17 Drows'd] Dos'd D, CB (Dosed *in*

CB); Dased *L*; Dazed *W²*   18 Spares . . .flowers *interlined above* < Spares for some slumbrous minutes the next swath > *D*   18 swath] sheath (*corrected by Keats to* swath) *CB*   18 twined] honied (*corrected by Keats to* twined) *CB*   20 laden] l< e > aden (*the correction made first by Woodhouse in pencil and then by Brown in ink*) *CB*   20 a] the *D, CB*   21 patient] patent *D*   22 oozings] oozing *D, CB*   25 While] When *W²*   25 barred . . . bloom] a gold cloud gilds *altered to* barred clouds bloom *D*   26 And touch] < And > Touching *altered to* And Touch *D*   26 with] *added above the line in D*   28 borne] < on the > borne *D*   29 or dies] and dies *D, L, W²*   30, 33 And] *written over* < The > (*the same alteration in both lines*) *D*   31 with treble] again full *D, CB*   32/33 < And new flock still > *D*   33 gathering] gather'd *D, L, W²* (Gather'd *made out of* Gathering *in D*).

2. The others include a great number of other sonnets by Shakespeare, especially 12, 15, and 33. Though there are echoes of Chatterton, and Thomson, they do not seem centrally important to the poem.

3. Cf. also VI, 280-283:

> [The ocean] with warm
> Prolific humour softening all her globe,
> Fermented the great Mother to conceive,
> Satiate with genial moisture.

All the passages I quote from *Paradise Lost* have been marked with a vertical line beside them in Keats's copy of the poem in the Keats Museum. When Keats has also underlined a phrase or a line, I reproduce his italics. To read *Paradise Lost* through Keats's eyes is to see it in part as a poem of Shakespearean characterization, but chiefly as a poem of luxuriant and opulent description, full of growth, change, ripening, delectable sweets, and golden profusion. The desolation is noted, but it does not usurp "*the sweet of life*" (VIII, 184, Keats's italics). Keats's underlinings in his Shakespeare also illuminate this ode; there are many markings of passages on autumn which delay or repudiate the death implicit in harvest, among them *Antony and Cleopatra*, v.ii. 86-88, and *The Tempest*, IV.i. 60-72, 114-115. He also marked ll. 134-135:

> You sun-burn'd sicklemen, of August weary,
> Come hither from the furrow and be merry.

(I quote from Keats's seven-volume *Dramatic Works* of Shakespeare, now in the Houghton Library.)

4. Cf., however, the "purple stars, and bells of amber" of the "real" flowers in *Calidore*, 137.

5. John Barnard's summary in the Penguin *Complete Poems* (p. 675) reports the movements of the poem in the general way in which they are always represented:

The stanzas can be seen as moving through the season, beginning with pre-harvest ripeness, moving to the repletion of harvest itself, and concluding with the emptiness following the harvest, but preceding winter. It also progresses from the tactile senses, to the visual, culminating in the auditory senses, and focuses first on the vegetable world, then on the human activity in gathering the harvest, and concludes in the world of animals, birds, and insects. It has also been read as a movement from morning to evening.

While this is roughly true, it is not very interesting unless countermovements are noted and both movements and countermovements are explained. Barnard's summary, "The interconnectedness of maturity, death, and regeneration is implicit throughout," seems to me dubious, since there is no regeneration and no death as such, unless one is prepared to speak of execution. The corn does not die, it is cut down; the apples do not die, they are pressed to juice. Nothing regenerates.

6. Keats is remembering, in the barrèd clouds, his early epistle *To My Brother George*, where he fears that all his contemplations of nature, because of his depression, will not yield up poetry:

> That I should never hear Apollo's song,
> Though feathery clouds were floating all along
> The purple west, and, two bright streams between,
> The golden lyre itself were dimly seen:
> That the still murmur of the honey bee
> Would never teach a rural song to me.

The "golden lyre" of Apollo is the setting sun. Elsewhere Keats refers to Apollo's "hot lyre" (*God of the meridian*, 228); and his association of sunset, Apollo, the "laurel'd peers" (who appear in the *Ode to Apollo* and the sonnet *To My Brother George*) and clouds surrounding the sunset—a constellation reappearing many times—justifies our seeing references to poetry in the sunset of *To Autumn*. The real point to be made is that the sun, visible in the epistle to George between its two bright streaks of cloud, is in the ode veiled from sight.

7. Some commentators have wished to have "bourn" mean "brook" (cf. Barnard, p. 676: "Almost certainly Keats means 'boundary', but 'bourn', meaning a stream, would make sense"). It hardly makes sense, however, to have sheep bleating from a stream, and a hilly stream at that. Sheep are sent up untillable land to graze.

8. Hartman, "Poem and Ideology: A Study of Keats's 'To Autumn,'" *Literary Theory and Structure*, ed. F. Brady, J. Palmer, and M. Price (New Haven: Yale University Press, 1973), p. 312; rpt. in *The Fate of Reading* (Chicago: Chicago University Press, 1975), pp. 124–146.

9. The word "clammy" comes from Dryden's translation of the *Georgics*, where it is used twice of bees' cells, just as Keats uses it:

> Not birdlime, of Idnean pitch, produce
> A more tenacious mass of clammy juice.
>
> (VI, 58-59)
>
> Those [bees] at home
> Lay deep foundations for the labor'd comb,
> With dew, narcissus leaves, and clammy gum.
>
> (IV, 236-238)

Keats had been reading Dryden during the summer while writing *Lamia*. John Arthos, in *The Language of Natural Description in Eighteenth-Century Poetry* (Ann Arbor: University of Michigan Press, 1949), cites, as paraphrases of honey, "a clammie humour of honie," from Holland's *Pliny* (1601) and also, from Marton's *Northampton* (1712), "that clammy, sweet, Honey-like Juice" (pp. 371-372). Arthos identifies "clammy" as one of the "epithets with suffix -*y*" common in eighteenth-century poetry, used especially to translate Latin terms (pp. 395-397). Keats uses the phrase to remind us of the georgic tradition, but uses it not of honey but of the honey-comb.

10. See my earlier discussion of these verbs, and other aspects of the language of the ode, in my review of Roger Fowler's *Language and Style* in *Essays in Criticism* 16 (1966), 457-463.

11. Hartman, *Fate of Reading*, p. 132.

12. Cf. Shakespeare, *Two Noble Kinsmen*, IV, i, a passage marked by Keats in his folio Shakespeare:

> The place
> Was knee-deep where she sat; her careless tresses
> A wreath of bull-rush rounded.

13. Like "clammy," "fume" is a word Keats borrowed from Dryden's *Virgilian Pastorals*. In the sixth of these, two satyrs find Silenus lying on the ground, "Doz'd with his fumes." Keats, who had been reading Dryden (see Brown's *Life* of Keats, in *The Keats Circle*, II, 67), first wrote in the draft of *To Autumn* that Autumn was "Dos'd with red poppies." Once he had corrected this, to "Dos'd with the fume of poppies," he must have heard the echo of the Dryden intoxication. He changed "Dos'd" to "Dased" ("Dazed") and finally settled on "Drows'd." The debt to Dryden makes it clear that the poppies are for Keats a metamorphosis of wine and other intoxicants invoked in earlier odes; they also serve, with their incense, as a last reminder of cultic worship. Of course this allusion points again to the Virgilian influence on the ode, an influence not only from the *Eclogues,* but also from the *Georgics,* both mediated in this instance through Dryden (cf. the "clammy" cells). Keats is also recalling Lemprière's account of Ceres "holding in one hand a lighted torch and in the other a poppy, which was sacred to her."

Lemprière's Ceres is half goddess, half agricultural laborer, like Keats's Autumn, but Lemprière's version is ungainly: "She appears as a countrywoman mounted on the back of an ox and carrying a basket on her left arm and holding a hoe, and sometimes she rides in a chariot drawn by winged dragons."

14. In envisaging a permanent death for the grain, rather than a self-renewing decay, Keats was I believe following Shakespeare's sonnet 12, in a passage he remarked on: "And Sommers greene all girded up in sheaves / Borne on the beare with white and bristly beard." But Keats will dissolve his natural forms, rather than create obsequies for them.

15. This detail may derive not only from the *Introduction to Entomology* noted in Allott's edition of the *Poems* (p. 653n.) but also from the Mutability Cantos (VII, xxii), speaking of the air which

> flit[s] still, and with subtill influence
> Of his thin spirit all creatures . . . maintaine[s]
> In state of life[.] O weake life! that does leane
> On thing so tickle as th' unsteady ayre,
> Which every howre is chang'd.

16. The verb "twitter" and other details come, as Allott notes, from Thomson, just as the rising and falling of the gnats come from an 1817 introduction to entomology, whose gnats "form themselves into choirs, that alternately rise and fall" (Allott, pp. 653–654, in the latter instance quoting B. L. Woodruff in *Modern Language Notes* [April 1953], 317–320). Keats's selectivity with respect to his sources is of course what is of interest; the entomologists go on to say that the gnats "may be seen at all seasons, amusing themselves with their choral dances," and Thomson's swallows "twitter cheerful, till the vernal months / Invite them welcome back" (*The Seasons, Autumn*, 846–847). Keats will have nothing amusing or cheerful, not to speak of vernal invitings.

17. There may well be other motions and submotions functioning in the poem: Virgil Nemoianu says rightly that the poem's "superposed curves" have not all as yet been described; he, for instance, sees "an 'upward' movement, from undifferentiated materiality to complex vitality, from vegetal to animal, from fixed and determined to relatively autonomous and arbitrary motility, . . . ascent on the evolutionary ladder" (pp. 205, 206). This latter notion does not sound Keatsian to me, but it is an example of a motion another critic would wish to defend. What we all agree on is that there are several motions, superimposed, and that "there is a richer polyvalence" in the poem "than is generally assumed" (p. 211). I cannot agree with Nemoianu, as my reading will show, that the poem exhibits in its syntax "a moving away from a living interaction of elements toward a purely mechanical sequence" (p. 208), nor that "whirring and bleating" are "'mechanical'

sounds," nor that the rhyme scheme progresses from a "good" irreducible one to one that is "mechanically reducible" (pp. 207, 211). Nor can I read the last stanza, as he does, as "a criticism of a mechanical late phase of democracy," nor see the first stanza as he does: "Lush grass, the heavy scent of flowers, the immediacy of buzzing insects—all form the sticky, stifling atmosphere that may be the hidden unsavory reverse of the glorious luminous fertility and mellow generosity of the natural-social symbiosis that a garden always is" (p. 206). Lush, sticky, buzzing, heavy-scented, and stifling are all the wrong adjectives for Keats's first stanza. Such wrongness of perception is endemic in Keats criticism, and urges on us all a more self-denying fidelity to what Keats actually wrote. My quotations are from "The Dialectics of Movement in Keats's 'To Autumn,'" *PMLA* 93 (1978), 205–214.

18. See my article arguing that the odes often exhibit a central node from which they radiate backward and forward, and that they are best seen as originating from that central *donnée*, rather than progressing in a linear fashion from one notion to the next. This fashion of composition-from-a-kernel is of course not peculiar to Keats, but has been more appreciated in novels than in poems. The article, "The Experiential Beginnings of Keats's Odes," appeared in *Studies in Romanticism* 12 (Summer 1973), 591–606.

19. The "benevolent pair," as I have called them, who are conspiring to load and bless the earth with fruit by their combination of warmth and moisture, are of course themselves eternal, and come, as I have said, from the Miltonic Jupiter who "impregns the clouds" and the sun "whose virtue . . . works . . . in the fruitful Earth." Being eternal, they cannot possibly be described as Paul Fry unpleasantly and jocularly describes them (*The Poet's Calling in the English Ode* [New Haven: Yale University Press, 1980], p. 267):

> The sun is now an older gentleman who seems in any case to be an immemorial companion of the matronly autumn. True, they have their mystification to practice on us, but nothing their conspiracy hatches could surprise or alarm us.
>
> Their old dodges are played out in a scene [etc. as Fry makes much of Keats's misspelling of "eaves" as "eves," a usage admitted, as he notes, by the OED]. The landscape played over by these genial cronies, Autumn and the sun, is a little like a human body, like the figures that will appear in the next stanza, except that strangely enough it seems very old. It has a thatch of hair that is frosted, silvered over in the eve, perhaps even the midnight, of its life. It is bent and mossed over like a crooked tree, laden with the fruits of experience. As the genealogical "of" in the first line suggests, Autumn is born from this whitened, filmy-eyed figuration that is faintly perceptible amid the happy plenty of the landscape.

This grotesque transmutation of the eternal pair is matched by Fry's transmutation of the bees into creatures "who are belike too stuffed and clammy to utter their cosmic sound," and by his unhappy pun which calls Keats's autumn "more serial than cereal" (pp. 268, 269). Other inventions (including "the dried rows of plants in the garden-croft," p. 271) and imported un-Keatsian metaphors ("the loose gathering of swallows, crisscrossing the light like black stars," p. 271) bring a degree of fantasy into literary criticism that is repellent to its function. Can anyone but Fry see a frosty thatch of silver hair or an older gentleman in this poem? If Keats had wanted black stars and dried rows of plants, would he not have inserted them? Fry, incidentally, also thinks the reaper is masculine (p. 269). While such errors persist, there is room for more careful debate.

20. Of course Keats distances and frames his pining knight both by placing him in the company of the other sufferers in his vision and by introducing a sympathetic questioner. But no one doubts that the poem is about powerlessness and deprivation.

21. Many of these words recall the earlier odes, of course.

22. Allott (*Poems*, p. 655n.) notes the underworld parallel (in *Aeneid*, VI, 309-312) to Keats's gathering birds.

23. By his employment of a double process—vegetative growth and agricultural harvest—Keats avoids the single linear process of Moneta's decline. I take this assertion of many coincident processes, all enacted in the poem, as Keats's single most triumphant imaginative leap.

24. The presence of the georgic flock in *Autumn* distinguishes it firmly from *Psyche*; in *Psyche*'s fanciful landscape there are nymphs but no sheep. The bleating lambs are clearly *Autumn*'s substitute for the lowing heifer in the *Urn*. The heifer may owe something to the bull (Taurus) on which April rides in the Mutability Cantos: "His hornes were gilden all with golden studs, / And garnished with garlands goodly dight."

25. Hartman, "Poem and Ideology: A Study of Keats's 'To Autumn,'" in *The Fate of Reading*, pp. 124-146.

26. It is perhaps not too fanciful to see the three scenes of *Autumn*, in their plastic grace, as a "natural" reworking of the three scenes on the urn. *Melancholy*, too, has three "scenes."

27. On Yeats, see de Man's "Symbolic Landscape in Wordsworth and Yeats," in *In Defense of Reading*, ed. Reuben A. Brower and Richard Poirier (New York: Dutton, 1962), pp. 22-37. On Keats, see de Man's "Introduction" to the *Selected Poetry of Keats* (New York: New American Library, 1966), p. xxxii.

28. The word "melody" of course is related to the word "ode," itself meaning

"song." It may be that Keats did not call this poem an ode because it is about music too complex to be called simply a song or a melody.

29. We know these things will happen because we see the full-reaped stubble plains; we are emphatically not permitted to see any future season, whether flowers springing again or swallows returning. One cannot deduce more than the poem allows, an axiom often honored in the breach.

Conclusion

1. Keats's increasingly sure view that art was different from nature, and his emphasis on work (by contrast to indolence or "spontaneity") as the prerequisite for the creation of art, even his choice, in his last ode, of an agricultural tool, the reaper's hook, as his symbol of the writer's intervention in the natural, make him one of the most clear-minded of the writers of the Romantic period. Ernst Fischer, in *The Necessity of Art* (London: Penguin, 1963, tr. Anna Bostock, p. 17), quotes Marx on the labor of the worker in words that seem entirely appropriate to Keats's view of the labor of the artist:

> We have to consider labour in a form peculiar to the human species. A spider carries on operations resembling those of a weaver; and many a human architect is put to shame by the skill with which a bee constructs her cell. But what from the very first distinguishes the most incompetent architect from the best of bees, is that the architect has built a cell in his head before he constructs it in wax. The labour process ends in the creation of something which, when the process began, already existed in the worker's imagination, already existed in an ideal form. What happens is not merely that the worker brings about a change of form in natural objects; at the same time, in the nature that exists apart from himself, he realizes his own purposes, the purpose to which he has to subordinate his own will.

2. "Concerning the Relation of the Plastic Arts of Nature" (1807), tr. Michael Bullock, quoted in Herbert Read, *The True Voice of Feeling* (London: Faber & Faber, 1953), p. 331.

3. *The Life of Forms in Art* (New York: George Wittinborn, 1948), p. 15.

4. Michel Foucault, *The Archaeology of Knowledge*, tr. A. M. Sheridan Smith (New York: Pantheon, 1972), p. 221.

5. *Poetics of Music* (Cambridge, Mass.: Harvard University Press, 1957), pp. 50–51.

Index

Woodruff, B. L., 322n16
Wordsworth, William, 128, 174,
215, 260, 265–266, 282; *The
Excursion,* 52, 85, 309n22; *Ode:
Intimations of Immortality,* 50,
59–60, 234, 236, 237; *Tintern
Abbey,* 31

Yeats, William Butler, 5, 34, 80,
107, 251, 272, 309n21, 316n2